I0644172

Images of Modern America

THE DECADE

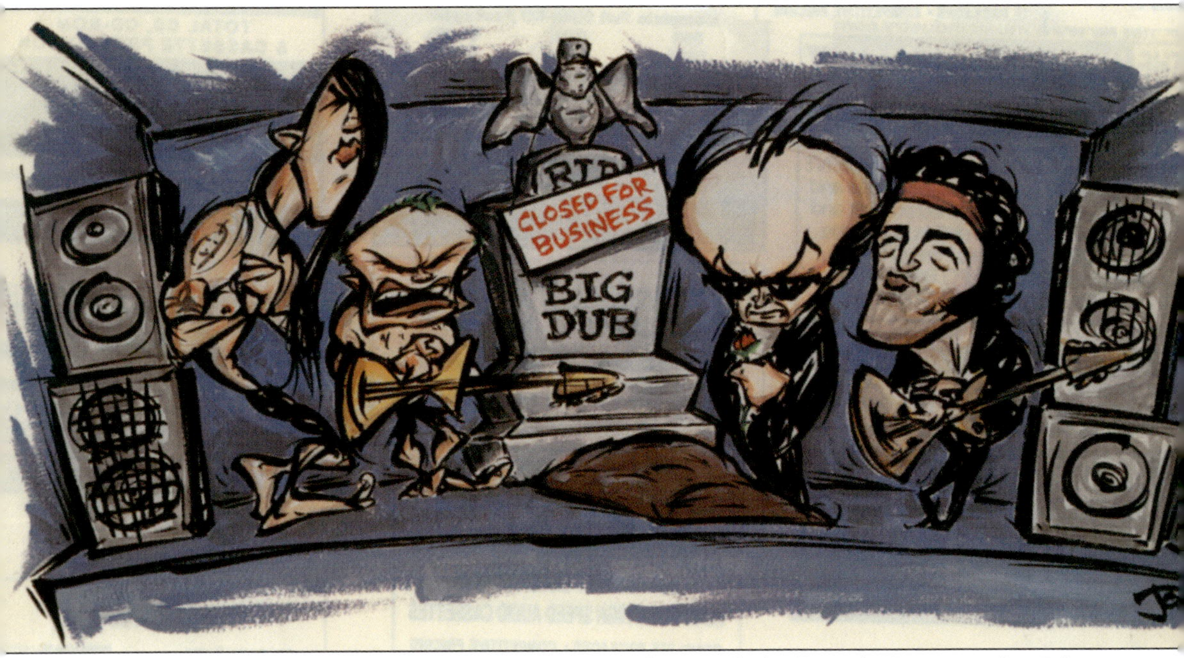

This comic was done by Joe Fournier during the closing of The Decade. It was used in *Musician* magazine beside an article written by Reverend Billy Wirths, and like the article, it embodies many aspects of life at The Decade.

Front Cover: The Decade album (courtesy of Xayne Berlinski and On a Roll Productions; see page 84)

Upper Back Cover: DiSilvio family (Dom DiSilvio)

Lower Back Cover (from left to right): Cyndi Lauper (courtesy of Sasha Koledin; see page 45), The Decade sign (Dom DiSilvio), Bon Jovi on The Decade stage (courtesy of Sasha Koledin; see page 49)

Images of Modern America

THE DECADE

Gabby Means
with foreword by Dom DiSilvio

ARCADIA
PUBLISHING

ISBN 978-1-4671-1720-3

Published by Arcadia Publishing
Charleston, South Carolina

Printed in the United States of America

Library of Congress Control Number: 2016931365

For all general information, please contact Arcadia Publishing:
Telephone 843-853-2070
Fax 843-853-0044
E-mail sales@arcadiapublishing.com
For customer service and orders:
Toll-Free 1-888-313-2665

Visit us on the Internet at www.arcadiapublishing.com

This book is dedicated to my late grandmother, Janet Chepes, without whom this book and my life would not have been possible.

Contents

ACKNOWLEDGMENTS

As a rising junior in college, I had the unique opportunity to spend the entire summer by my grandfather's side, interviewing the people he has come to know as family, and learning about the business that provided him a legacy in the Pittsburgh music world. That being said, I cannot say I personally spent a ton of time drinking and listening to live music in The Decade—I wasn't legal back then, just five months old when it closed. Yet, I feel ever grateful to be the one to tell this story. I got the chance to record folklore, a generation's memories of youth, an essential era in the time of Pittsburgh music, and above all, my grandfather's life. I cannot promise that every detail is a cold, hard fact, as memories undoubtedly fade and change over time, but what I can guarantee is that my grandfather and I did our best to encapsulate what The Decade was and what it meant to the people who loved it.

Unless otherwise stated, the photographs in this book are from Dom DiSilvio's personal collection.

FOREWORD

I saw a quote the other day, and I think it's very fitting here: "It's amazing the number of great people in my life that I wouldn't have ever met if it wasn't for music." Let there be no mistake, this book—written by my eldest granddaughter Gabby, about a rock 'n' roll bar on the corner of Atwood and Sennott Streets—would not have been possible without the people who made the bar what it was. Gabby and I came up with this idea, and through her constant badgering, we wrote a book together to memorialize everything that occurred within those walls. The Decade's last days were in 1995, the year the author was born, and so this book could not have happened without all of the performers, employees, regulars, crazies, friends, and family that we interviewed in the process. When you talk to people you haven't seen or heard from in a while and it's like you talked to them yesterday, it's how you know they're great friends. This process taught me many things, but above all, that friendship isn't relegated to time. I am very moved and happy about the family I have gained because of The Decade, and I cannot say enough to express my love for these people. Enjoy this book and all of our stories, and thank you again to everyone who helped make all of this possible.

—Dom DiSilvio

INTRODUCTION

Dominic Nicholas DiSilvio (henceforth referred to as "Dom") was born on May 18, 1939, in Pittsburgh to surgeon Dr. Dominic and teacher and writer Zarelda (Mazza) DiSilvio. Selectively mute until the age of four, he did not speak a word until the day he definitively stated, "I want a cookie." Dom was a character from day one, and he always knew exactly what he wanted. Through his mother's teaching, Dom's skills on the piano reached prodigious levels by age 11; however, after her premature death, he refused to ever play the piano again. Despite clear association to his mother, he cultivated his love for music and retained a deep appreciation for it throughout his entire life.

Dom recalls that the Pittsburgh radio persona Porky Chedwick—known in Pittsburgh as "Daddio of the Raddio" and the "Boss Man"—had a huge influence on his musical interest. Driving around in convertibles with the top down, Dom listened to Chedwick's vibrant personality and distinctive voice call out, "This is Pork the Tork, your platter-pushin' papa." Additionally, annual summer vacations in southern New Jersey landed Dom in a rock 'n' roll mecca. Time spent in bars like Bay Shores, Tony Marts, The Attic, Dunes Til Dawn, and Mothers left him with an insatiable thirst for the live music scene.

During college, Dom studied at the University of Pittsburgh ("Pitt"). Around this time, he hosted what he referred to as "picnics," but what are today known as keg parties that usually featured a local band. Naturally, being the entrepreneur Dom was, and still is, he instituted a cover charge at said picnics. During his sophomore year he joined the Pi Kappa Alpha fraternity—informally known as "Pike"—and as the social chairman, Dom not only gained more freedom with which to host events, but also the financial means to do so.

After college, Dom spent some time in graduate school, but much to his parents' dismay, he opted to drop out and open a bar. As a fresh college graduate, Dom, along with his partners Paul Turbavich and Johnny DePhillips, opened Fat Daddy's on Baum Boulevard; a bar that, per Dom's request, would highlight live musical acts. Fat Daddy's helped start the trend of live music before a majority of its peers in the Pittsburgh bar scene. Owning a bar located between Shadyside and Oakland at such a young age, Dom's clientele at Fat Daddy's was comprised of friends from his fraternity, college students, and regulars from other local bars. "Being the youngest, not the most intelligent or sophisticated," Dom explains, "after a Saturday night, we would spend all of the money we earned at an after-hours club on Walnut Street called The Hollywood Social Club."

This period in his life proved monumental for other reasons when Dom went on a blind date with the woman who would later become his wife, the mother of five of his children, and his esteemed business partner, Janet Chepes. Born in Smithfield, Pennsylvania, Janet was strong and sensible yet gentle and selfless, and instantly stole Dom's heart.

Before Fat Daddy's closed and Dom and his partners went their separate ways, they began hosting a few national acts; this foreshadowed some of the acts that would play The Decade several years in the future. The small venue hosted big names such as Richard Otto, Sarah McLawler, and Cozy Cole (known for the 1958 hits "Topsy 1" and "Topsy 2").

After Dom realized he was not yet the businessman he thought he was, having five children over a span of six years affirmed his decision to put rock 'n' roll emporiums on hold.

One

From Humble Beginnings

In 1972, after the birth of their children Gina (1964), Caesar (1965), Domenique (1966), Dante (1968), and Juliet (1969), Janet and Dom DiSilvio finally found a new opportunity to accomplish their mutual goal when, with the help of real estate partner Mario Noce, they bought the property at 223 Atwood Street in Oakland. The building was previously the Oaklander Hotel, which once hosted Honus Wagner along with other early Pittsburgh Pirates baseball players. This hotel, located in the shadow of Forbes Field, had also been a bar with apartments on the second, third, and fourth floor, a restaurant called Atwood Gardens, and a pizza joint uniquely named The Pizza Pub before Dom and Jan laid claim.

Due to internal problems, Dom and Jan signed a liquor license under the name "Samuel Noce." As Dom tells the story, the "infamous and benevolent" Pennsylvania Liquor Control Board cost Dom and Jan the opportunity to sell alcohol during an entire Pitt football season, and because of these "scoundrels," the young couple did not acquire a liquor license until December 1973. They opened officially as a restaurant, but despite Jan's wariness, Dom knew that he wanted it to become a bar where he could take another shot at hosting live musical acts. The name of the bar was derived from Dom and Jan's love of the 1950s, which they believed to be the decade of true rock 'n' roll. This, combined with the 10 years of marital bliss they had shared up to that point, led to the obvious choice: The Decade. When Dom was asked whether it was ever truly just a restaurant, he laughed and said, "My wife and my father thought it was a restaurant, but I could see that it would be something else . . . a rock 'n' roll saloon."

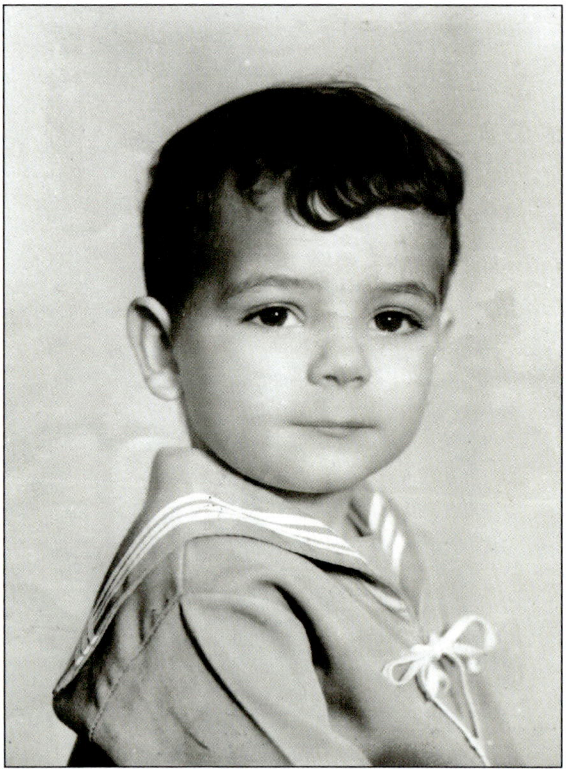

Along with his younger siblings Natalie (DiSilvio) Baker and Richard DiSilvio, Dom was born to two highly educated parents. Unusual for the time, both held degrees: father Dominic had earned a bachelor of science and a doctor of medicine from the University of Pittsburgh. He was chief of surgery and spent the last years of his life as a historian and writer. Zarelda held a master of science in teaching and home economics from Carnegie Institute of Technology and Columbia University. She hosted a radio cooking show and wrote for a homemaking advice column under the pen name "Prudence Penny."

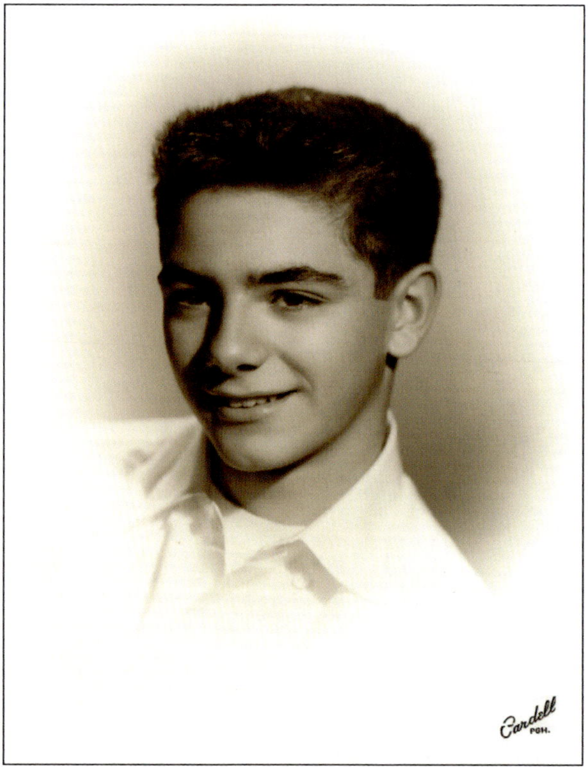

Dom attended high school at Central Catholic, the catholic preparatory school for boys in Pittsburgh, and then walked a few streets over to study at Pitt. There he joined Pi Kappa Alpha and, as their social chair, hosted his infamous "picnics." He charged a cover fee for these picnics to offset his costs after he blew his entire year's budget from the fraternity within the first few weeks of the semester. (Photograph by Cardell Pittsburgh.)

Dom has often associated his early interest in music with Pittsburgh radio personality Porky Chedwick (left). Chedwick, unfazed by the racial segregation of the 1940s, chose music without bias. His radical nature combined with his friendly demeanor and relatability to a new generation of radio listeners made him a fan favorite in Pittsburgh and one of Dom's foremost musical influences. Chedwick apparently had such a strong influence over his fans that when he called out, "blow your horn," the entire city of Pittsburgh resounded by honking. (Courtesy of Raphael J Monti.)

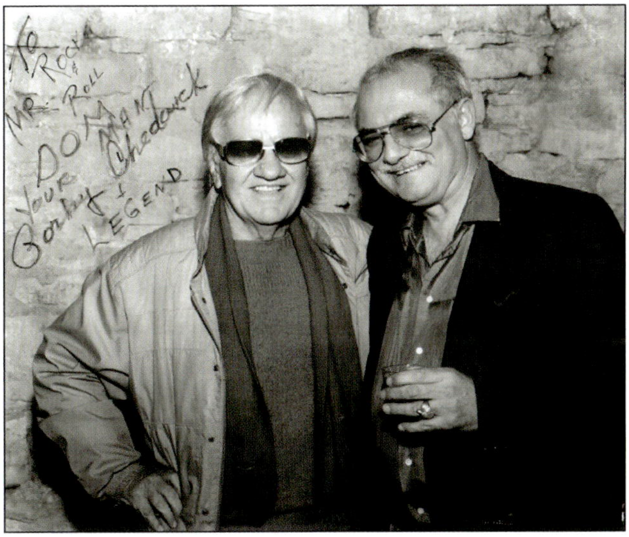

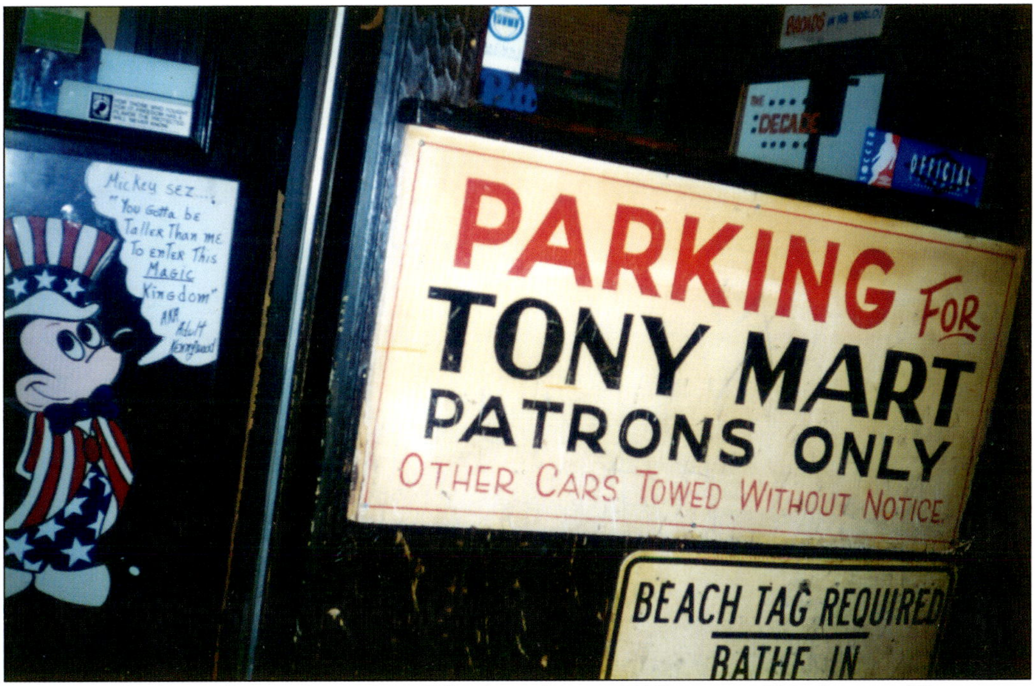

New Jersey had Bay Shores, Tony Marts, The Attic, Dunes Til Dawn, and Mothers, and Dom came to appreciate the live music scene on his annual summer vacations. True to form, the underaged teen began to sneak into the New Jersey bars with his friends when he was only 15 years old. Pittsburgh had yet to have its live music renaissance, and so, for Dom and his friends, the New Jersey bar scene was an entirely new and influential experience where they got the chance to see greats like Bill Haley and Conway Twitty. This Tony Marts sign hung in The Decade as an ode to Dom's business role model.

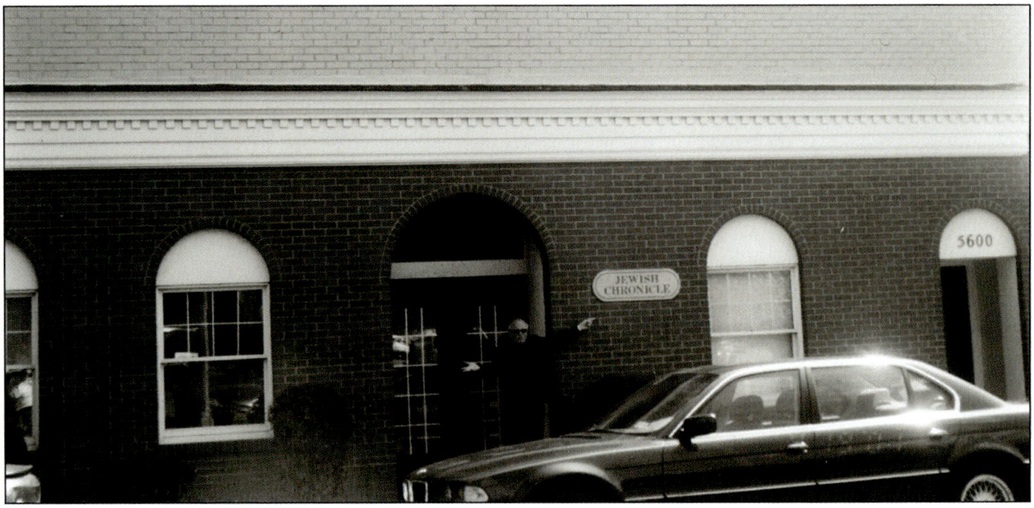

With his friends Paul Turbavich and Johnny DePhillips, Dom opened his first venture into the bar business, Fat Daddy's. He attempted to bring live music to the forefront; however, the bar, located in the building pictured above, literally and metaphorically buckled under the burden of this endeavor. Down in the basement where the beer was kept, the ceiling swayed under the weight of the crowds the national acts would draw. Dom recalls overhearing performer Cozy Cole complain to one of his band members that he was paid in change, and the band member replied, "At least your change was rolled," and that is when Dom knew the bar was headed toward an inevitable end. Pictured below are two of Fat Daddy's performers, Sarah McLawler and Richard Otto.

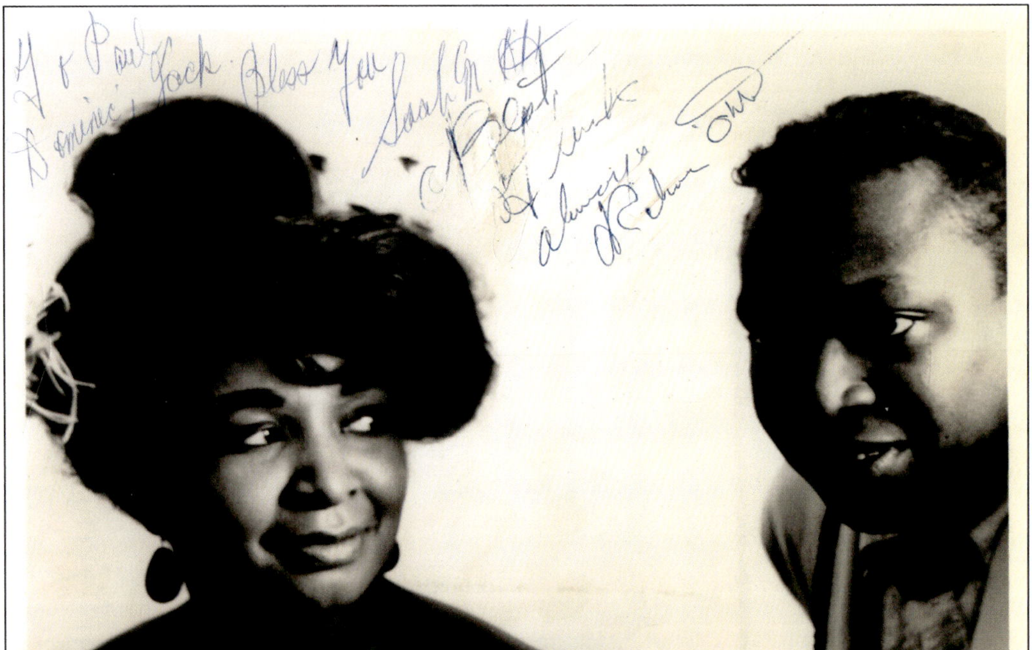

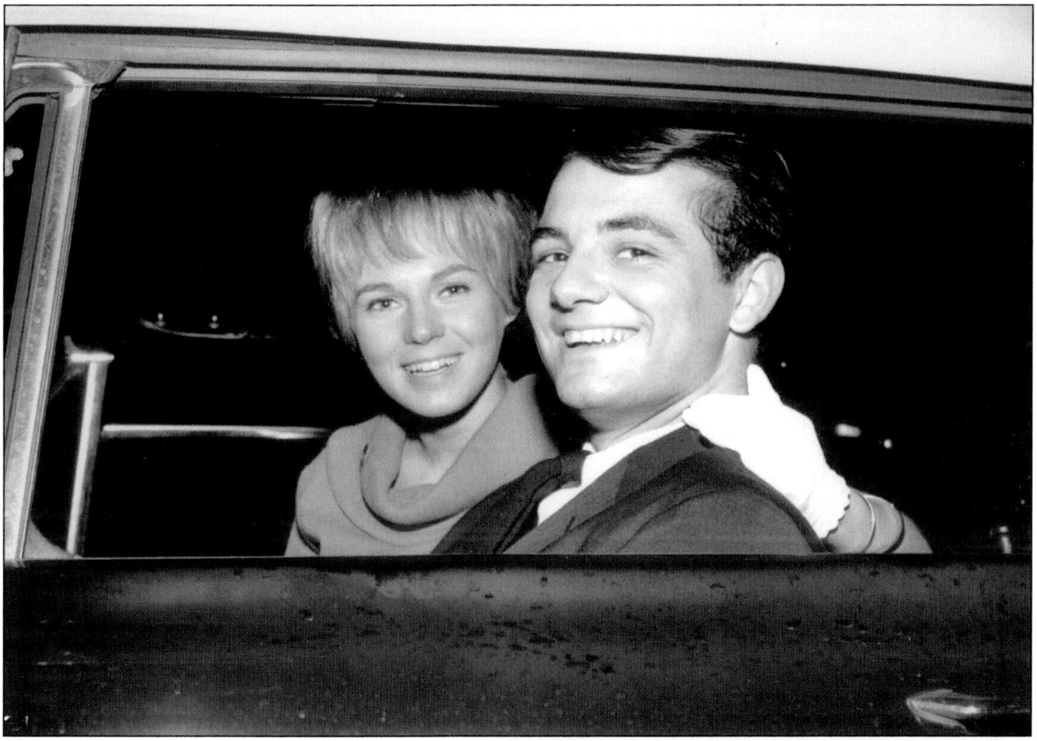

Set up on a blind date by either Dom's business partner Paul Turbavich or their mutual friend Stu Feldman, Dominic Nicholas DiSilvio and his first wife, Janet "Jan" Lee Chepes, were married in April 1963. Over the next six years, they would raise five children and open The Decade. Even after their divorce in 1978, Dom and Jan remained close friends and always continued to run the bar as a successful team.

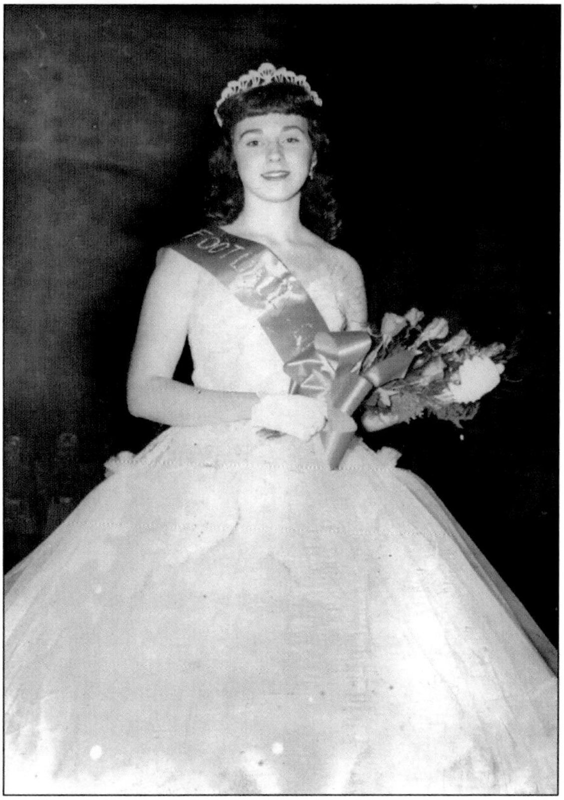

Jan was born in a small town called Smithfield, Pennsylvania, on April 16, 1941. Also the oldest of three, Jan was always a caretaker. As a level headed, pragmatic, soft-spoken woman, she proved the perfect foil to the ever-mercurial Dom. Throughout their marriage, she constantly brought his far-reaching goals down to earth. During the years that the bar struggled to survive on nightlife alone, Jan's highly successful, well-run kitchen—a true metaphor for herself—supported Dom's bar quietly from behind the scenes.

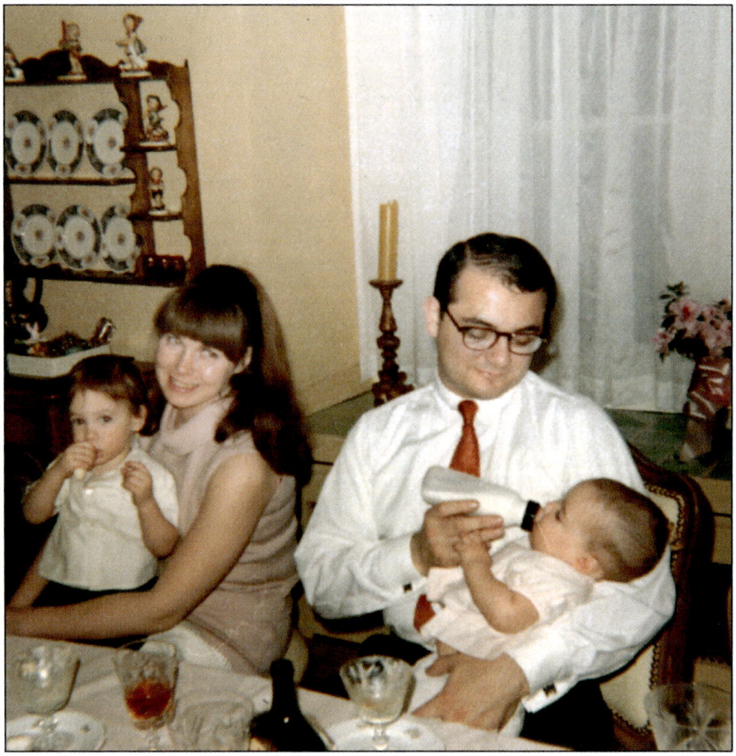

While putting off his rock 'n' roll endeavors, Dom chose more practical means of supporting his wife and five children. He dipped into several other business ventures, including a Squirrel Hill pizza joint, a mortgage company, and a window washing business, before returning once more to the Pittsburgh bar scene. His children (pictured below from left to right) Domenique, Caesar, Gina, Juliet, and Dante spent a quintessential childhood on Saline Street in Squirrel Hill, and all five eventually worked shifts at The Decade during their adolescence and college years.

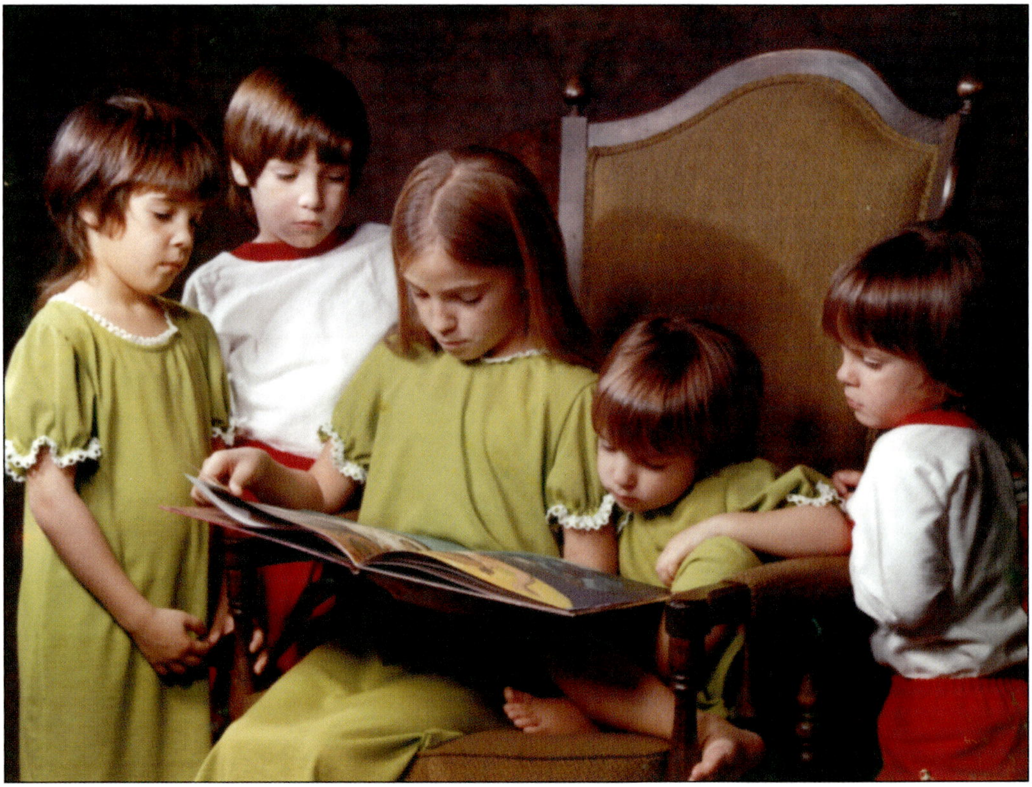

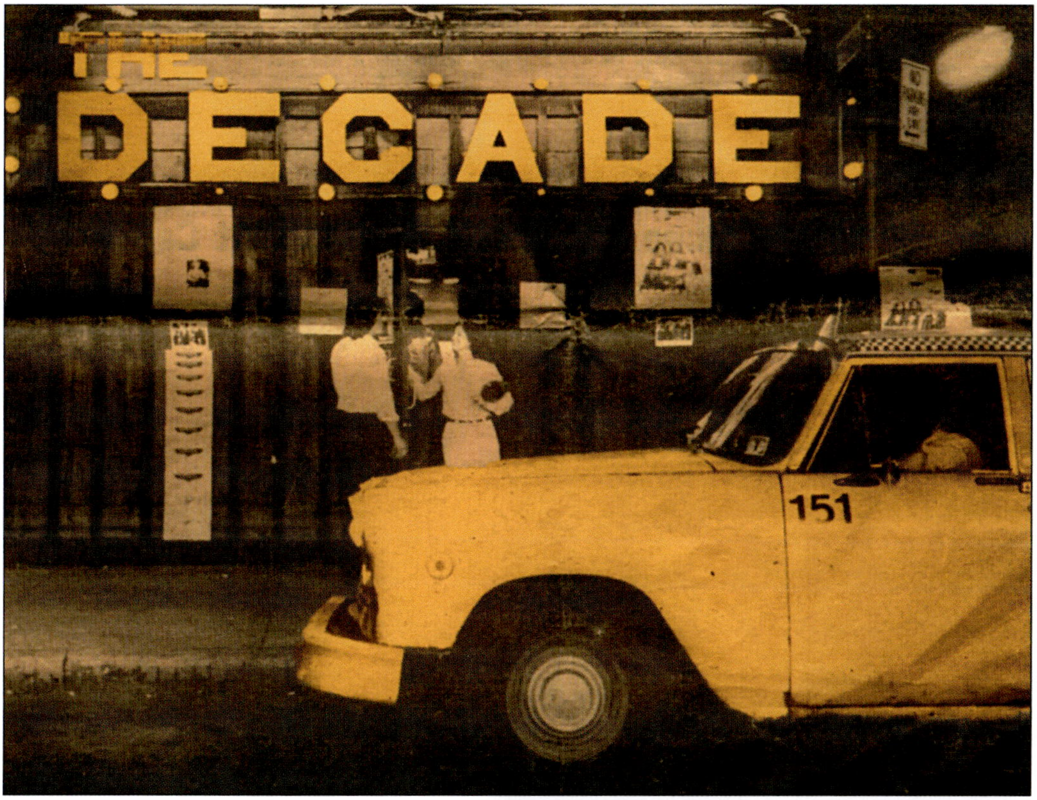

Dom and Jan, with the help of businessman Mario Noce, purchased the building on the corner of Atwood and Sennott Streets. It had lived several past lives as the Oaklander Hotel, other bars, and finally The Pizza Pub before it became The Decade. The couple knew the location would be ideal for what they intended to accomplish, as it was in the center of Oakland and on a corner; it couldn't get much better than that. (Courtesy of Gary Tweed.)

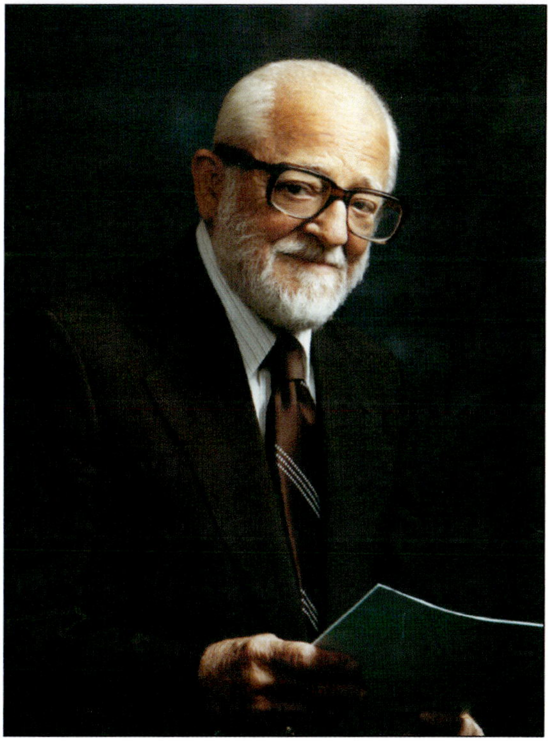

Dom's father, Dr. Dominic DiSilvio, chief of surgery at the Saint Margaret Memorial Hospital, had high hopes for the future of his eldest son. However, when Dom dropped out of graduate school to open a slew of rock 'n' roll bars, he had some doubts. When The Decade opened, Dr. DiSilvio, under the assumption that The Decade was less rock 'n' roll bar and more family-style restaurant, told Dom "I like your restaurant son, but it's a little loud." (Photograph by Elson Alexandre.)

Phone 621-4393

Specialities

Mug of homemade soup	.85
Mug of homemade chili	1.15

Salads

Italian salad w/ prov, ham & salami	2.25
Decade salad w/ prov, ham, salami amer. cheese, bacon & turkey.	3.15
Small tossed	1.10

choice of Russian, French
Italian or Roguefort dressing
(Roguefort extra)

Entrees

Spaghetti w/ 2 meatballs & salad	2.90
Spaghetti w/clam sauce & salad	2.90
Devonshire w/french fries & salad	4.30

Above items served
with garlic toast

Available Mon. thru Fri.
untill 7:00 p.m. only

THE DECADE
Bar & Restaurant 223 Atwood

Sandwiches

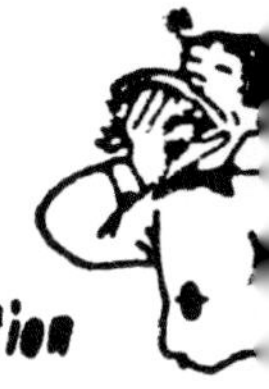

DECADE DAGWOODS

Try your own combination

Dagwood burger	1.7
Dagwood cheeseburger	1.9
Dagwood baconburger	2.1
Dagwood hot sausage	2.1
Dagwood tunafish	2.0
Dagwood meatloaf	1.8
Dagwood jumbo fish	2.1
Dagwood double egg	1.8
Dagwood prov, swiss or amer.	1.8
Dagwood ham	2.1
Dagwood bacon	2.1
Dagwood turkey	2.0
Dagwood salami	1.9
Dagwood capicola	2.1
Dagwood roast beef	2.1
Dagwood corned beef	2.5
Dagwood steak	2.1
Dagwood cheese steak	2.4
Dagwood ham or bacon & egg	2.4
Dagwood ham or bacon & cheese	2.4
Dagwood corned beef & egg	2.[illegible]

Lettuce, tomato, dressing and fr
are served on the Dagwoods...
other extra's - onions, pickles,
hot peppers, cheese, etc. 25¢

Please specify "hot or cold"

"try a blondie"

In keeping with the 1950s theme, Jan designed a menu featuring sandwiches called "Dagwoods," after the quirky husband from Chic Young's comic *Blondie*, which was popular at the time. The kitchen specialized mainly in sandwiches, but it also served spaghetti—an ode to Dom's Italian

In the ♡ of oakland

Side dishes

21 shrimp in a basket	3.15
French fried mushrooms	1.50
French fried onion rings	1.50
French Fries	.85
Cheeseballs	1.50

Pizza

	plain	extras	everything
4 cuts	1.45	.20 ea	2.60
8 cuts	2.80	.35 ea	4.80
16 cuts	5.20	.60 ea	8.50

Beverages

	small	large
Coffee	.35	.50
Iced tea	.35	.50
Soft drinks	.35	.50
Hot tea	.35	.50
Milk	.35	.50

Desserts

Homemade cheese cake	.90
w/strawberries	1.15

Ask your waitress for daily dessert specials

Thank you for your patronage

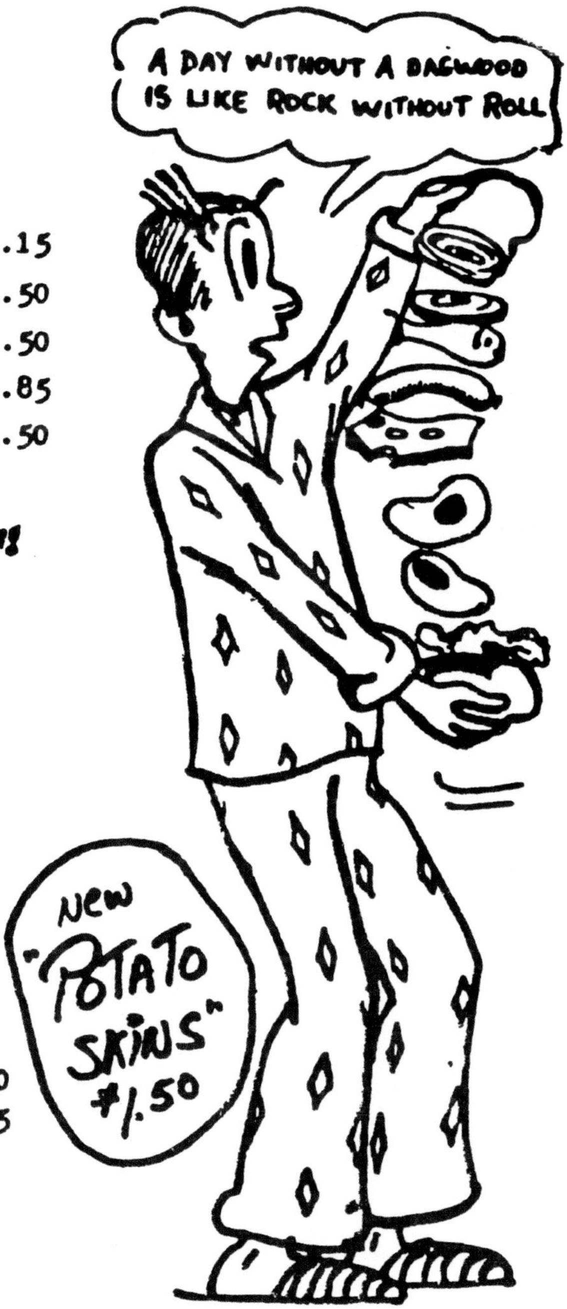

heritage—that Jan made with Dom's grandmother's recipe. Back in 1973, one could snag a burger and a soda for under $2. Later on, at the height of kitchen business, the staff put out as many as 250 lunches in a mere two-and-a-half hours.

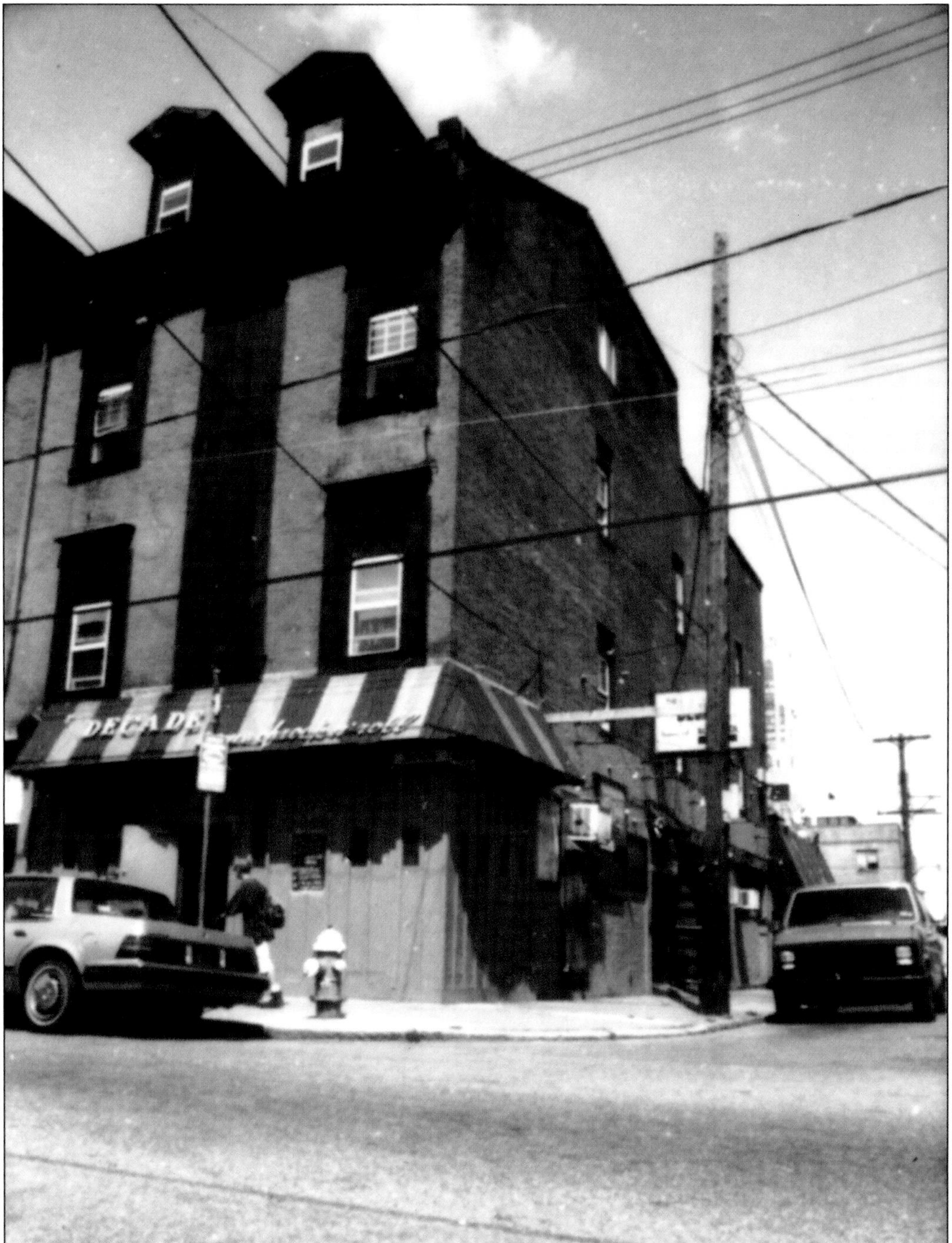

No one knew that the corner of Sennott and Atwood Streets would later be the birthplace of Pittsburgh rock 'n' roll. It was a fluke timed perfectly. The man who took this photograph, Iron City Houserockers' roadie Jay Flory, encapsulates the serendipity of it all: "It was a Greek tragedy; everything about the human condition was at The Decade. Everyone was entranced by youth, and it was a microcosmic moment in time that can't be repeated. If you weren't there, you'll never understand it fully. It was home. It was personal. It was irreplaceable."

Two

The Pittsburgh Music Scene

Without a stage upon which to practice their original music, many local bands found themselves in a rut. Creativity was at a stalemate as Pittsburgh musicians were expected to churn out Top-40 covers during their live performances to appease blue-collar audiences. One of the earliest bands that broke out of this mold was Diamond Reo. The "Diamonds" were originally comprised of Frank Cruzi, Bubs McKeg, Norman Nardini, and Robbie Johns; Pittsburgh guitar legend Warren King was added later. In 1974, the trio of King, Nardini, and Czuri began writing original music for the band but had difficulty finding a venue that condoned this display of creativity.

As soon as he could, Dom began booking live acts at his neighborhood bar, but he generally stuck to local bands and only hosted them on the weekends. He and Jan advertised in the *Pitt News* and made phone calls to bands they found through the newspapers. It was primarily a grassroots operation slowly gaining popularity through word of mouth until bands began to come in on their own. Two of these initial acts were The Neighborhoods and Corbin Hanner.

Things seemed to be gelling for the gig-thirsty musicians and the performer-hungry bar owners. Unfortunately, life seemed to have other plans for Dom and Jan. Just as live music started to take shape at The Decade, Dom spent a year-long hiatus in the slammer, and in doing so, he left Jan in charge of running both their household and their bar. Considering the unnecessary pressure that booking bands would cause Jan, Dom chose to put his live music aspirations on hold for just one more year. However, Jan defied his expectations and began booking acts on her own. As it turns out, several of the bands she booked without Dom ended up being some of The Decade's most favored acts; namely, Gravel and the Iron City Houserockers.

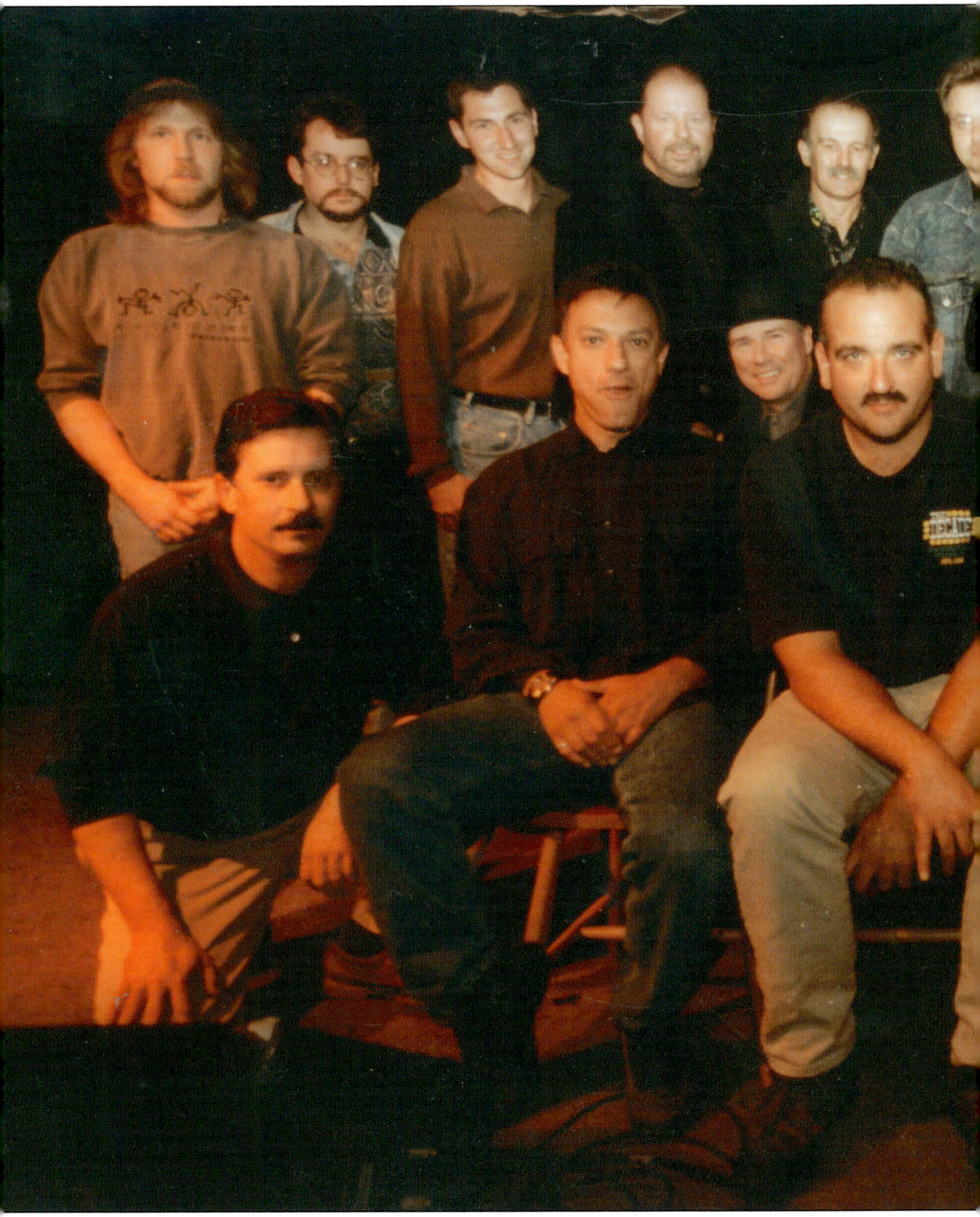

An important component of the Pittsburgh music scene was the interchangeability of musicians among the local bands. The scene was comprised of many great performers who would rotate between bands throughout their careers. During the time in which The Decade was around,

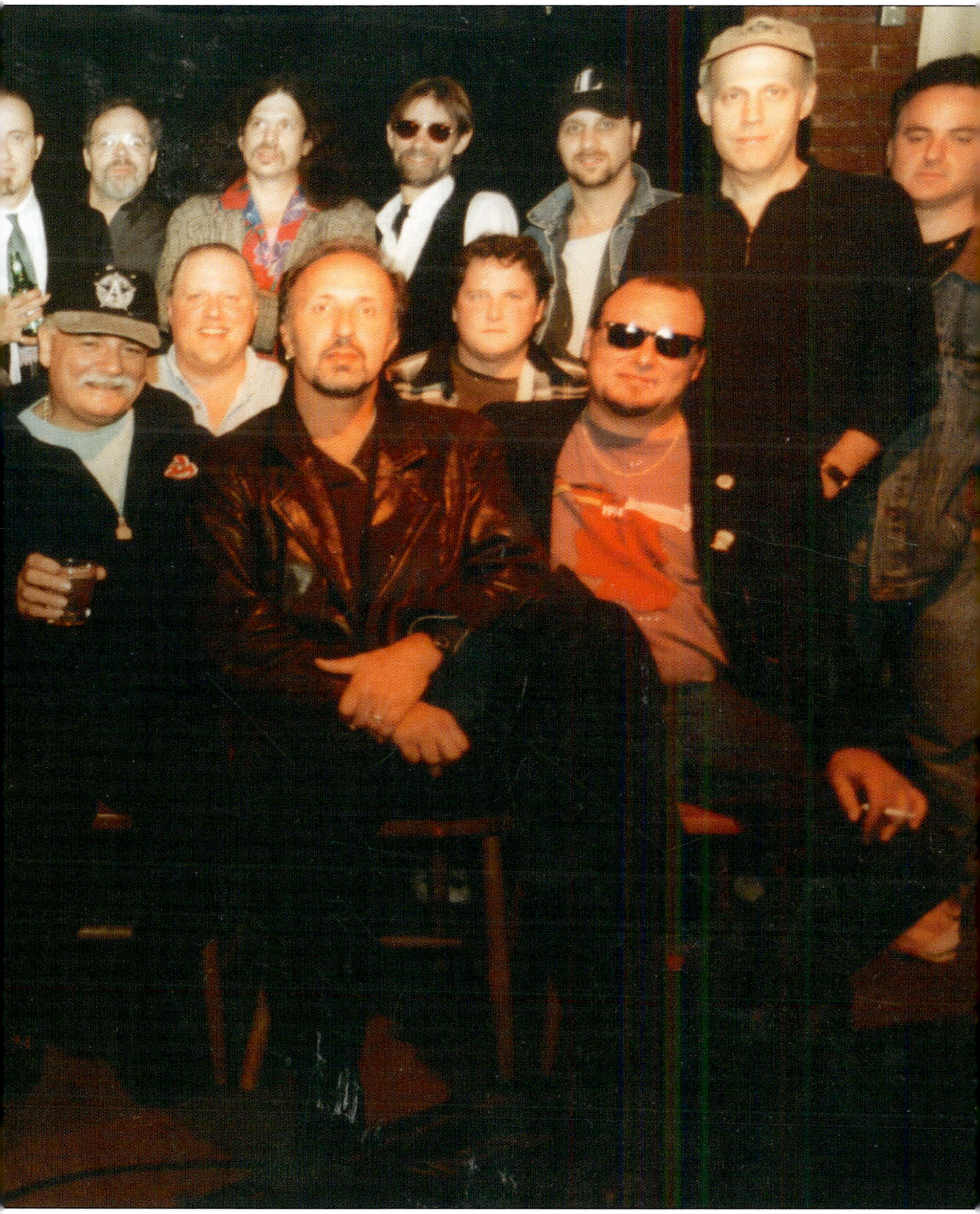

Pittsburgh was fortunate enough to have four bands with record deals as well as a plethora of other great bands. Pictured here are many of the musicians who made up the local music scene, as well as some fans at a Decade reunion hosted at Buffalo Blues.

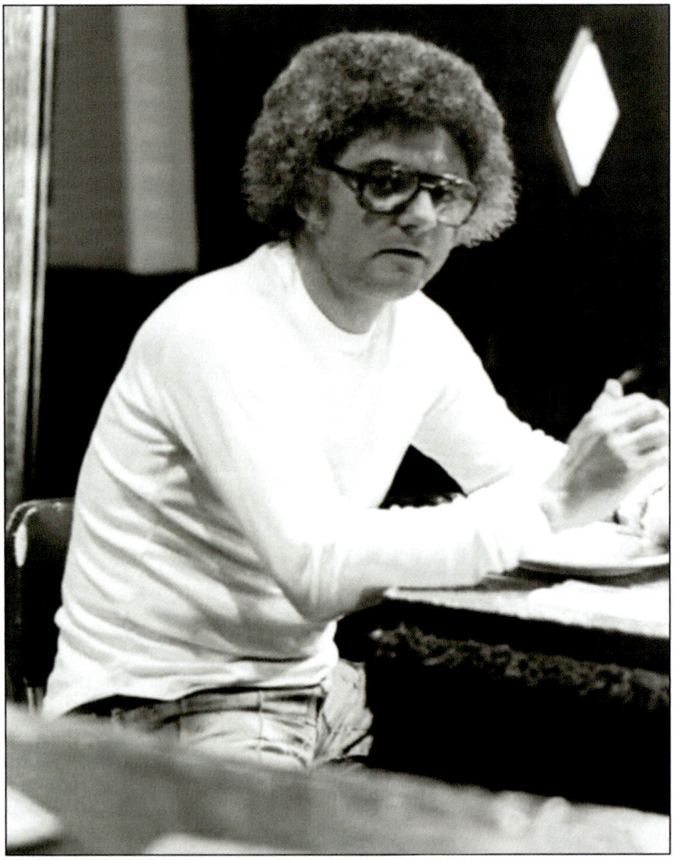

Very shortly after Dom (left) and Jan (below) decided to start booking live, local music acts, Dom went away on a year-long vacation paid for by the state. The year was 1977, and Jan was left in charge of a prepubescent business venture as well as five prepubescent children. Dom held some concerns that booking bands would be too difficult for his wife to handle on her own. Contrarily, Jan booked several of The Decade's most popular bands during the time that he was "in the can." The image below is of Jan in the small Decade office. It was a cramped spot, tucked away under the stairs, where she made menus, booked bands, and handled payroll. Dom always preferred to work at the bar where he could make his phone calls and handle business amidst the chaos.

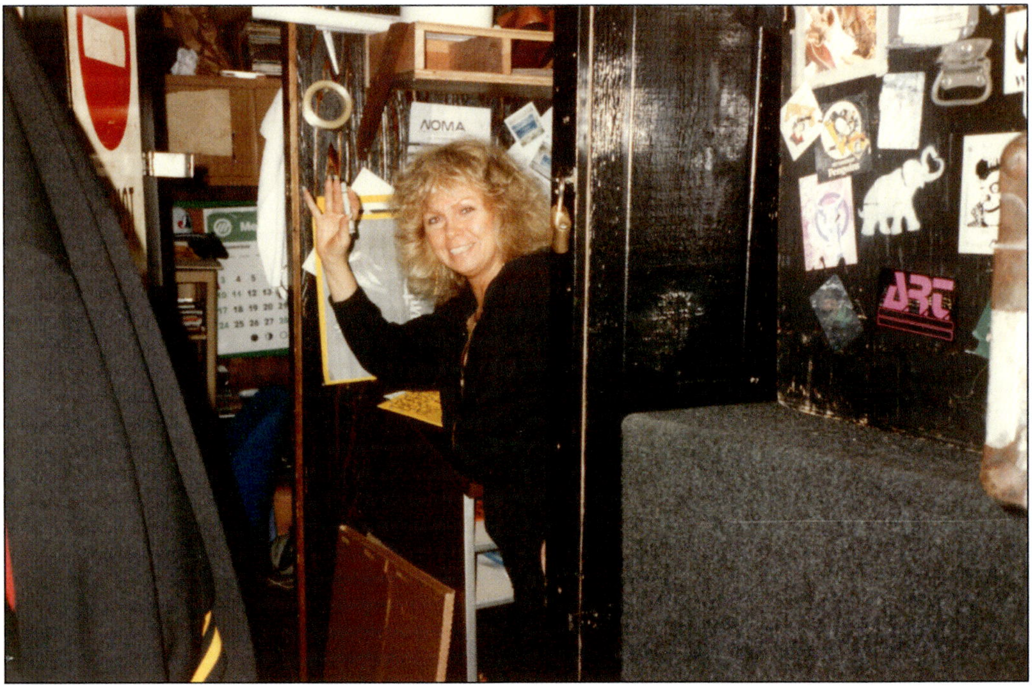

Decade regular Dewey Gurall accurately sets the scene of this chapter in his Decade memoir: "Feverishly moving glasses out of the way so they wouldn't get crushed by a table-walking Warren King, while he played another jaw-dropping extended guitar solo on 'Peter Gunn' during a hot Silencers gig. Or Norman Nardini railing against everything from ex-girlfriends to politicians to Freddie Mercury while the Tigers—the thumping bass of Ray Gunn, Whitey Cooper's drums and exceptional backing vocals, and most of all, the outstanding guitar of Paul Shook—rocked hard behind him." This was The Decade's local music scene.

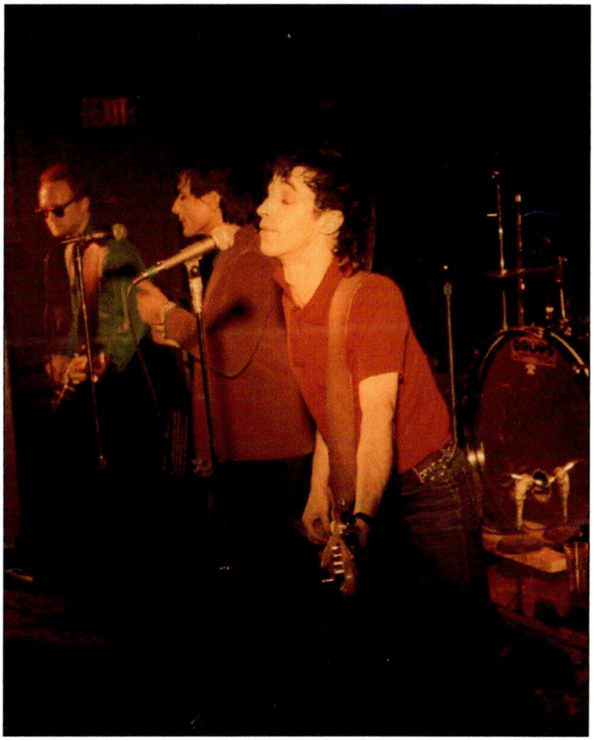

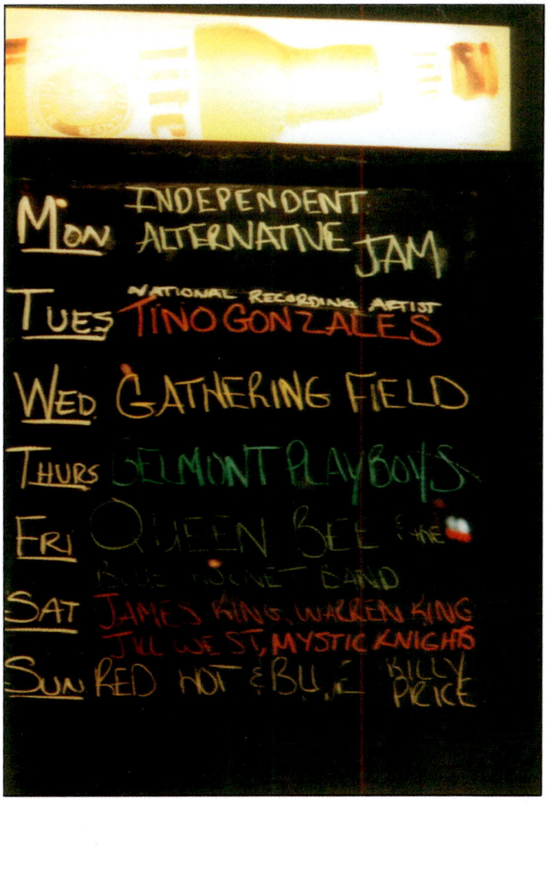

The chart that hung on The Decade wall was updated weekly to let fans know when their favorite band was playing. However, there was a general pattern; for several years at a time, a specific band would have a monopoly over a certain night. For a long time, both Thursdays and Saturdays were held by what could be thought of as The Decade house band: the Iron City Houserockers.

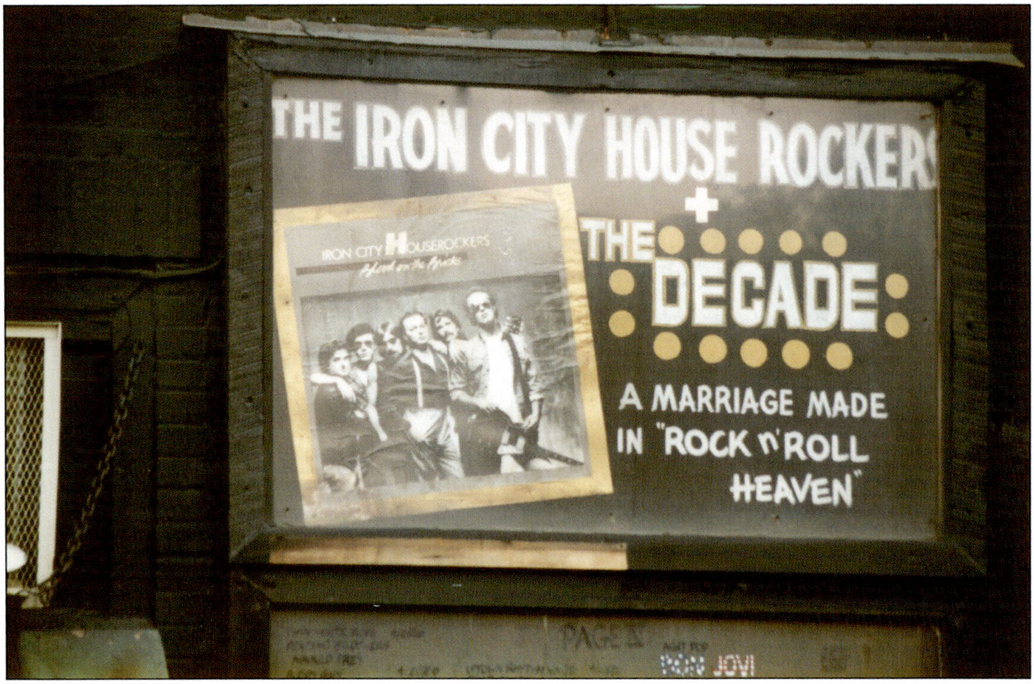

The Iron City Houserockers began their career in an upward battle, striving to play original music while holding a regular gig at Gazebo; they intended to record original music instead of playing covers. When the Brick Alley Band (what the Houserockers went by back then) walked into The Decade and performed for Jan one fateful day, she knew she had struck gold. "Dom will love you because you're so greasy," Joe Grushecky, the guitarist and lead vocalist of the band, remembers her saying. Jan knew it was the perfect fit for their bar; Grushecky knew it was the perfect fit for the band. It was a marriage made in rock 'n' roll heaven.

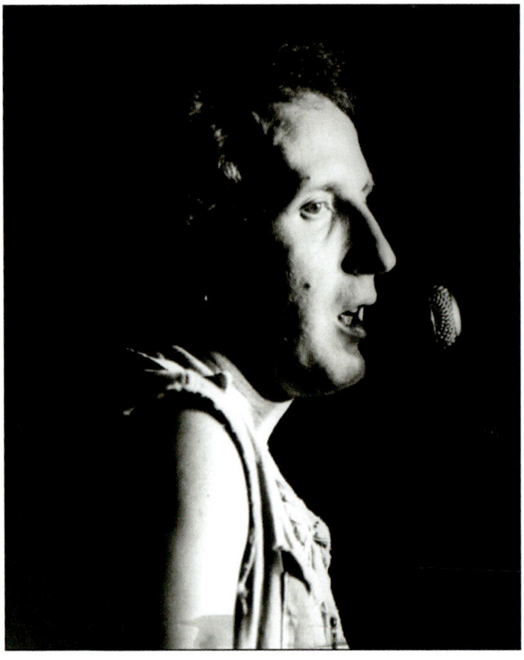

Steve Popavich signed the Houserockers to MCA Records through a company called Cleveland International. At this point, the Houserockers were playing regularly at The Decade on Thursday nights, recording new songs on Fridays in Cleveland and returning to Pittsburgh for their Saturday night show; they were motivated, ambitious, and a little bit crazy. In 1978, Grushecky even postponed his honeymoon due to a previously-scheduled gig at The Decade. (Courtesy of Raymond Wuslich.)

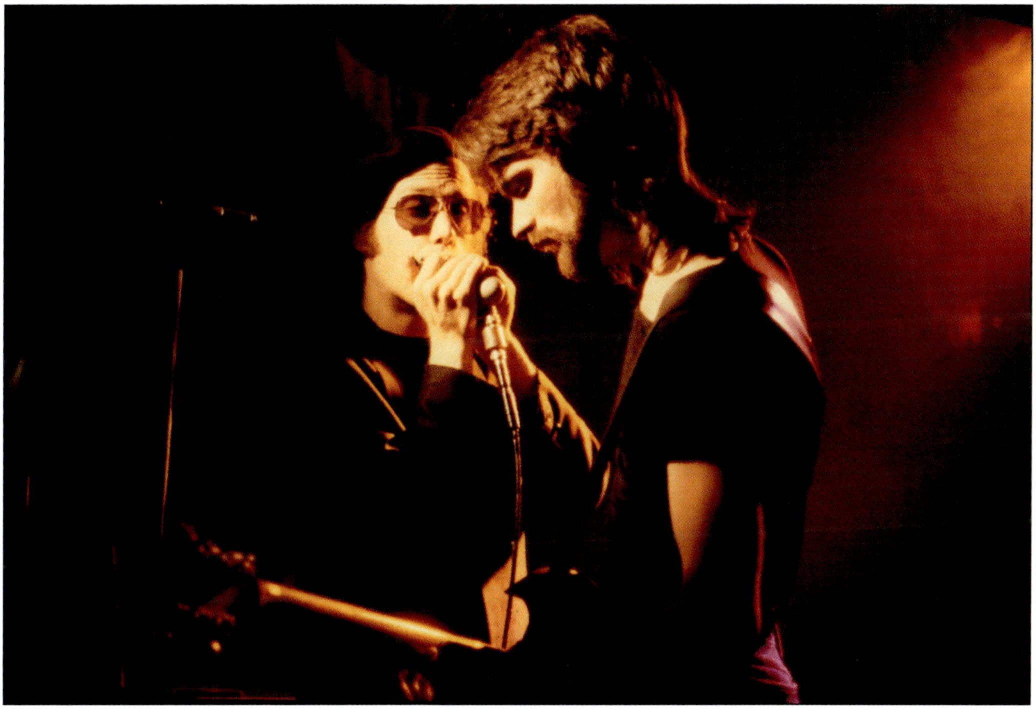

The combination of The Decade and the Houserockers proved a perfect storm; everything came together in a culmination of mutual respect and affection. As far as they went and as popular as they got, the Houserockers never denied any of Dom's requests. Grushecky equates playing The Decade to playing a home game, further claiming that "nothing could be as good," as he has not hung out in a bar since. The Decade embodies the youth years of the Iron City Houserockers; it allowed the band to become who they are, and it gave their music a point of view. (Courtesy of Mike Chedwick.)

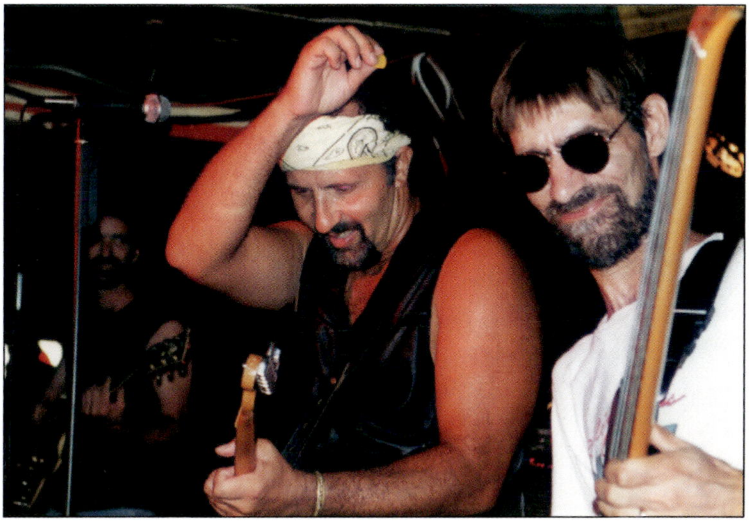

The Iron City Houserockers continue to play today. The lineup that regularly played The Decade included Joe Grushecky (guitar and lead vocals), Art Nardini (bass), Ned Rankin (drums), Gilbert Snyder (keyboards), Marc Reisman (harmonica), and Gary Scalese (guitar). Grushecky and Nardini are pictured here.

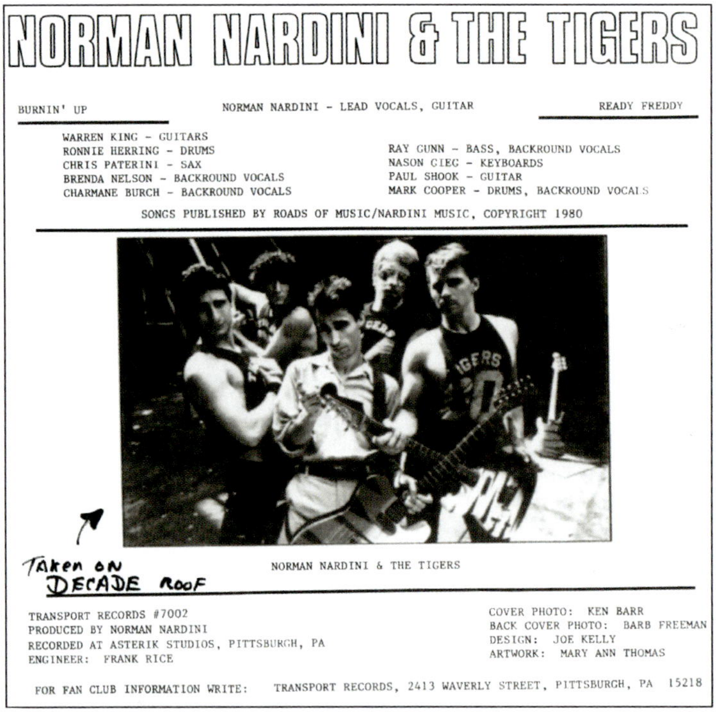

NORMAN NARDINI & THE TIGERS

BURNIN' UP

NORMAN NARDINI - LEAD VOCALS, GUITAR

READY FREDDY

WARREN KING - GUITARS
RONNIE HERRING - DRUMS
CHRIS PATERINI - SAX
BRENDA NELSON - BACKROUND VOCALS
CHARMANE BURCH - BACKROUND VOCALS

RAY GUNN - BASS, BACKROUND VOCALS
NASON GIEG - KEYBOARDS
PAUL SHOOK - GUITAR
MARK COOPER - DRUMS, BACKROUND VOCALS

SONGS PUBLISHED BY ROADS OF MUSIC/NARDINI MUSIC, COPYRIGHT 1980

Taken on DECADE Roof

NORMAN NARDINI & THE TIGERS

TRANSPORT RECORDS #7002
PRODUCED BY NORMAN NARDINI
RECORDED AT ASTERIK STUDIOS, PITTSBURGH, PA
ENGINEER: FRANK RICE

COVER PHOTO: KEN BARR
BACK COVER PHOTO: BARB FREEMAN
DESIGN: JOE KELLY
ARTWORK: MARY ANN THOMAS

FOR FAN CLUB INFORMATION WRITE: TRANSPORT RECORDS, 2413 WAVERLY STREET, PITTSBURGH, PA 15218

Norman "Norm" Nardini played regularly with his band, the Tigers, which initially included Robbie Johns and Warren King with drummer Derrick Edwards and bassist Ray Gunn; however, Warren eventually left the band and began playing with Frank Czuri and the Silencers, which led Nardini to reform his band. The new lineup included Altoona-born Nason Gieg on keyboards and bass, the "very handsome" Paul Shook on a left-handed guitar, Ray Gunn on bass, and Whitey Cooper on drums. Nardini was known to surround himself with hunks. (Photograph by Ken Barr.)

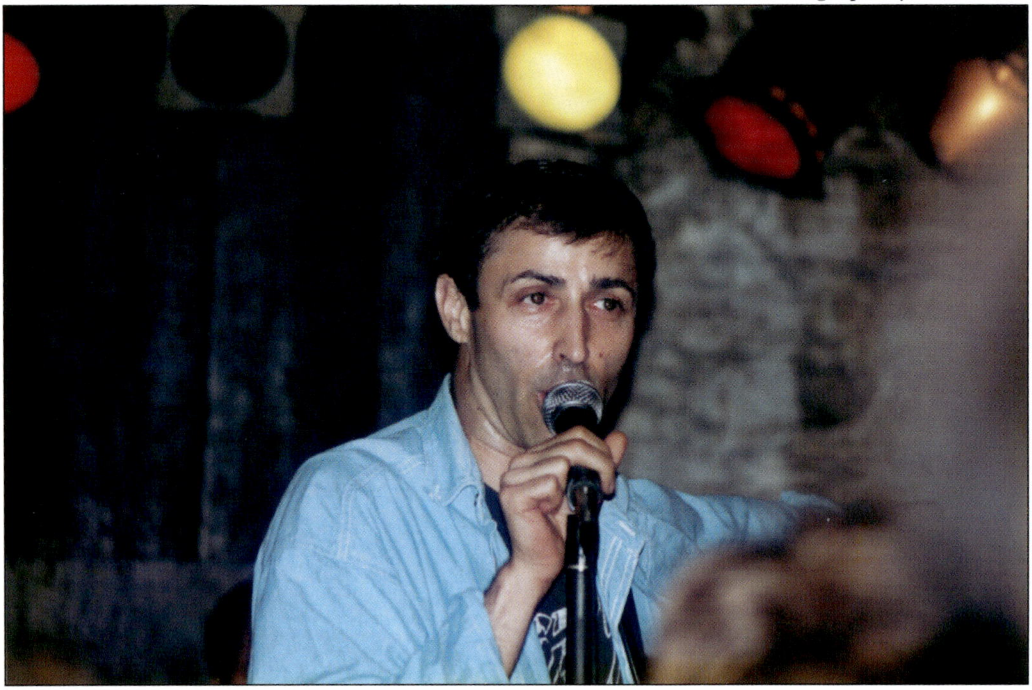

Along with his fellow Pittsburgh musicians, Nardini agrees that The Decade helped his career flourish. It gave him a chance to compete on stage with national acts in front of the Pittsburgh audience. He reminisces, "We were young and beautiful and we owned the world." The Decade was the "official headquarters for Pittsburgh music;" everyone wanted to play there. "But local color," Nardini claims, that's what The Decade had in abundance.

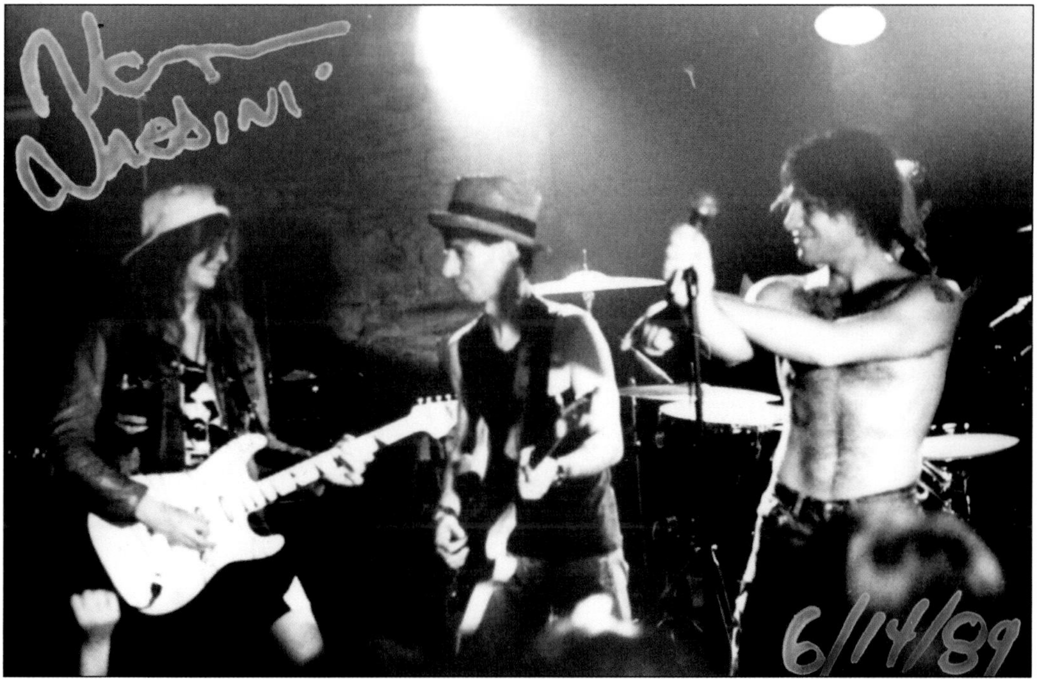

One of Norm's most memorable moments occurred one night when he was not performing but just hanging around the bar with his bandmates. Nardini spotted an attractive girl and made eyes with her before she growled, "Nardini," in a suspiciously deep voice. The attractive girl turned out to be a man and finished her conversation with Norm by requesting a kiss. One never knew who they would run into at the bar. Norm is pictured above with rock legend Bon Jovi and below with fellow Decade favorite Billy Price.

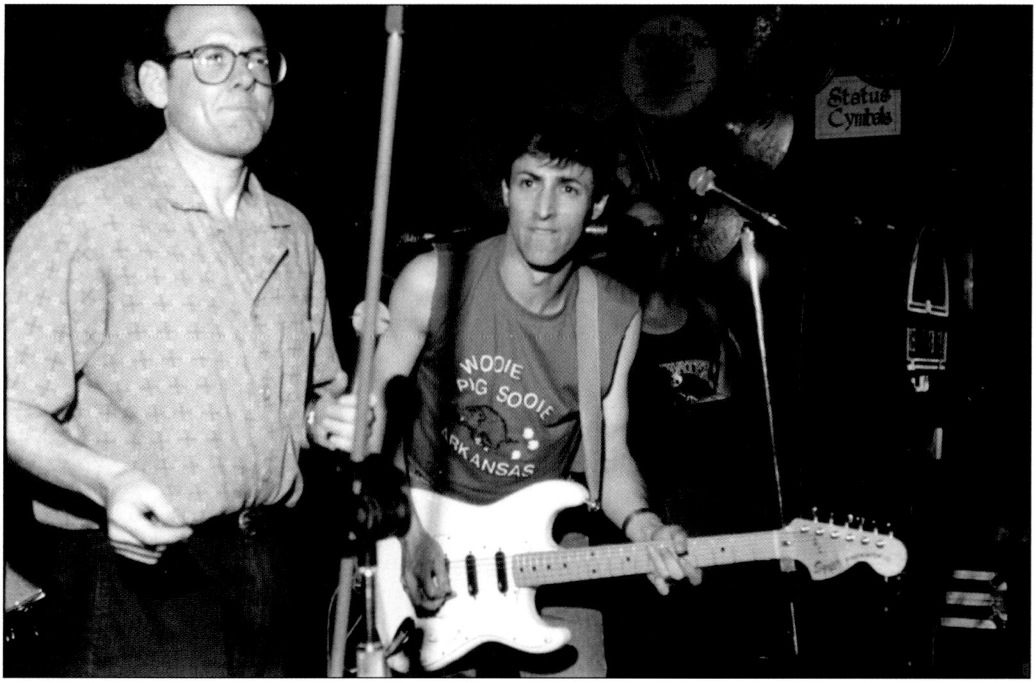

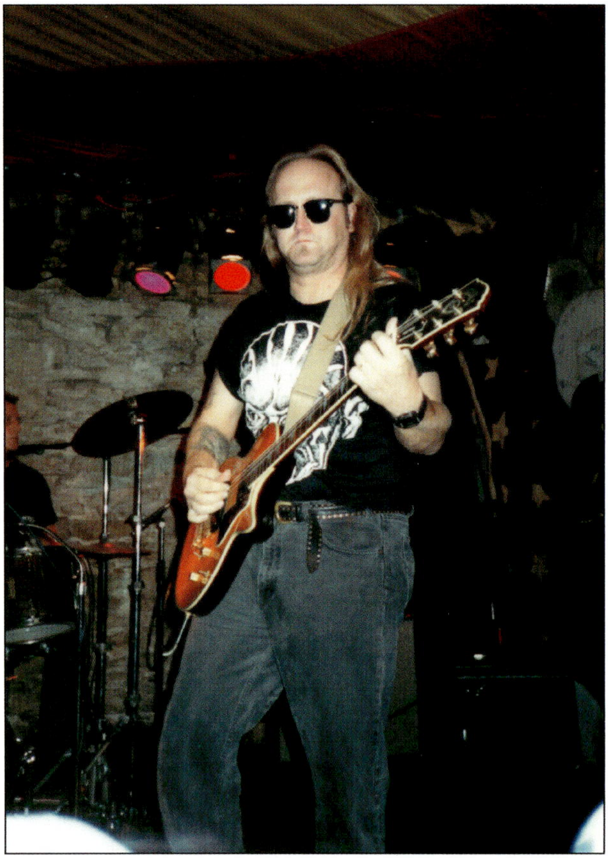

As far as Dom is concerned, Warren King was one of the top-three guitarists to ever play at The Decade and, in his opinion, to ever come out of Pittsburgh. As legend has it, the higher he got, the better he played. King was the type of guy who would rather turn his shirt inside out than wash it; he couldn't care less about keeping up appearances, but in The Decade, he was a legend. Unfortunately, King passed away from cancer on January 29, 2010. "The Kingfish" is missed dearly and remembered well for his time spent playing in a plethora of Pittsburgh bands, including Diamond Reo, Norm Nardini and the Tigers, the Silencers, Red Hot and Blue, and the Mystic Knights.

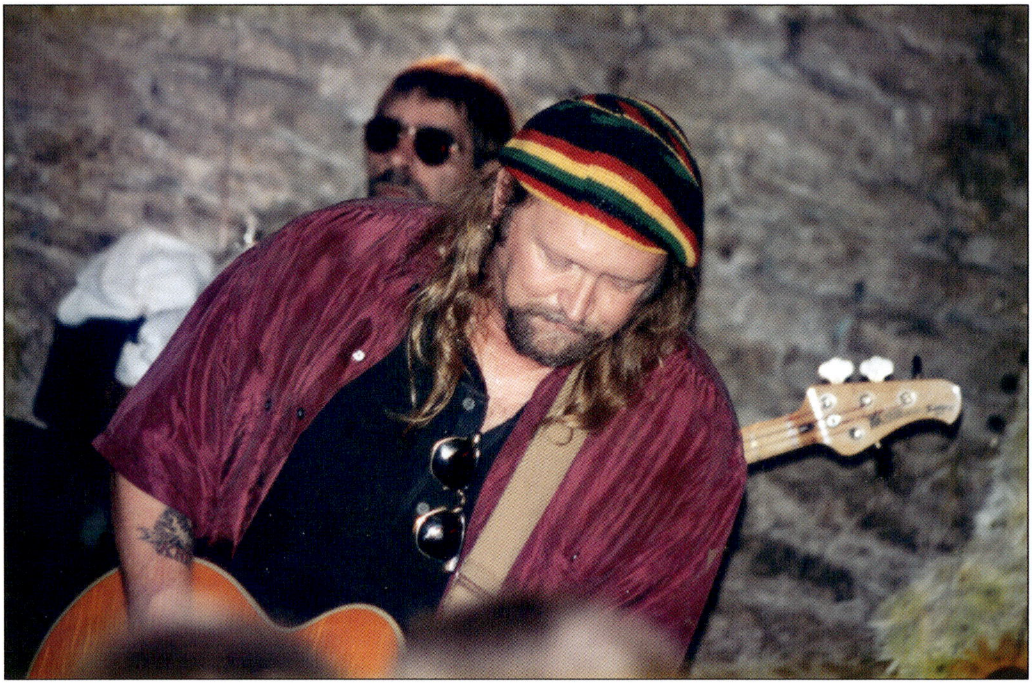

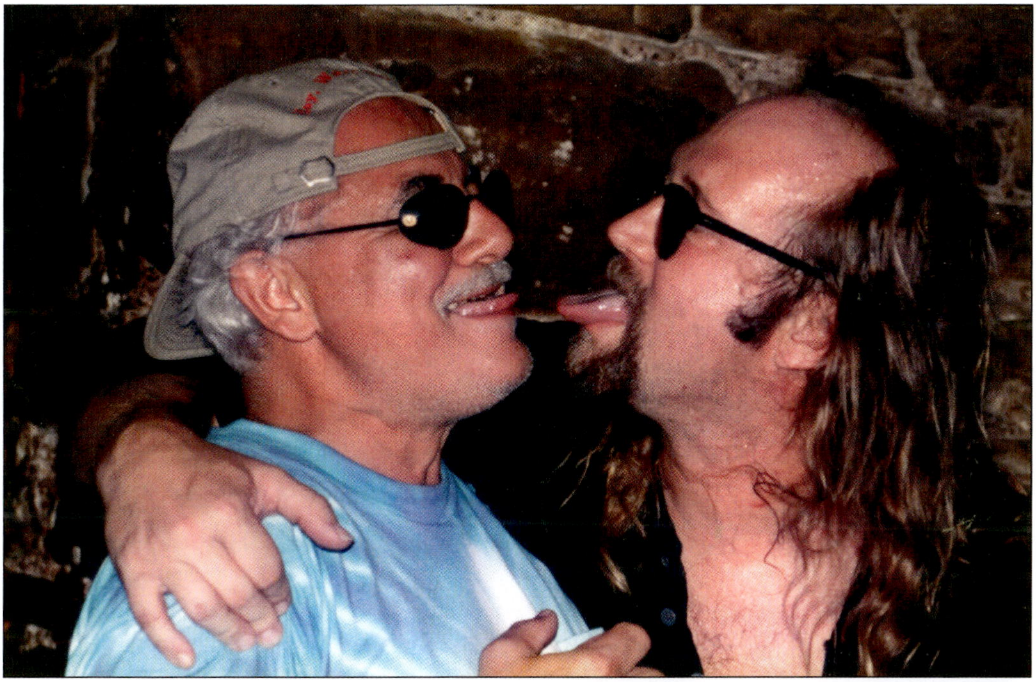

Many of the Pittsburgh musicians remember King fondly. Norm Nardini recalls that he "had as much fire as any guitar player I've ever seen in my life, and I've seen them all; you couldn't take your eyes off of him." An avid fan of Warren's antics, Dom remembers many wild moments with the guitarist. For example, a specific radio interview for WYEP during which he and Warren drank an entire fifth of Jack Daniels—apparently the interview was very in-depth. On the closing night of The Decade, King gave Dom his white guitar (right) claiming he would have given him his wife if he could have.

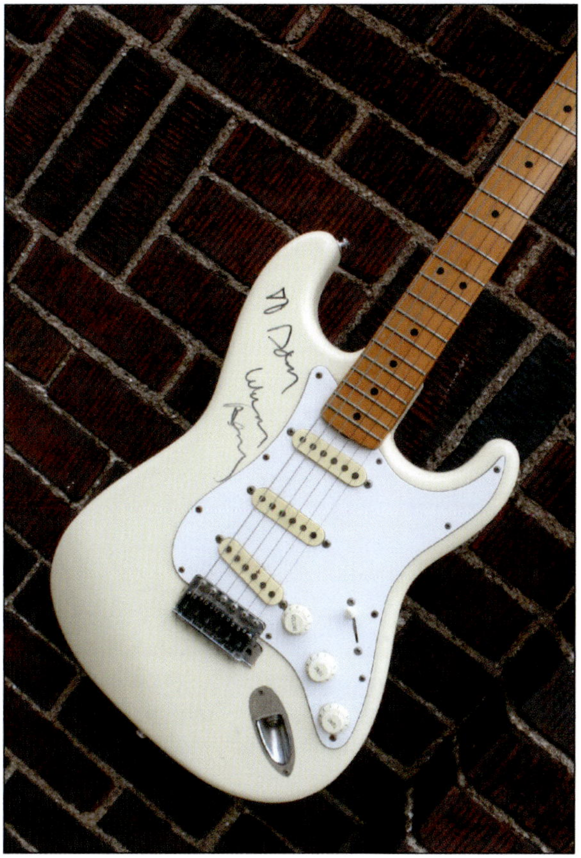

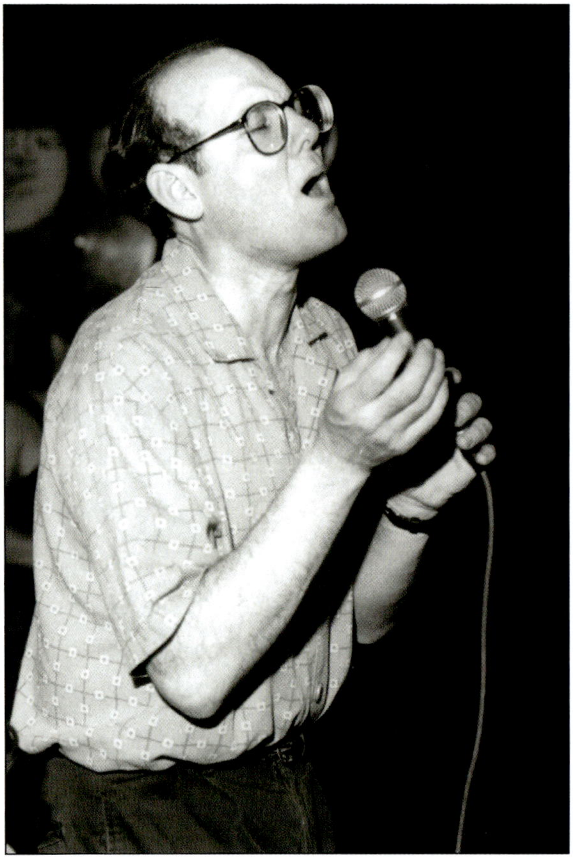

Billy Price remembers his time on the Decade stage fondly. It wasn't like performing anywhere else. He describes it as "funky" and noisy, as the crowd was always having a good time, even if it wasn't because of the band. The audience was situated right in the performers' lap, so there was a real ability to connect with them. Price played every Sunday night. He likens playing at The Decade to playing in a subway depot: "full of constant activity and life."

Price's manager Tom Carrico thought to invite R&B/blues singer Otis Clay (pictured below with Price) to play some shows with Billy Price and the Keystone Rhythm Band. In addition to being huge fans of Clay, the Keystone Rhythm Band had been performing several of his songs at the time. After plenty of convincing, Clay decided to play with them and went on to play many more shows over the years. He ended up playing with Billy Price at The Decade on an especially notable night (see chapter five).

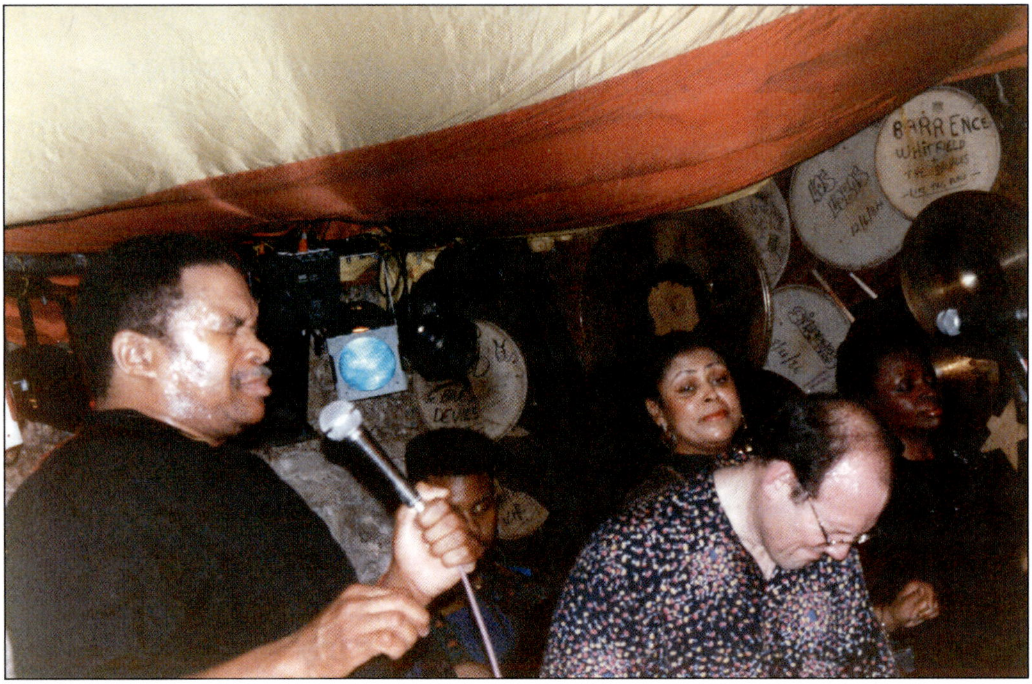

The first time the Silencers were scheduled to play The Decade was in August during one of Dom's vacations to the Jersey Shore. The day before Dom left, he was packing (one of his least favorite activities) when the band's keyboardist Dennis "D.T." Takos called and cancelled the gig. Dom said he was not going to threaten them, but if they did not play, he might set their van on fire; the Silencers took the risk and cancelled the gig anyway. Dom did not burn their van, but did harbor resentment, so the next two shows the Silencers played were pro bono. It did not take long before the cantankerous bar owner fell in love with the group and completely forgot his arson plot. The group included Frank Czuri (vocals), Warren King (guitar), Ron Byrd Foster (drums), Dennis Takos (keyboards), and Michael Pella and Michael Cercone (bass). (Below, courtesy of Mike Chedwick.)

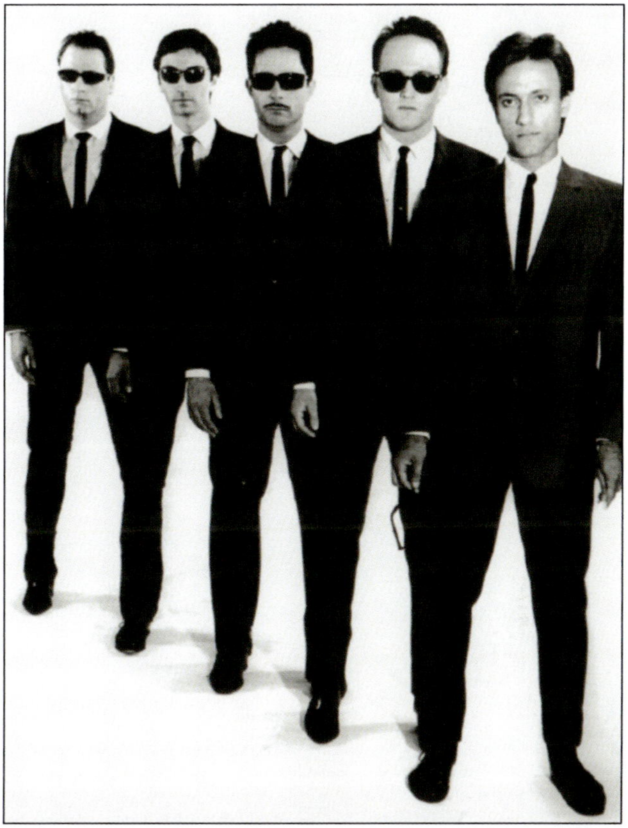

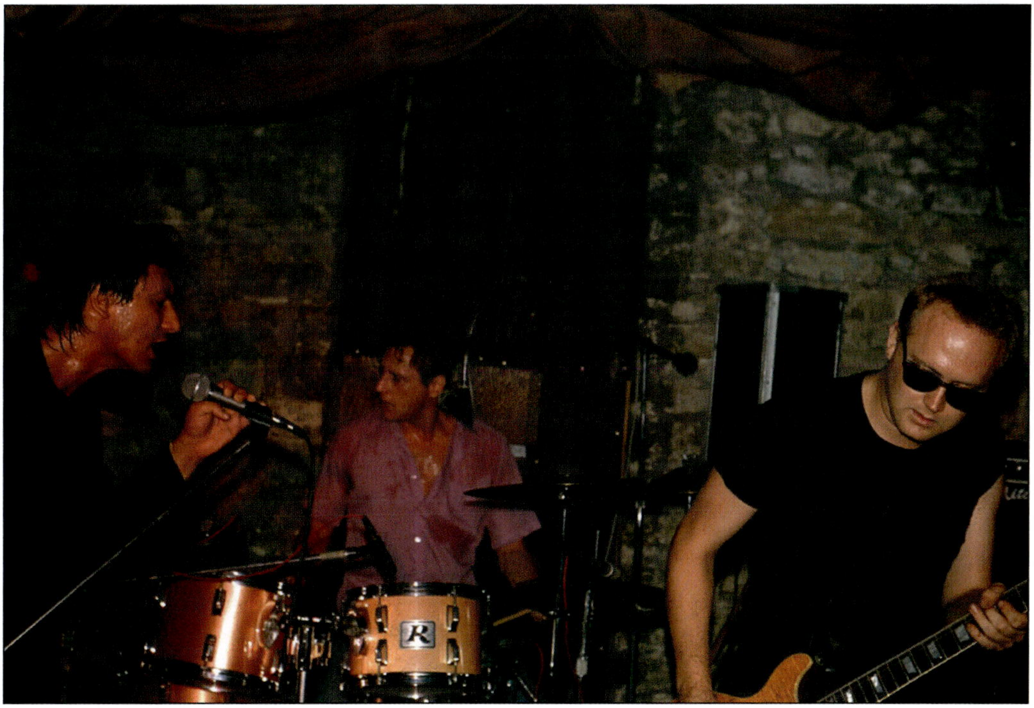

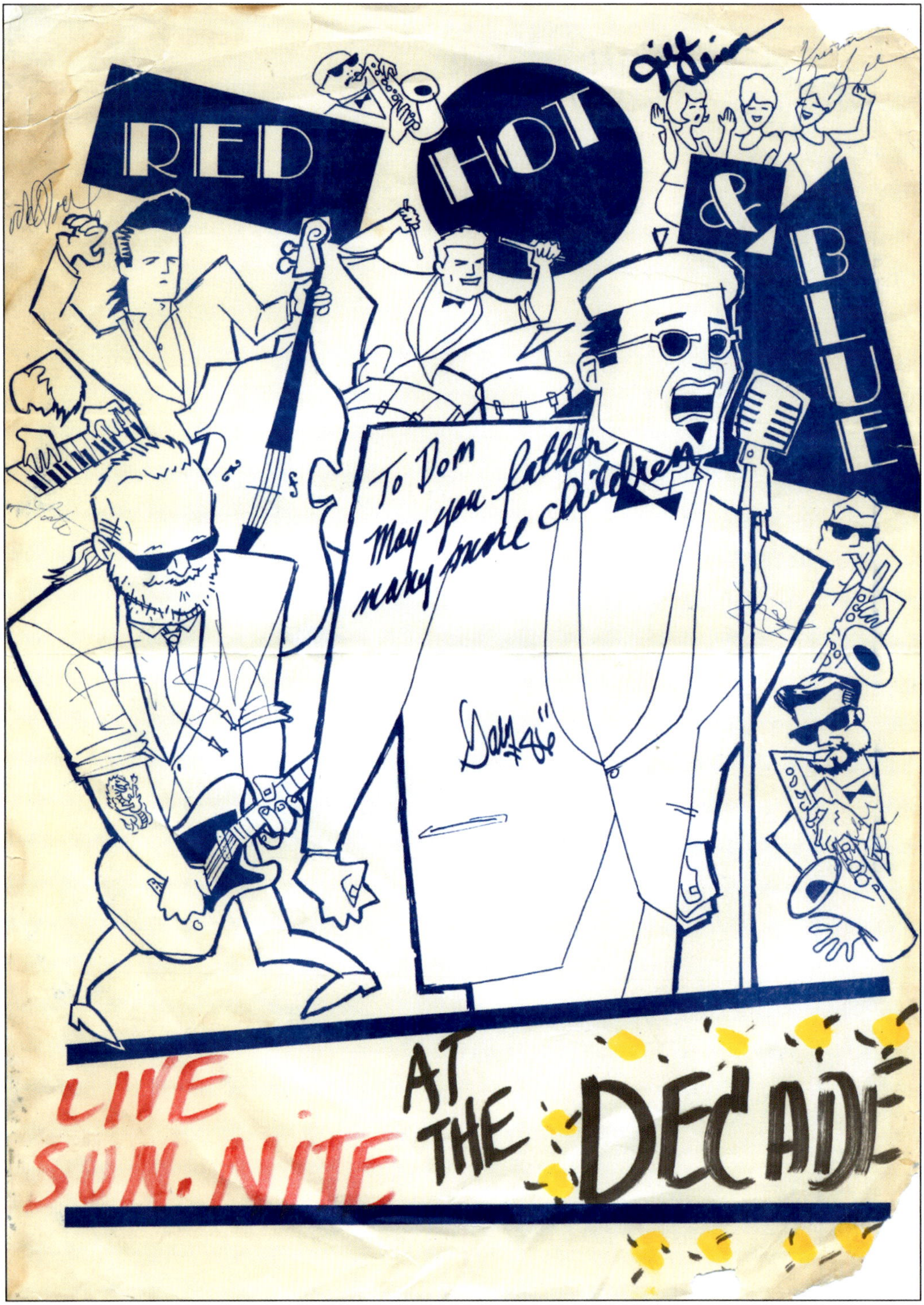

Red Hot and Blue was comprised of lead singer Gary Belloma, guitarist Warren King, bass guitarist Mick O'Toole, drummer Ronnie Foster, and saxophonist Robbie Klein. Belloma's "pure sound" made him one of Dom's favorites; the two had a very loyal mutual relationship.

Eddie and the Otters formed one night at Chatham College to entertain a toga party. They soon became the Peter's Pub house band until, as front man Ed Townsend puts it, "Someone better came along to take our place." Townsend describes his band's style as a "simulation of *Animal House*;" they took themselves lightly and aimed to please the crowds who wanted to drink, have a good time, and dance to songs they knew. They found that outlet in the community that ran on "Iron City and Jack Daniels" at The Decade.

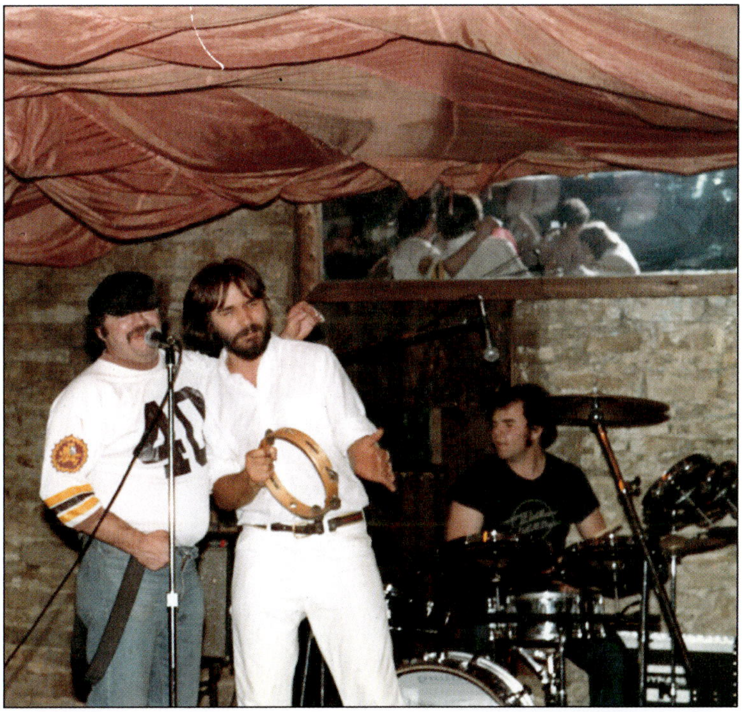

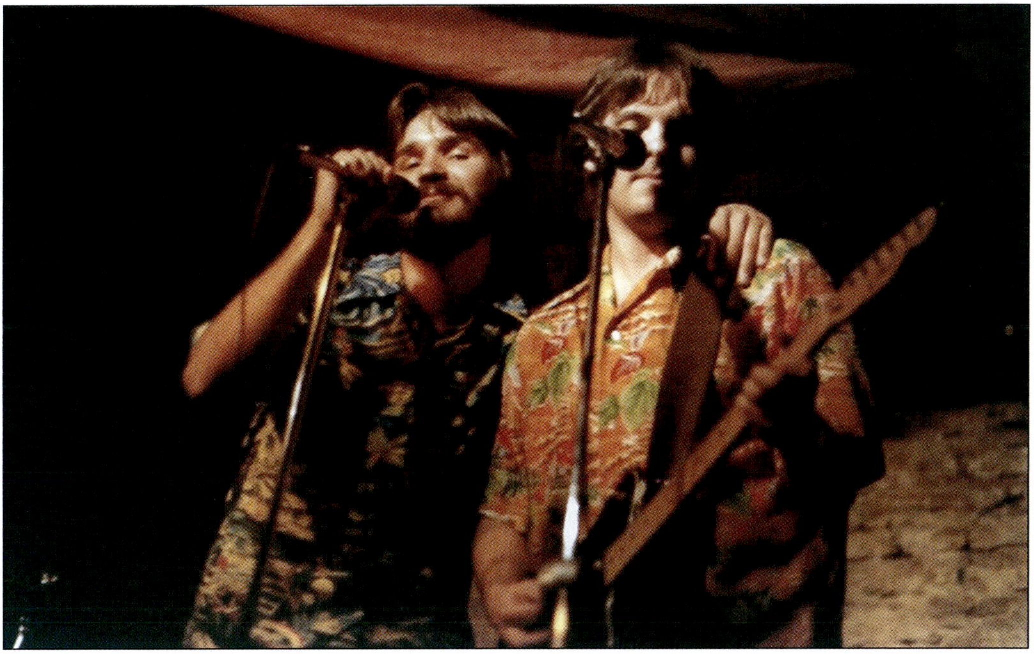

Ed Townsend (left) and Doug "Deluxe" Gebhard (right), from the fun-loving band Eddie and the Otters, consistently graced the stage. Other Otters included Jim "Jimmy Ramone" Spitznagel, Jim "Surfin'" Bird, Mike Kolesar, Steve Fisher, Billy O'Connor, Diane Ford, and Jonathan Neuhaus. Whenever Townsend was not jamming out on The Decade's stage, he was actually in the seminary on track to become a minister. Today, both Gebhard and Townsend are Presbyterian ministers. Go figure.

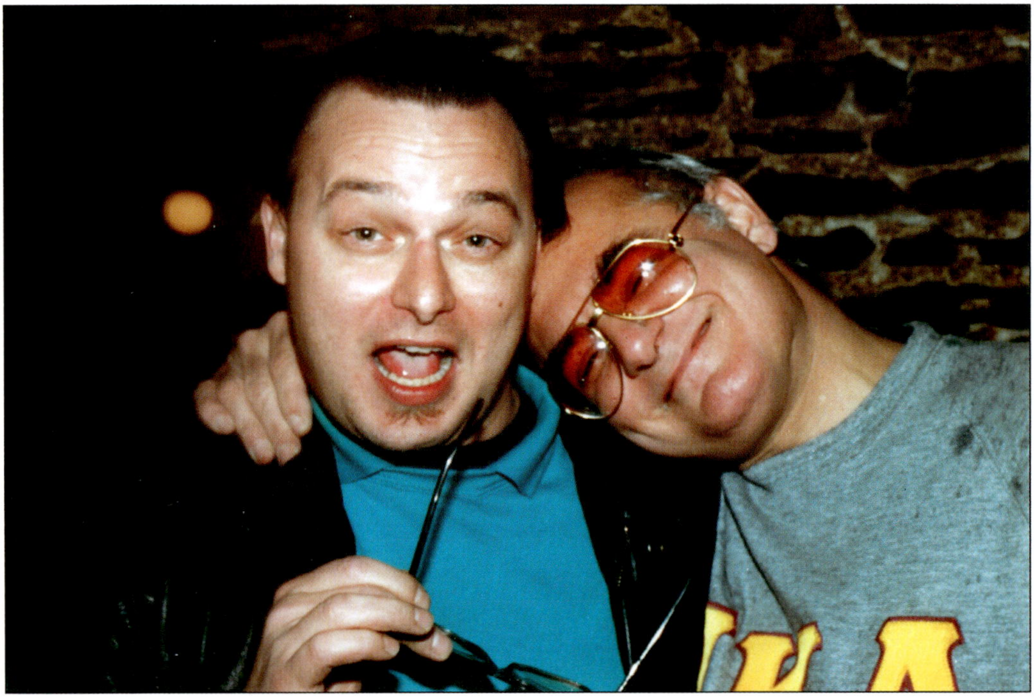

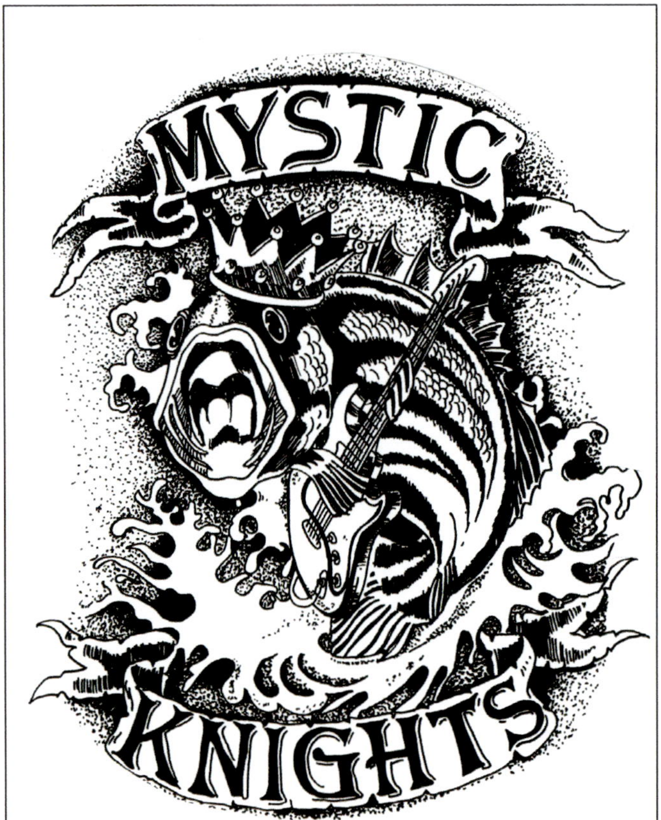

In one of many concerted efforts to redesign Monday nights at the bar, Dom decided to create an all-star Decade band with the help of his good friend guitarist Warren King. Musicians from several different Pittsburgh bands left their respective groups to play in Dom's Monday night experiment, which would eventually be known as the Mystic Knights of the Sea—or the Mystic Knights for short—and the members included Bryan Bassett, Warren King, Gil Snyder, Ron "Byrd" Foster, Chizmo Charles, and Zack Wiesinger. Bassett, of Wild Cherry and Foghat, was thrilled to get the chance to play alongside one of his musical heroes: Warren King. Bassett loved performing in the all-star band because The Decade was "the center of the Pittsburgh musical universe; when bands weren't playing, that's where they went to see other bands."

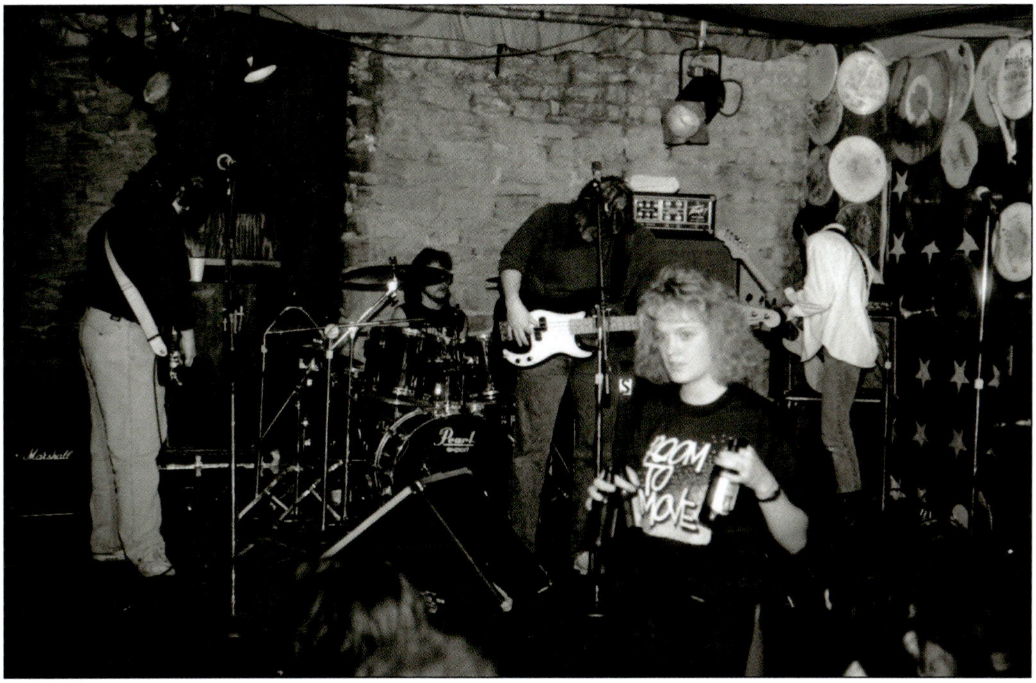

Don Czek, frontman for Room to Move, was only around 18 years old when he started listening at the door of The Decade and pestering doorman Danny Means and Dom's son, back bartender Dante DiSilvio, incessantly asking what it took to play at the bar. Ironically, he was too young to get in the The Decade, despite being the same age as the bouncer and bartender. Dante decided to take advantage of Czek's perseverance and gave him a trial gig at the DiSilvio kids' Halloween party. Room to Move set up amps in the college students' house, and the performance was so loud that the police came to shut the party down. Dom's son Caesar, the owner of the house, was dressed as a bee and hid on the roof. The police engaged in a zealous search for "the bee," eventually finding and booking him along with all of the other boys. This odd event did in fact pave the way for many Room to Move gigs at The Decade. (Courtesy of Kurt Weber.)

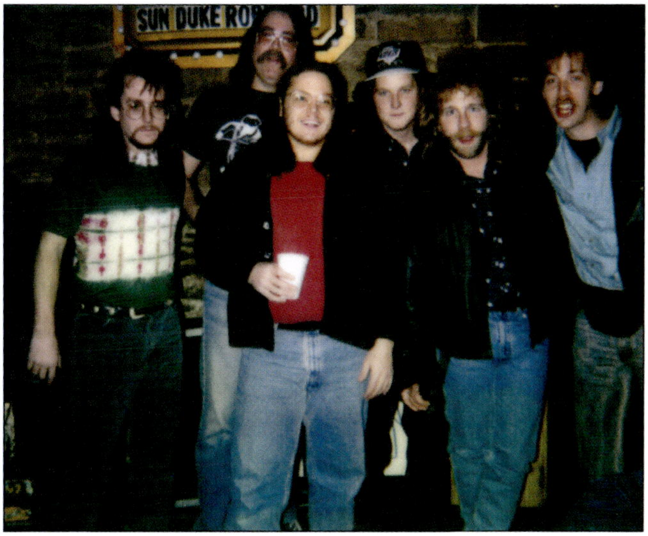

Room to Move was comprised of Don Szejk on vocals and guitar, Joey McGuire on bass, Joey's brother Sean "Shaggy" McGuire on drums, and Taylor Sinclair on guitar. Former members included Mike Choby on bass, Mike O'Toole on bass, and Mark Anderson on guitar. Joey recalls that his time at The Decade "schooled him as a musician." It was his second live gig ever, and having been given only a week to learn the songs, he was "scared shitless." His brother Sean had to remind him to breathe so he didn't pass out. (Courtesy of Krissy Leonard.)

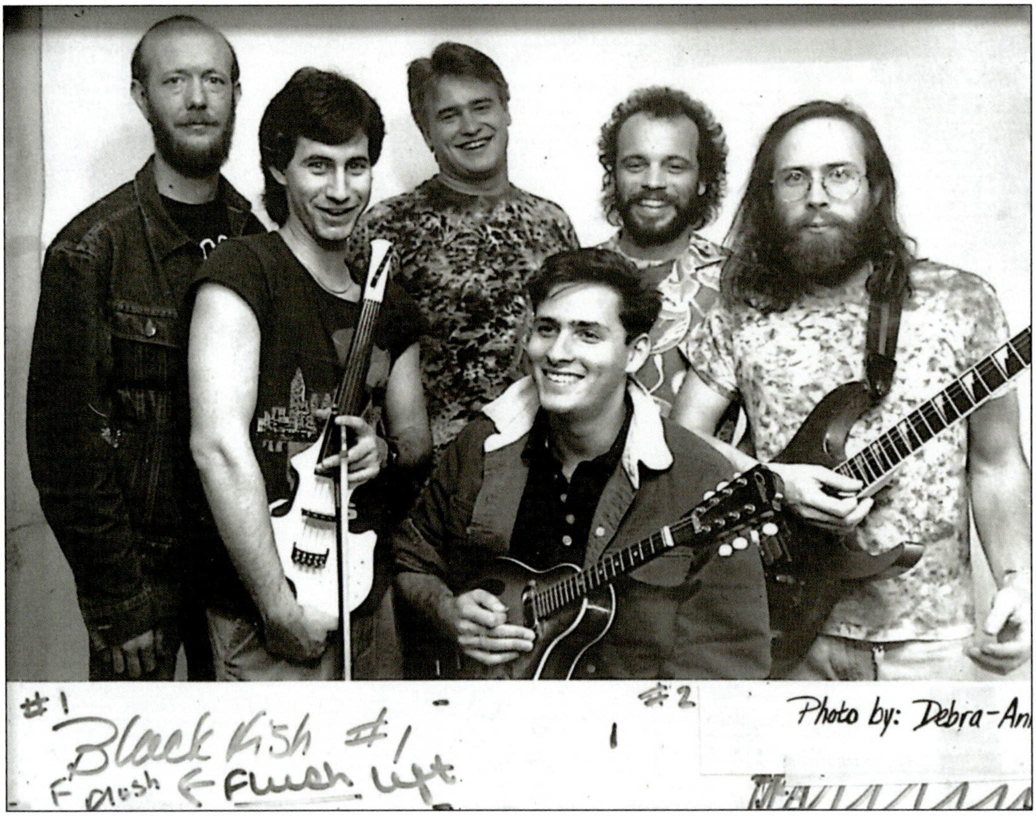

Pictured here is the most well-known version of Black Fish—the Pittsburgh Black Fish that played at The Decade on a regular basis. TJ Spina, childhood friend of the DiSilvio children, played alongside Darren Jarvis, John Milnes, Dave "Olde Bones" Westcott, Scott Lipsitz, and Bruce Lebovitz. Spina recalls the day the band planned to move to San Francisco after getting a record deal. Dom took Spina on a fatherly walk and urged him to finish college so he would have something to fall back on since his band "wasn't all that good." Dom was never known to mince words. Nevertheless, the band was one of his favorites.

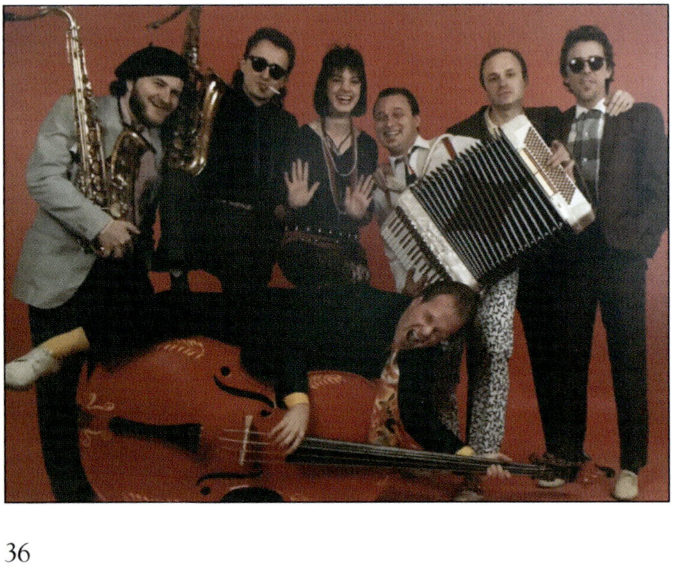

Sharon Pavone (center) followed her first husband, Glenn, when he left Virginia to play with Billy Price and the Keystone Rhythm Band. She left her home and her band behind but quickly found both at the place that she says "housed magic." While playing with her band Bon Ton Roulet, Sharon got the chance to open for—and play with—many great stars because, as Dom said, "she commanded the stage," so if a big star came, he wanted Sharon to perform.

Many other local bands graced The Decade stage. In fact, there are too many to count, but some of the other treasured groups included The Clarks, the S.P.U.D.S, 8th Street Rox, the 8 Balls, the Automatics, Trash Vegas, Torn and Frayed, the Pep Boys, Robbie Klein, King Solomon, and many more. (Courtesy of Kurt Weber.)

It was not just musicians who started their careers at The Decade; many photographers and journalists found topics and a point of view at the neighborhood bar. Scott Mervis, a longtime writer for the *Pittsburgh Post-Gazette*, got his first journalism job at *In Pittsburgh Newsweekly* due to a piece he wrote for the *Pitt News* about a Houserockers show at The Decade. He remembers what a tease the live music scene was for underaged kids at the time. Due to this injustice, he also recalls operating on his cardboard driver's license in order to sneak into the bar. Journalists like Mervis and Mary Robb Jackson gave the bar much appreciated ink during its early days. (Courtesy of Kurt Weber.)

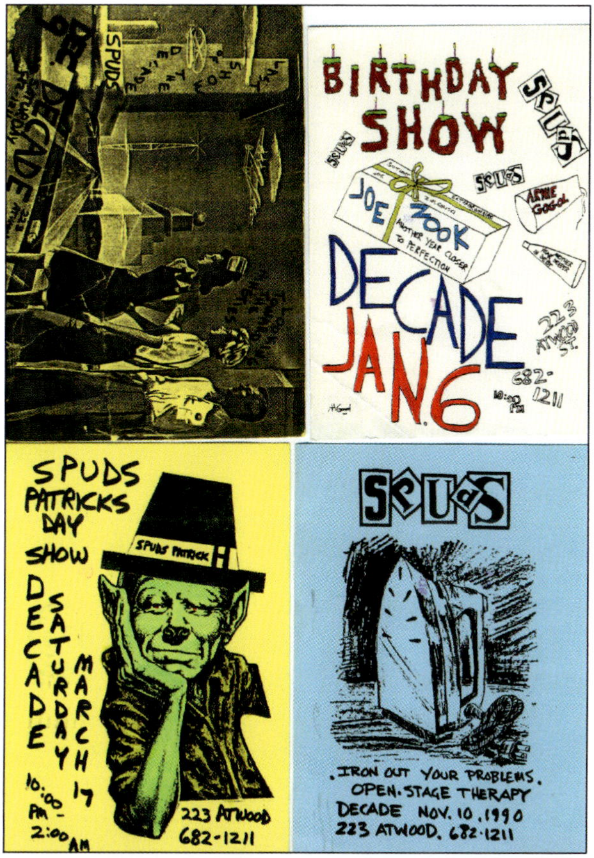

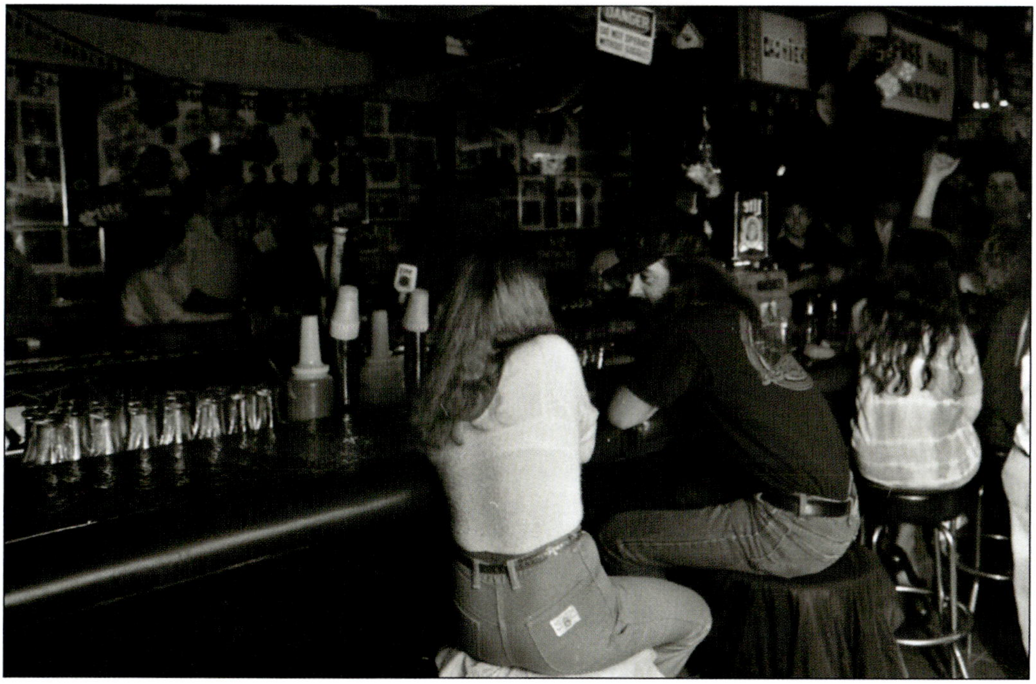

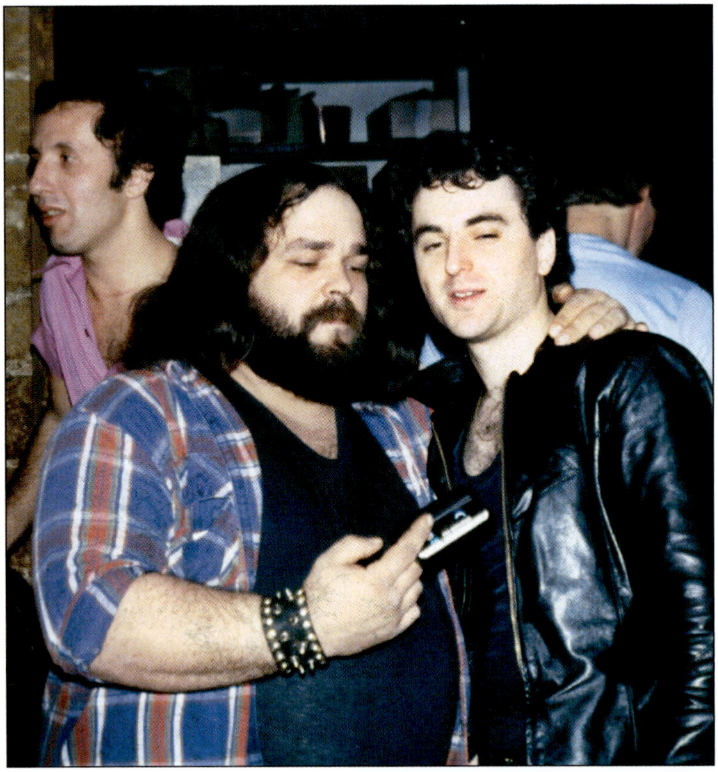

The Iron City Houserockers needed a soundman, and Bob Boyer stepped up to the plate. He was not only a soundman and a roadie, but also a songwriter; in fact, he is a cowriter on the Houserockers song "Old Man Bar/ Junior's Bar" with Gilbert Snyder. According to his longtime friend Jay Flory, The Decade was home to Bob Boyer; he had no family, and so the bar was everything to him—it even became his final resting place, an odd fact that will be covered later. (Courtesy of Mike Chedwick.)

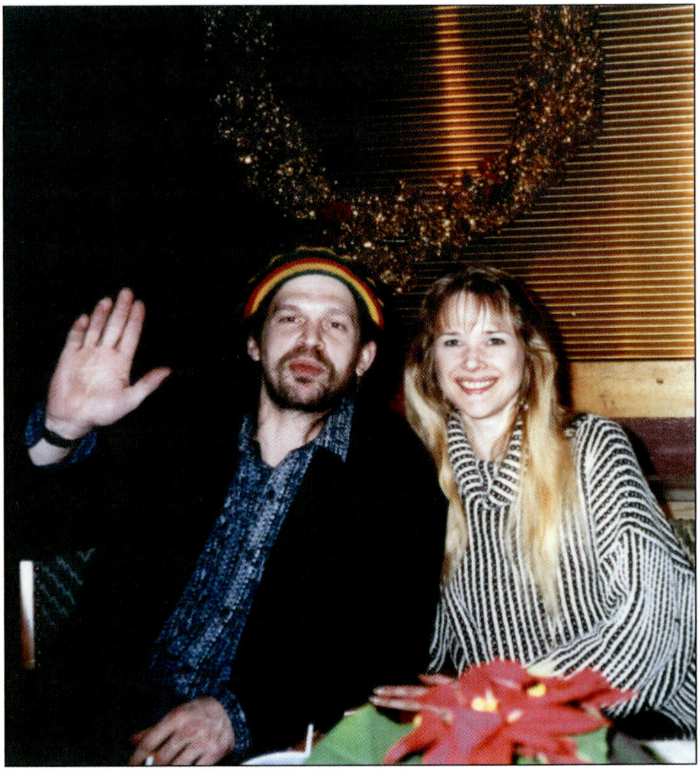

An issue of *Details* magazine reports on the immense talent of Decade soundman Eddie Smith. They boil it down to the simple phrase, "The soundman knows what he's doing."

Three

NATIONAL ACTS, THE DANNY KRESKY ERA, AND OTHER MUSIC GENRES

By 1978, after five years of business, Dom had single-handedly made a name for The Decade in Oakland. He had just fallen into a groove with the local acts when he received a call from California-bred music promoter Danny Kresky.

After finding luck with a Rod Stewart show at the Syria Mosque, Kresky's company, Pacific Presentations, sent their new hire, Kresky, to scope out the scene of a little blue-collar town called Pittsburgh, Pennsylvania. Relocating, he found the city to have a monopoly-ridden promotion arena, so he staged a coup on the industry and instantly created a name for himself by bringing Elton John to the Civic Arena. Yet, Kresky shifted his efforts from focusing solely on superstars after realizing how advantageous working from the ground up could be—enter Dom DiSilvio.

Kresky asked Dom if he was interested in bringing a few national acts to the puny five-by-seven-foot Decade stage. Ending the phone call with a curt "no, thank you," Dom expected to never hear from Kresky again; he had yet to comprehend the incredible opportunity he had just flatly rejected. Meanwhile, in the year that passed before their next interaction, Danny Kresky Enterprises continued to promote huge acts in the city of Pittsburgh, so eventually, Dom returned Kresky's call.

The California promoter's expertise in the realm of celebrity, combined with the Pittsburgh bar owner's business tactics, allowed The Decade to become a prosperous music venue despite its size. Together, they built the stage a little bit bigger and brought in smaller, round tables, and claimed a room upstairs for the band, but more importantly, in doing this, they gave an underdog Pittsburgh bar the capability to host live music and appeal to national acts. Kresky claims that during his entire tenure as The Decade's promoter, from 1978 to 1984, no musician ever lamented the rather tight, generally cramped circumstances of the bar or even protested the weight-bearing pole that stood obtrusively off stage right. Some acts came through the door without even booking the joint just to see what the hype was about. As Ed Townsend from the local band Eddie and the Otters explains, "You left your ego at the door when you played The Decade".

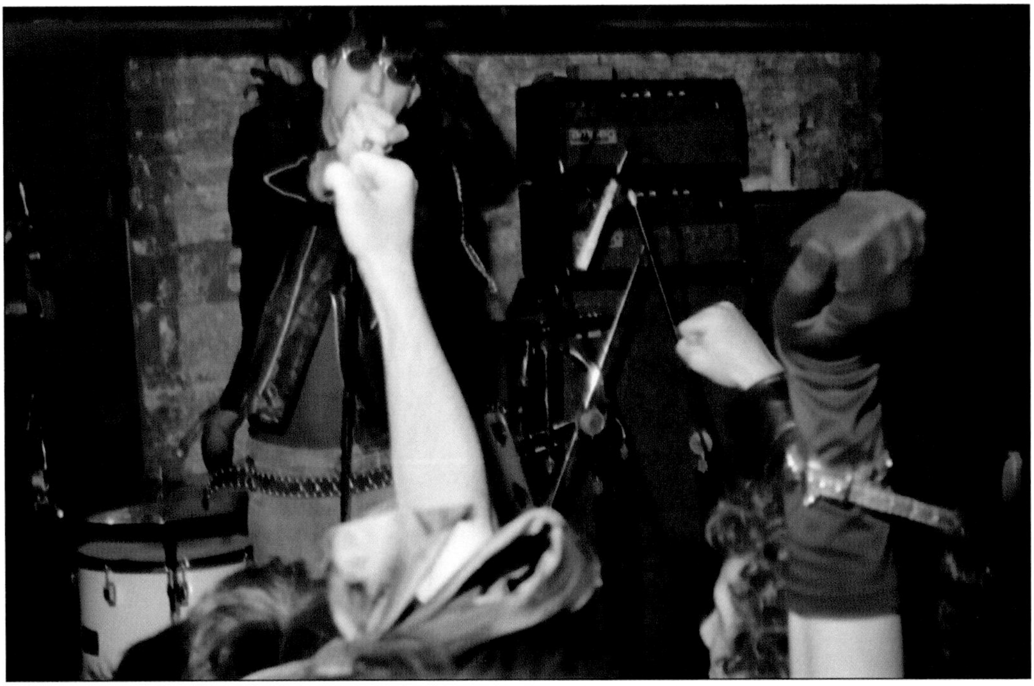

When Kresky booked The Decade's first national act, Maria Muldaur—famous for her hit single "Midnight at the Oasis"—Dom was ecstatic. But when Muldaur didn't show, he threw his hands up in frustration, doubting Kresky's competence as a promoter. However, the very next Decade show Danny Kresky booked was an up-and-coming punk band called the Ramones. The Ramones became the first and only national act to play The Decade two nights in a row, on March 6 and 7, 1979. (Courtesy of Larry Rippel.)

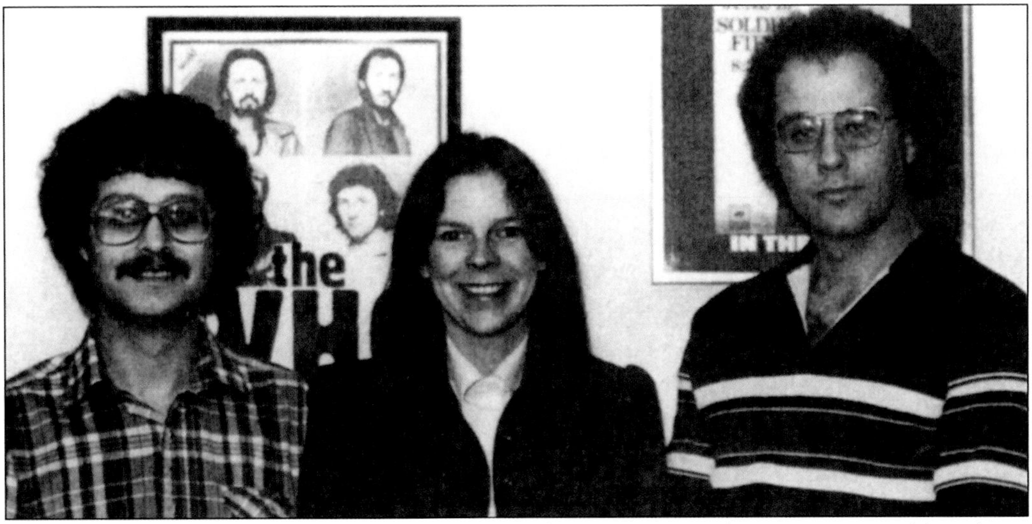

Danny Kresky worked with his team at Danny Kresky Enterprises. The operation would not have been what it was without Marc and Susan Sternberger, pictured here with Kresky (right). Susan recalls the work she and her late husband did with Danny: "We worked hard at promoting those shows, had a good time in the process, and in my opinion, helped accelerate the careers of many an artist between 1979 and 1984".

As Kresky continued to promote big name acts at places like the Civic Arena, he utilized his position to assist The Decade. When advertising for big bands, he would use the bottom eighth of the advertisement to promote smaller shows at The Decade. He would do the same thing with radio spots, using the last few seconds of the bigger band's paid air time to help out Dom and the smaller bands. This ad from the 20th anniversary is a lot bigger than the ones Danny used in the early days when advertising money was scarce—or nonexistent.

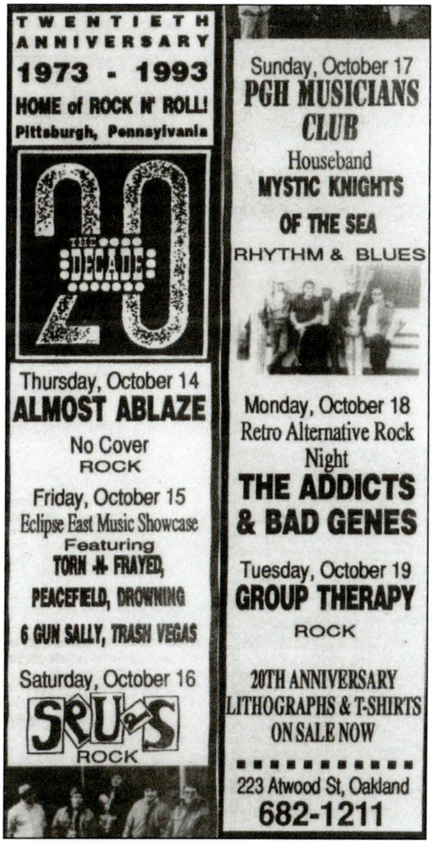

David Johansen, one of The Decade's first national acts, was a monster success. After Stillwater and the Ramones played within a three-month period, Kresky and Dom were flying high. Every agent in Pittsburgh wanted their new acts to play at The Decade. The combination of a good sound system and stage made The Decade the perfect spot, and Dom was the perfect club owner for this type of venue. Success on the national level became inevitable.

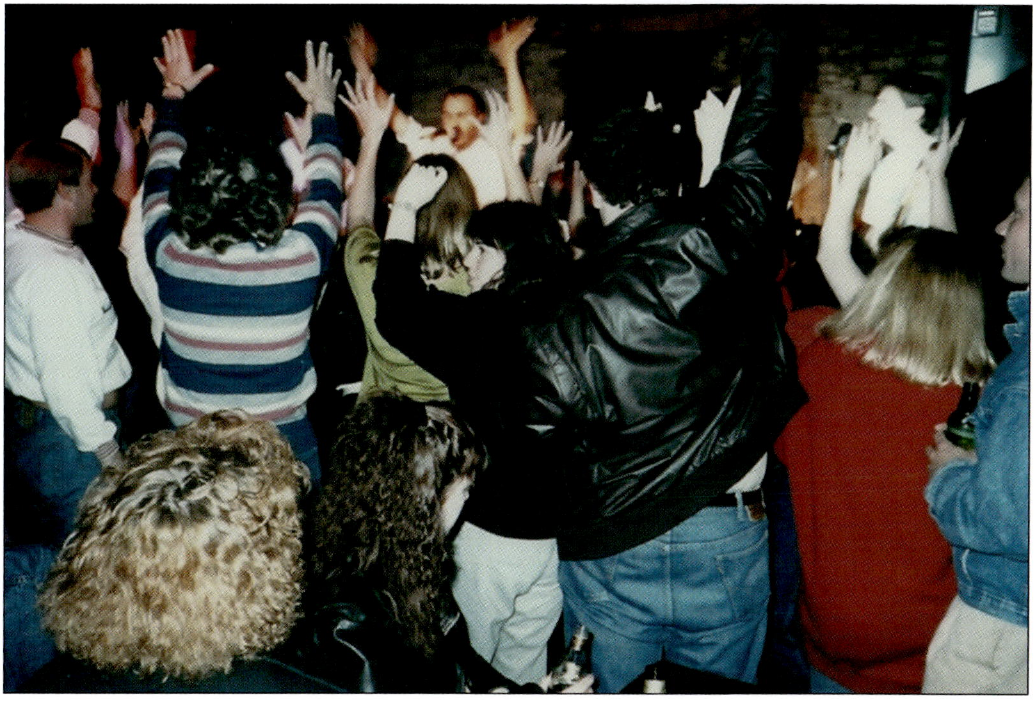

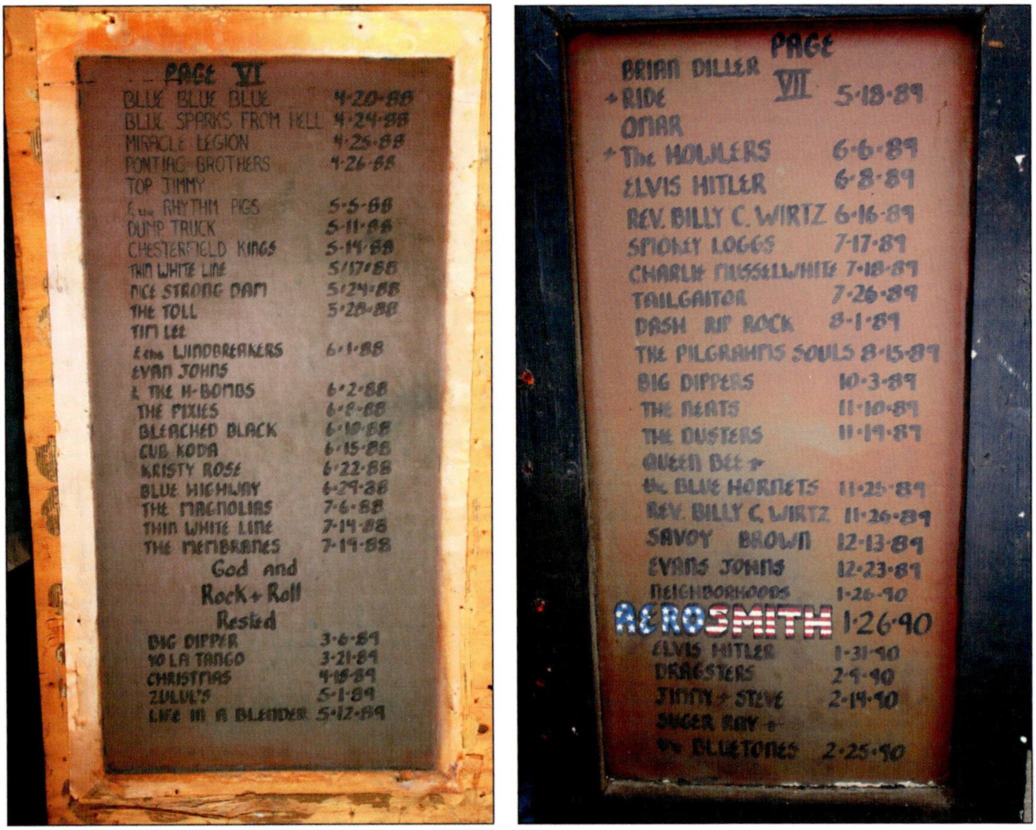

The famous copper signs hung outside of The Decade and listed every band that played at the bar. Jan updated them weekly. Copper was a well known aspect of The Decade aesthetic, as the tables and bar were both made of pounded copper. Dim lighting from the ceiling coated in old t-shirts enhanced the color of the pounded copper bar, which was cleaned regularly with soda water. The signs, a permanent, physical record of the bands that came through, also serve as an artifact, preserving a part of the eclectic style of the place. These particular signs track the period between 1988 and 1990 and include popular Decade regular the Toll, along with the very popular band Aerosmith, as well as a few Decade favorites such as Reverend Billy C. Wirtz, Queen Bee and the Blue Hornets, and Neighborhoods, plus radio personalities Jimmy and Steve, among many others.

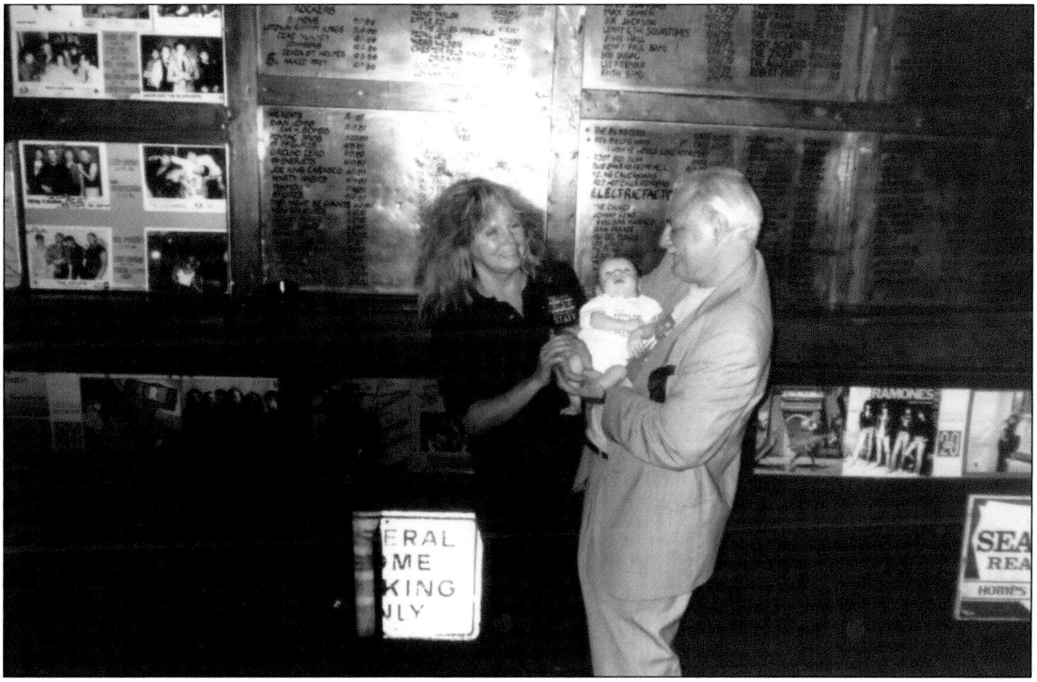

From 1979 to 1984, Danny Kresky promoted many national acts at The Decade, such as the Headpins, the Fuzztones, Gun Club, the Restless, Honeymoon Suite, Zebra, Divinyls, Stevie Ray Vaughn and Double Trouble, Artimus Pyle, the Roaducks, Alan Holdsworth, Helix, Cyndi Lauper, Fingerprintz, the Lydia Taylor Band, McGuffey Lane, the Rings, Doug and the Slugs, Ziggurat, U2, Carsickness, Snopek, the Rockats, the Jags, Robert Fripp and the League of Gentlemen, Spider, Nervus Rex, Benny Mardones, Angel City, Ellen Shipley, Tantrum, the Romantics, the Pretenders, Tony Sciuto, Stillwater, Steve Forbert, the Ramones, the Fabulous Poodles, Brownsville, the Police, Desmond Child & Rouge, Legs Diamond, Max Demian, Joe Jackson, Mark Tanner, Lenny and the Squiggtones, John Hall, Henry Paul Band, Bob Dubac, Lee Ritenour, the Faith Band, Bill Bruford, Herman Brood and his Wild Romance, Billy Falcon, Blackjack, David Johansen, Pat Benatar, Tom Johnston, 20/20, and the Beat.

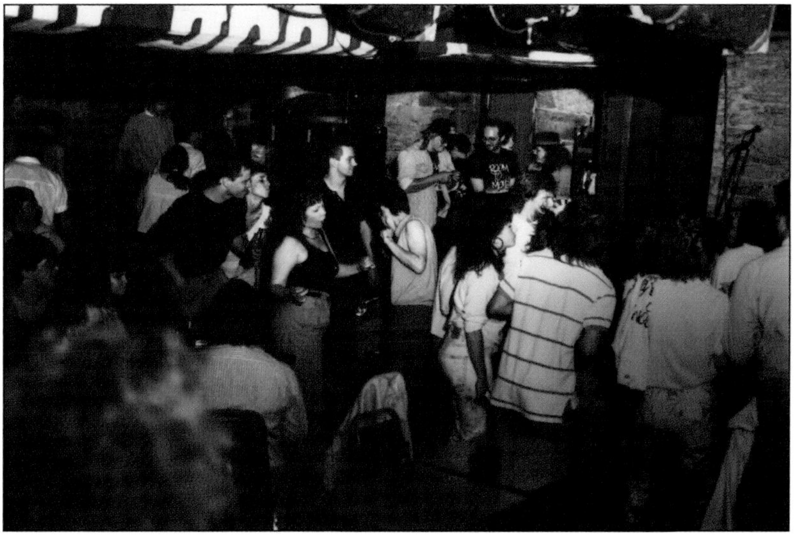

AMERICAN FEDERATION OF MUSICIANS OF THE UNITED STATES AND CANADA
(HEREIN CALLED "FEDERATION")

ICM

INTERNATIONAL CREATIVE MANAGEMENT, INC.

A MEMBER OF THE Josephson TALENT AGENCY GROUP

RIDER(S) ATTACHED HERETO IS (ARE) HEREBY MADE PART OF THIS CONTRACT

40 West 57th Street
New York, N.Y. 10019
(212) 556-5600

8899 Beverly Boulevard
Los Angeles, Calif. 90048
(213) 550-4000

Whenever The Term "The Local Union" Is Used In This Contract, It Shall Mean The Local Union Of The Federation With Jurisdiction Over The Territory In Which The Engagement Covered By This Contract Is To Be Performed.

THIS CONTRACT for the personal services of musicians on the engagement described below is made this 25 day of October, 1984, between the undersigned purchaser of music (herein called "Purchaser") and the undersigned musician or musicians.

1. Name and Address of Place of Engagement: The Decade/ Pittsburgh, PA.

Name of Band or Group: RED HOT CHILI PEPPERS

Number of Musicians: 3+1

2. Date(s), Starting and Finishing Time of Engagement: 11/5/84--Artist Rider/Artist to receive 100% Top Headline Billing, and to close show/Purchaser to provide and pay for first class sound and lights, Per Artists specifications/Purchaser to provide and pay for support talent, TBA, and is subject ,

3. Type of Engagement (specify whether dance, stage show, banquet, etc.): subject to artist's approval/Artist to receive sound check/Artist to perform 45 to 60 minutes/All checks except deposit check, must

4. Compensation Agreed Upon: $ be made payable to Moebetoblame music/(Deposit check is to be made payable to ICM)-----$750 Flat Guarantee/TIX:$5/CAP:325/PG:$1,625
(Amount and Terms)

5. Purchaser Will Make Payments As Follows: A deposit of $187.50 due 10/29/84, balance due prior performance.
(Specify when payments are to be made)

DEPOSITS: $ 187.50-25% (Certified Check, Money Order, or Bank Draft) payable to International Creative Management, Inc. as agents upon signing of contract.

BALANCE To be paid in United States currency (Certified Check, Money Order, Bank Draft, or cash) to leader on or before conclusion of engagement.

6. No performance on the engagement shall be recorded, reproduced or transmitted from the place of performance, in any manner or by any means whatsoever, in the absence of a specific written agreement with the Federation relating to and permitting such recording, reproduction or transmission. This prohibition shall not be subject to the arbitration provisions set forth in 7 below and the Federation may enforce this prohibition in any court of competent jurisdiction.

7. Breach of Contract – Arbitration of Claims:
(a) It is expressly understood by the Purchaser and the musician(s) who are parties to this contract that neither the Federation nor the Local Union are parties to this contract in any capacity except as expressly provided in 6 above and, therefore, that neither the Federation nor the Local Union shall be liable for the performance or breach of any provision hereof.
(b) This contract, and the terms and conditions contained herein, may be enforced by the Purchaser and by each musician who is a party to this contract or whose name appears on the contract or who has, in fact, performed the engagement contracted for
(Continued on reverse side)

THIS CONTRACT SHALL NOT BE BINDING UNLESS SIGNED BY ALL PARTIES HERETO.

IN WITNESS WHEREOF, the parties hereto have hereunto set their names and seals on the day and year first above written.

Ed Traversari/DiCesare-Engler Productions	Mike Balzary	47
Print Purchaser's Full and Correct Name (If Purchaser is Corporation, Full and Correct Corporate Name)	Print Name of Signatory Musician	Home Local Union No.
Signature of Purchaser (or Agent thereof)	Signature of Signatory Musician	
4423 Bigelow Blvd.		
Street Address	Musician's Home Address	
Pittsburgh, PA. 15213		
City State Zip Code	City State Zip Code	
Telephone	Telephone	
	Reid Anderson	000006
	Booking Agent	Agreement No.

Return All Signed Copies to: INTERNATIONAL CREATIVE MANAGEMENT, INC. as Agent for the Musicians

12/81 FORM C-1

The Red Hot Chili Peppers, fresh off of the August release of their second album, *Freaky Styley*, also took The Decade stage. On October 1, 1985, the Peppers' show, according to *Fornication: The Red Hot Chili Peppers Story*, "turned into a small-scale riot." The book also claims that "their set . . . ended by demolishing an 80-pound bag of popcorn with the help of a hatchet and an enthusiastic audience . . . combined with the Peppers' now obligatory 'socks on cocks' routine, their frat-boy-heavy crowd—tonight coated in popcorn and sweat—went apeshit."

When Cyndi Lauper performed at The Decade, it was about a week before "Girls Just Want to Have Fun" hit. Confused, Dom called up Sharon Pavone of Bon Ton Roulet and asked if she wanted to open for "Estee Lauder." Pavone replied that she was "unaware Estee Lauder was a singer."

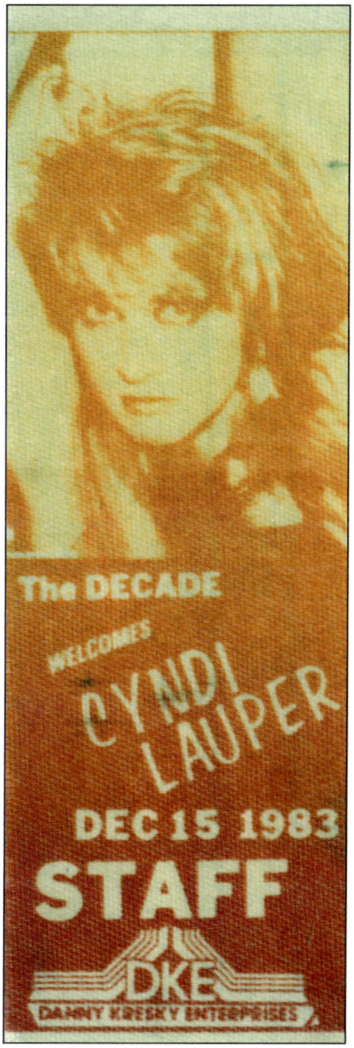

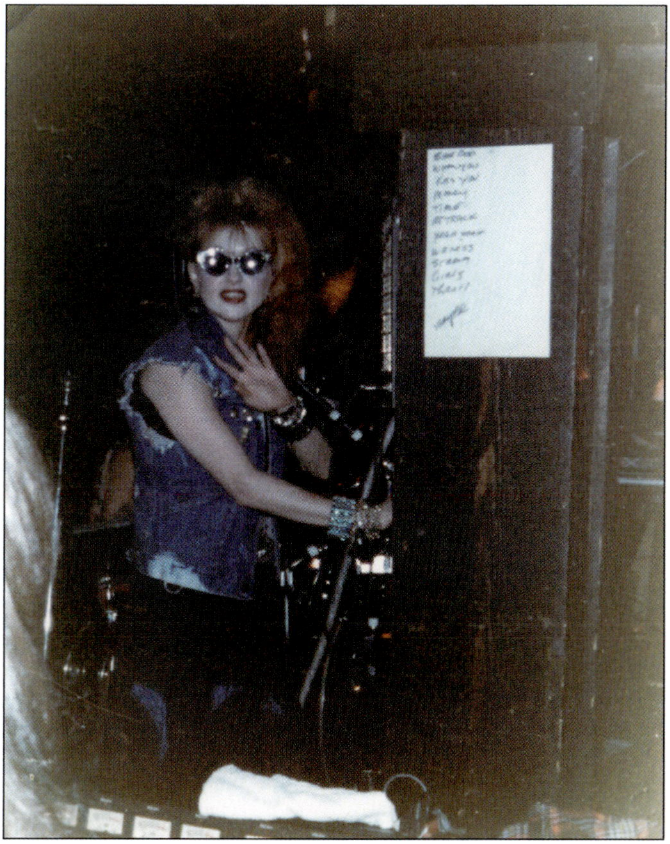

Lauper's set list on December 15, 1983, included "She Bop," "When You Were Mine," "I'll Kiss You," "Money Changes Everything," "Time After Time," "Yeah Yeah," "Witness," "I'm Gonna Be Strong," "Girls Just Want to Have Fun," and "What a Thrill." She hung around all night at the bar. A year later, when she returned to Pittsburgh, she sold out the Civic Arena.

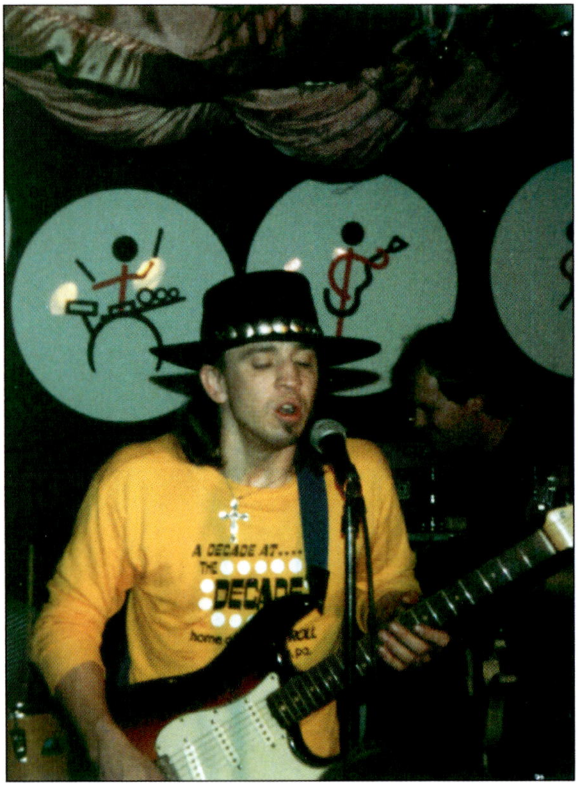

On one of his many trips to New Orleans, Dom traveled off the beaten path and found himself in a dirt-floor club where he listened to one of the greatest guitarists he had ever heard. Introducing himself to the man, he asked how far north he had ever gone to perform. Stevie Ray Vaughan answered pensively, "We've been as far as Atlanta." Dom paid him $500 for his performance at The Decade, and Vaughan played several other times before the venue closed its doors. Vaughan and Dom maintained a close friendship over the years, as the guitarist was a very down-to-earth guy who enjoyed spending time at both The Decade and Dom's after-hours club, The Castle.

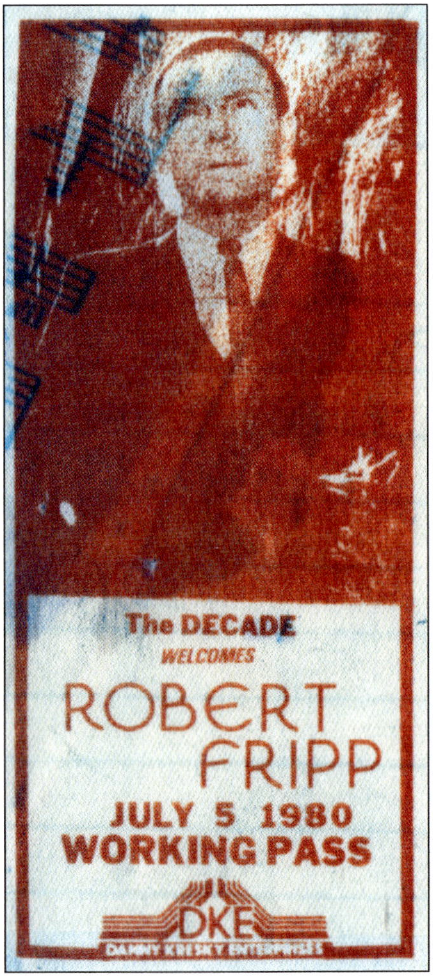

Legendary guitarist Robert Fripp jammed out at the corner of Atwood and Sennott Streets when he was trying out smaller venues. He was hanging out with Barry Adamson when Dom walked up to him and handed him a League of Gentlemen photograph and asked him to sign it. Fripp went into the kitchen and returned without the photo. Dom asked where it was, and Fripp said he had hidden it and that if Dom could find it, he could hang it on his wall. The musician was notoriously stingy with his autograph and told the bar owner that the only other person he had signed for was the queen. Dom found the picture and proudly hung it on his wall for many years.

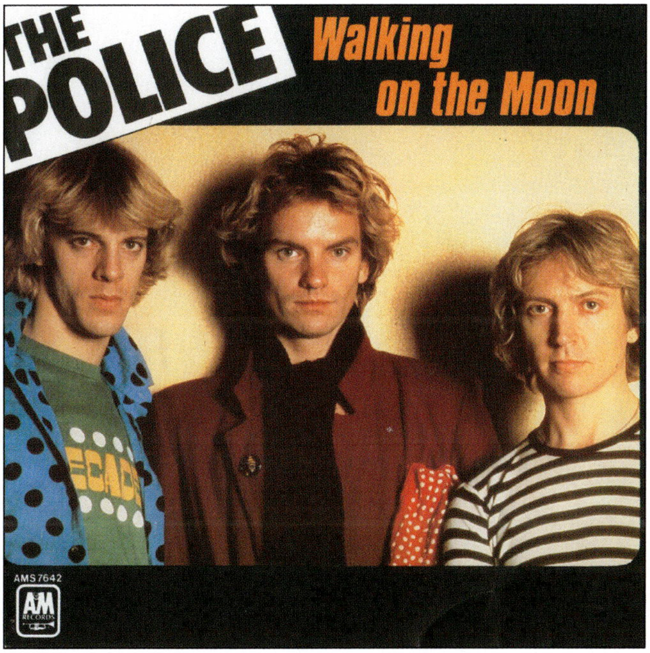

The Police performed "Roxanne" on The Decade stage, though the show was nearly cancelled. Unpopularity tempted Kresky and Dom to call off the gig, until "Roxanne" hit the airwaves the day before the band was supposed to play. The show went on, and people poured into The Decade to get a glimpse of them. Kresky recalls the irony in the amount of police outside during the Police's show inside. They actually ended up playing "Roxanne" twice because they didn't have enough material for a full set. Drummer Stewart Copeland is wearing a green Decade t-shirt on the cover for the single "Walking on the Moon."

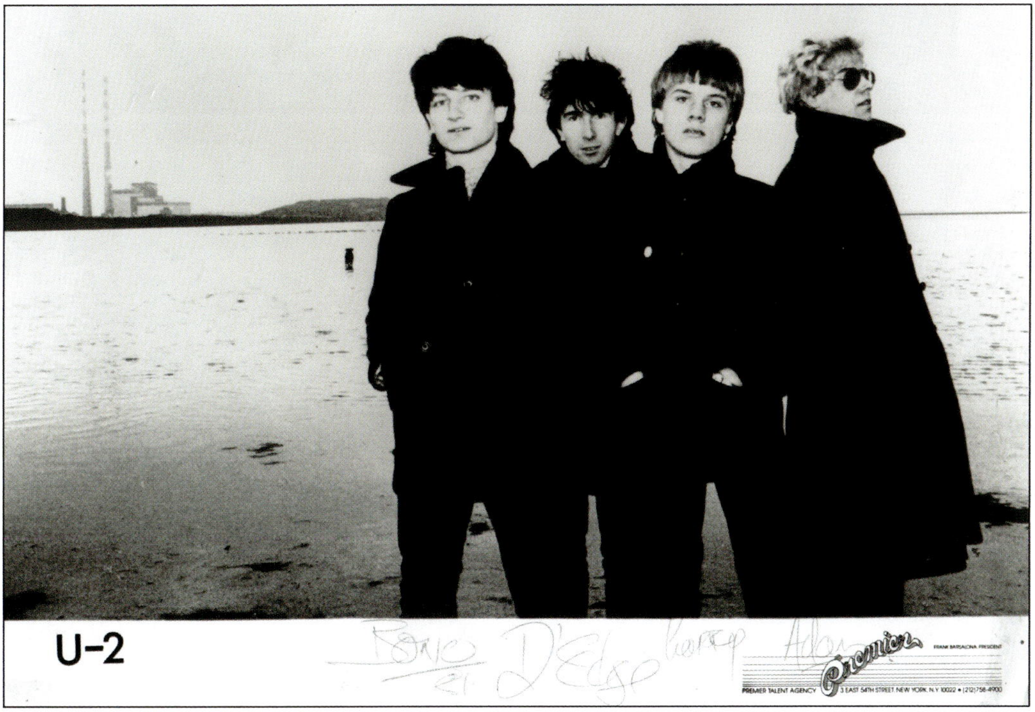

Local band Carsickness opened for U2 on April 21, 1981. Lead singer Steve Sciulli recalls drinking all of U2's beer that Dom had set aside, as U2 was going through a Christian phase at the time and had sworn off booze. Sciulli also remembers incorrectly singing along to U2's number-one hit amongst college students at the time, "I Will Follow," singing instead "I will swallow" loudly, much to the band's dismay. In 2011, when U2 played at Heinz Field, the band asked the crowd what bar they had played in back in the 1980s, and the crowd roared back, "The Decade!"

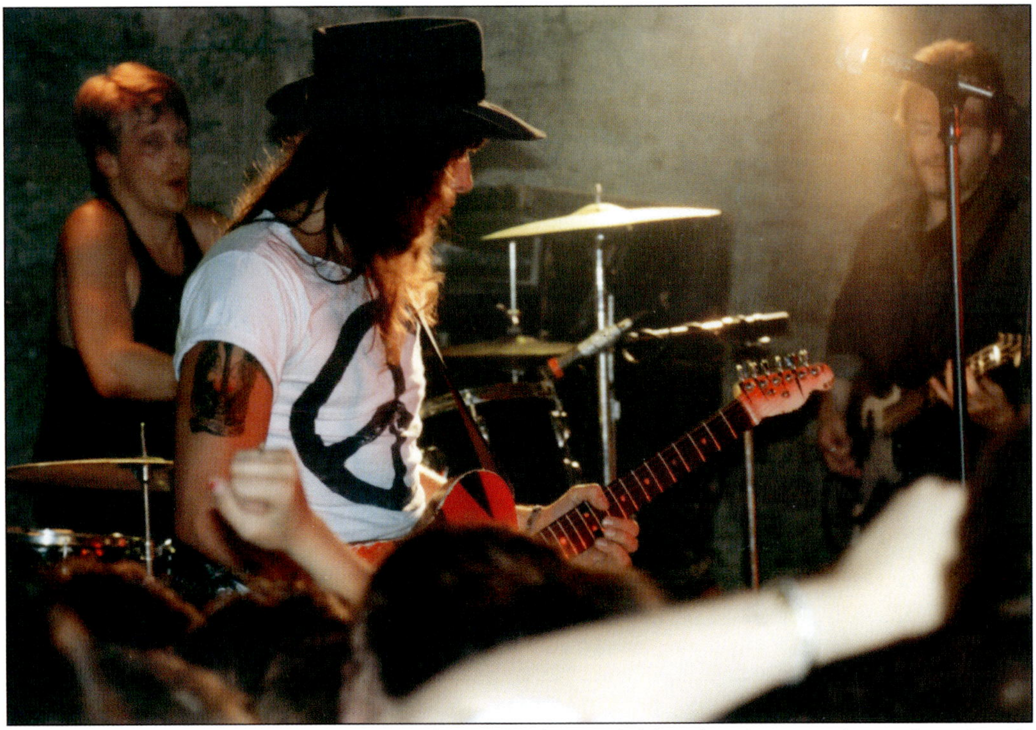

Because of the popularity the bar gained from both its solid local and national acts, huge bands began stopping in to see what the fuss was about. Aerosmith dropped in one night just to check out Dom and Jan's little place on Atwood Street. Visitors and staff never knew who could show up, and in a day before cell phones, it was all the more exciting to hear about a celebrity appearance through the rumor mill. One of the most memorable times this happened was when Bon Jovi showed up. Rich Sambora, his guitarist, is pictured here.

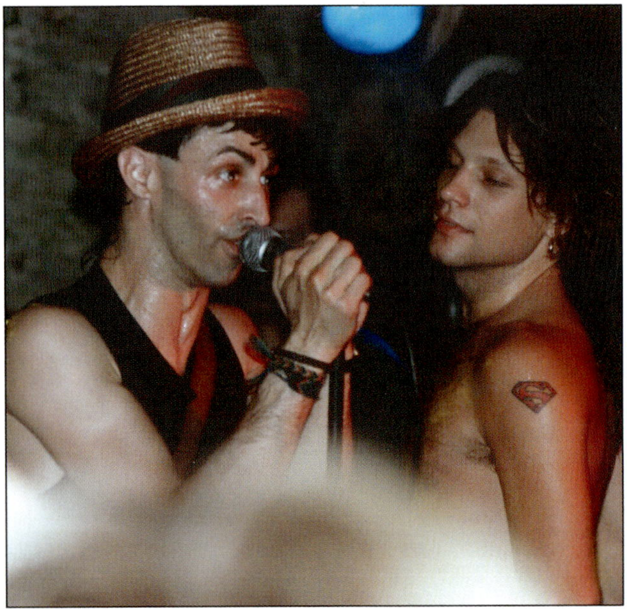

New Jersey–native Jon Bon Jovi found his Pittsburgh counterpart in Norman Nardini. When thinking back, Nardini explains that one had to earn their stripes at The Decade. It was a place that was attracting the gods of the music industry. Jon Bon Jovi was just a "street guy," so it was not beneath him to play at The Decade. He performed at the Civic Arena and swung by The Decade afterwards. Nardini brought Bon Jovi to The Decade because he knew he would be able to show him real rock 'n' roll and real people and, most of all, because "Jon wanted to be there."

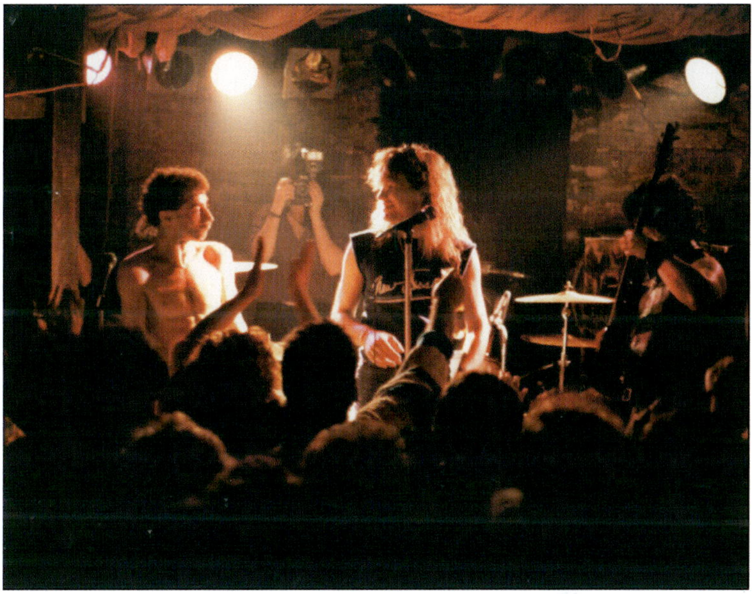

When asked about his time at The Decade recently, Bon Jovi related it to his hometown bar in New Jersey: "Like the Fast Lane in Asbury Park, The Decade was a sacred place where dreams came alive." In just a few visits on The Decade stage, Bon Jovi encapsulated the bar perfectly.

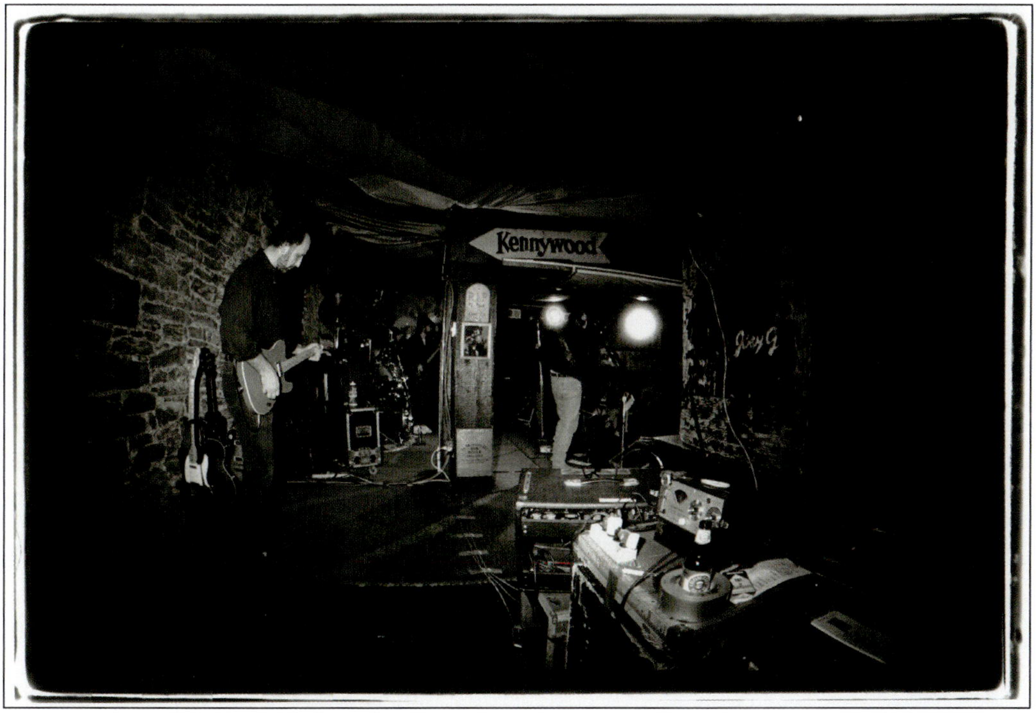

Steven Van Zandt of Bruce Springsteen and the E Street Band helped produce the Houserockers album *Have a Good Time (Get Out Alive)*. Van Zandt introduced Bruce Springsteen to Joe Grushecky, and the two hit it off. After driving around one night in Pittsburgh, and post hot dogs at "The O"—The Original Hot Dog Shop, Grushecky suggested they go down to The Decade. Gilbert Snyder and Bon Ton Roulet were playing at the time, and Sharon Pavone graciously invited Springsteen on stage. When he hopped off stage, he told Grushecky, "This is your Stone Pony." (Courtesy of Richard Kelly.)

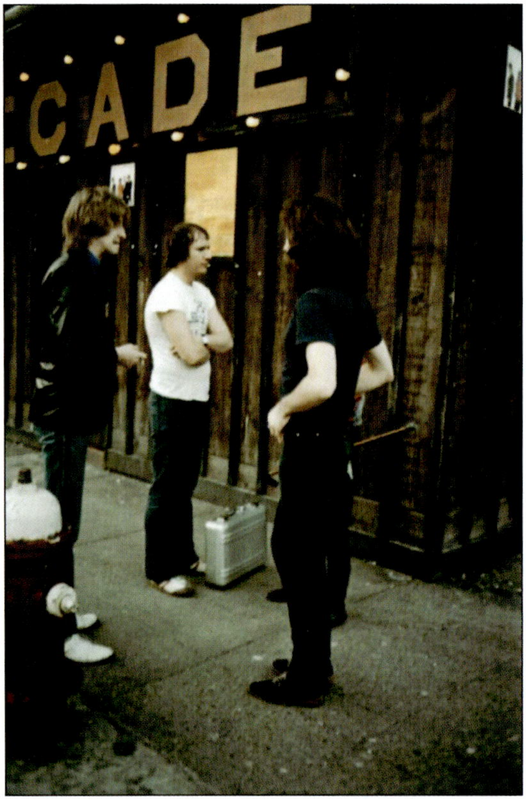

Mike Kolesar, drummer for Eddie and the Otters, recalls opening for the Pretenders on March 19, 1980. The crowd was huge, the bar was jammed beyond capacity, and tables and chairs had to be removed to make room in the tiny club. The Otters played a high-energy one-hour set, but when they came off the stage, they were told to get back on and play a second set, which to them seemed suspect and highly unusual. The insatiable crowd, hungry for the Pretenders, became restless and began screaming for their band. After finishing their set for a second time, the Otters returned backstage to find out that the Pretenders' bassist, Pete Farndon, needed a fix of heroin before performing that night. Thirty minutes into an already contentious show, police and a fire marshal showed up claiming code violations due to the large crowd—a regular occurrence at the bar. Kolesar remembers hiding in the back with his drum set.

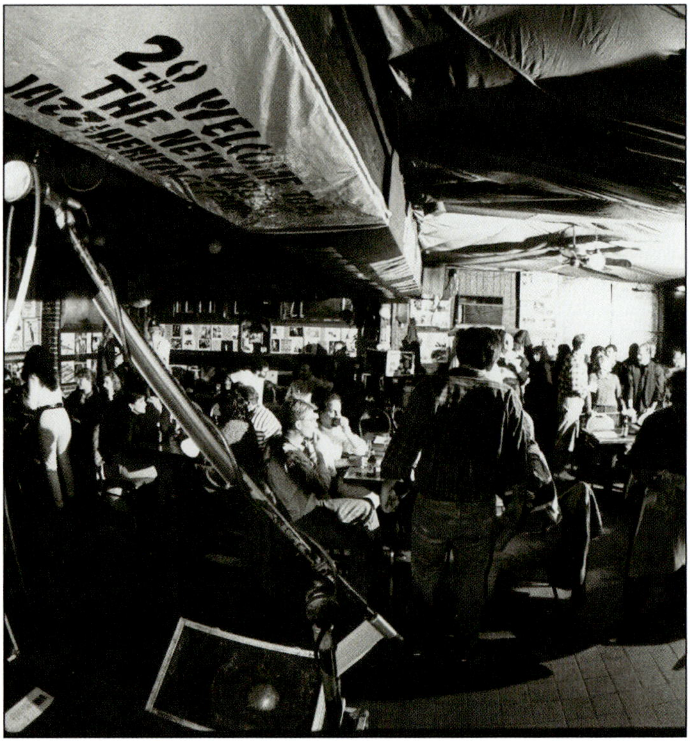

Comedian Sam Kinison was scheduled to perform a routine at The Decade in 1986, but his manager cancelled last minute to book him at rival bar Graffiti. When Kinison uncovered this injustice, he went over after his show to do an hour-long set at The Decade. There, he pumped himself up with jumping jacks and donned his usual beret and duster. After a quick discussion with Kinison that night, Dom's eldest daughter, Gina, and her husband, Danny, visited the *Saturday Night Live* set the next week to see Kinison, claiming to be on his guest list. They were not, but they still got to see the show live. (Courtesy of Richard Kelly.)

Reverend Billy C. Wirtz—musician, Decade enthusiast, entertainer, writer, and radio personality (with an emphasis on personality)—penned an article in *Musician* magazine entitled "Last Call at The Decade" and quipped, "There was no VIP seating, no 'light' menu. Hell there was usually no toilet paper. The dressing room was outside and up a flight of treacherous stairs. There was a column in the middle of the stage. . . . It was dark, hot, and reeking of sweat and stale Iron City beer, but no one seemed to mind. After all, it was home." At right are the lyrics to a song he wrote called "The Ballad of Dom."

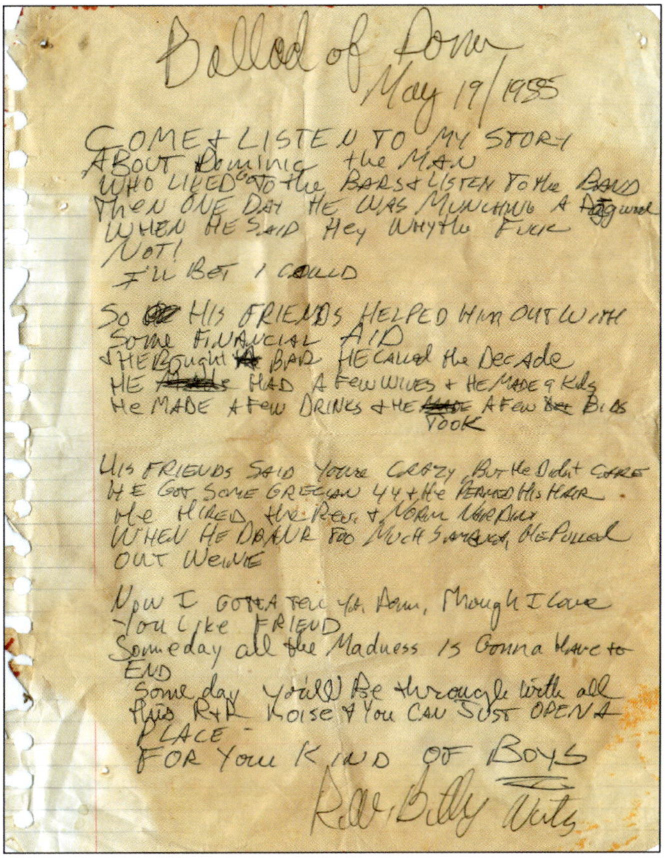
Ballad of Dom
May 19/1955

COME & LISTEN TO MY STORY
ABOUT Dominic the MAN
WHO LIKED to the BARS & LISTEN TO the BAND
Then ONE DAY HE WAS MUNCHING A [illegible]
WHEN HE SAID Hey Why the Fuck
NOT!
I'll BET I COULD

SO HIS FRIENDS HELPED Him OUT With
Some FINANCIAL AID
& HE Bought A BAR HE Called the DecAde
HE HAD A Few Wives + He MADE 9 Kids
He MADE A Few DRINKS & HE TOOK A Few BIDS

HIS FRIENDS SAID You're CRAZY, But He Didn't CARE
HE GOT SOME GRECIAN 44 & He PERMED His HAIR
He HIRED the Rev. + Norm Nardini
WHEN HE DRANK TOO MUCH SAMBUCA, HE Pulled
OUT Weenie

Now I GOTTA TELL YA Dom, Though I Love
You Like FRIEND
Someday all the Madness Is Gonna Have to
END
Some day you'll Be through with all
this R&R Noise & You CAN JUST OPEN A
PLACE
FOR Your KIND OF BOYS
Rev. Billy Wirtz

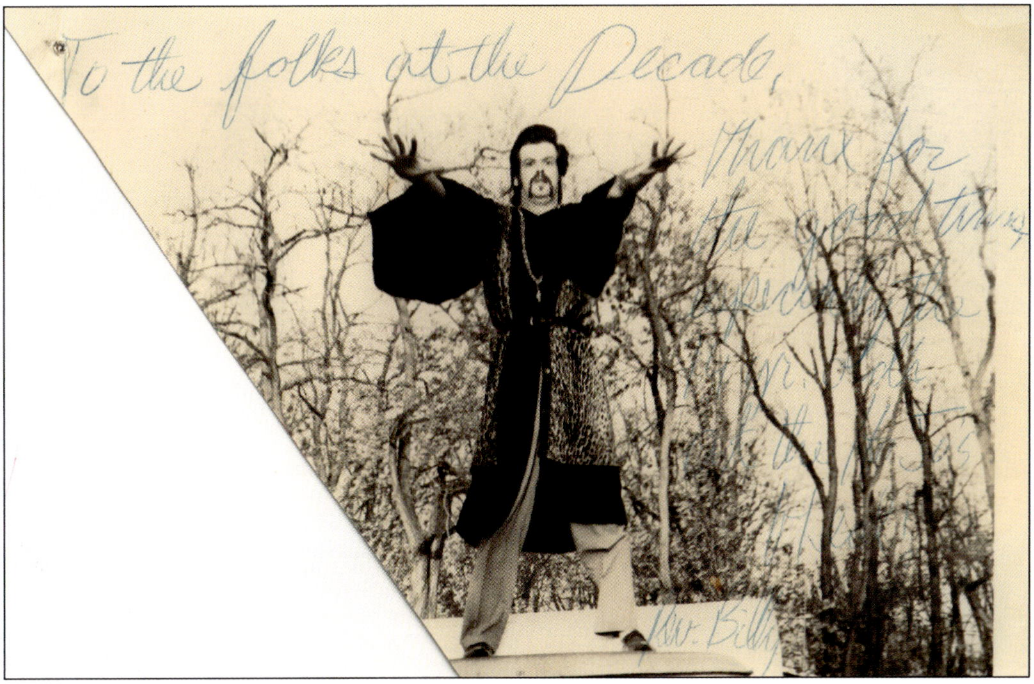

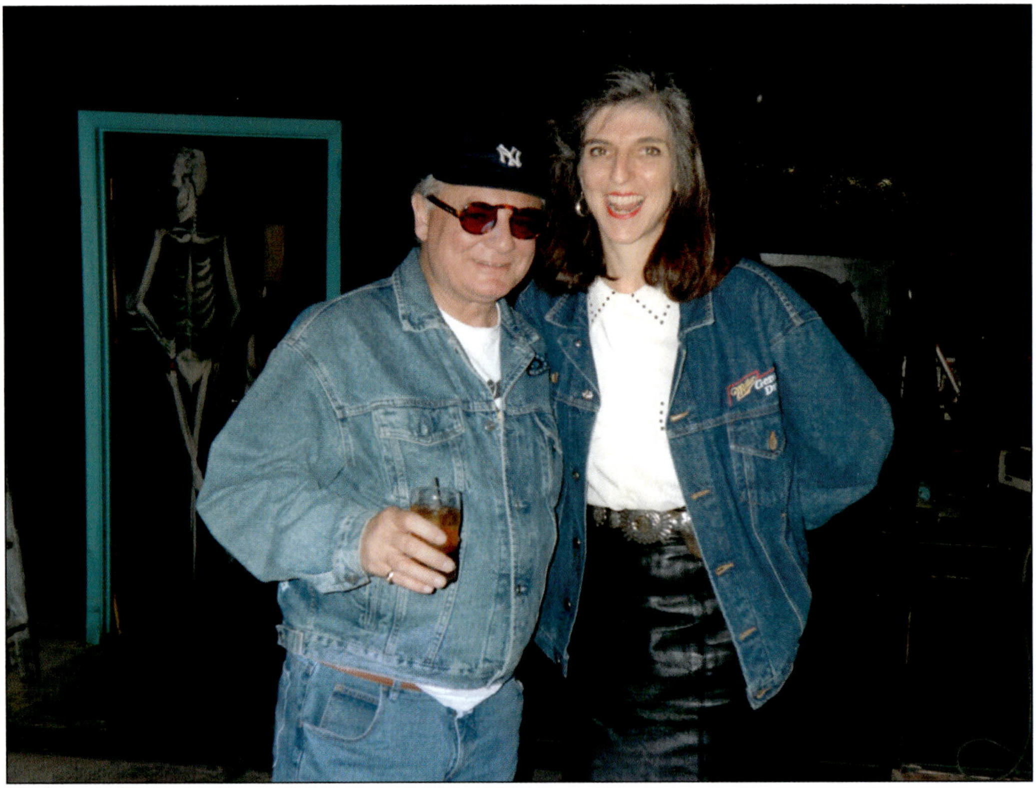

AMERICAN FAMOUS TALENT CORP
504 W. ARLINGTON PL.
CHICAGO, IL. 60614
312-880-6666

DEPOSIT RECEIVED
Date:
AMOUNT:

№ 6345

ARTIST ENGAGEMENT AGREEMENT

THIS AGREEMENT for the personal services of musicians on the engagement described below, made this 10th day of March 19 86 between Marc Sternberger for Electric Factory Inc. (purchaser) (herein referred to as Purchaser) and Marty Salzman (leader) (herein referred to as Artist)

1. PLACE OF ENGAGEMENT: The Decade (Name) 223 Atwood St. (Address) Pittsburgh, PA (City) (State) (Zip)
NAME OF BAND OR GROUP: BUDDY GUY
2. DATES OF ENGAGEMENT: daily or weekly schedule and daily hours: April 20, 1986
3. JOB DESCRIPTION: club (Event, Club) hours or sets: 2/60's between 10:30pm and 1:30am
a.) load in: 5pm b.) sound check: 7:30pm c.) stage size:
d.) lights provided by: club e.) sound provided by: club
f.) opening act provided by: n/a
g.) stage manager (or) club manager: h.) phone #:
4. ARTIST/INDEPENDENT CONTRACTOR: Marty Salzman (leader)
shall at all times have complete supervision, direction and control over the services of his personnel on this agreement and expressly reserves the right to control the manner, means and details of the performances of services to fulfill the entertainment requirements:
a.) Leader represents that the performances listed are available to perform the engagement. If a performer should be unavailable, leader shall arrange for a replacement.
b.) The Artist executes this agreement as an independent contractor, not as an employee of the Purchaser. Responsibility for appropriate payments of payroll taxes and charges under applicable federal and local law will be assumed by the artist.
5. CONTRACT PRICE: $1000.00
a.) ticket price b.) deposit: $500.00 c.) due no later than w/signed contract
d.) deposit payable to: AMERICAN FAMOUS TALENT e.) contract price should be paid as follows: Balance in CASH to leader at end of engagement.
6. AGENT PROVISIONS:
a.) The undersigned agent is acknowledged to have fully performed upon the commencement of this engagement. He shall not be liable for the default of a Purchaser or the non-performance of the Artist. No changes in the contract affecting agent's commission shall be made without the written approval of the agent.
b.) The percentage of commission is included in the gross price of this engagement and shall be held in trust by leader as fiduciary and forwarded to agent due by following Wednesday after performance. Delinquent commission shall accrue interest at 1% (one percent) per month, and if litigation is necessary for collection, attorney's fees shall be paid by debtor.
c.) If leader or key personnel of this musical group is rebooked into this or any establishment owned or controlled by the Purchaser (including chain buyers of music) within 365 (three hundred sixty-five) days from the termination of this agreement, leader shall be jointly and severely liable for payment to AMERICAN FAMOUS TALENT CORPORATION of commission at the rate due and owing or paid for previous engagement.
d.) If agreement has not been signed by artist or purchaser, but the performance in terms of the agreement has been executed this shall be deemed to be an acceptance of all of the terms contained in this agreement.
e.) It is hereby agreed that the undersigned Artist is an independent contractor and not an employee of the undersigned Purchaser and the signing of this agreement does not create an employer/employee relationship. It is further agreed that no employer/employee relationship exists between the Agent, AMERICAN FAMOUS TALENT CORPORATION and the Artist or between the Purchaser and the Agent.
f.) Artist(s) warrants and represents that Artist(s) has not executed any agreement with any other Agent(s) wherein Artist(s) would be obligated to pay commissions to any other Agency(s) relating to Artist(s) performance at the aforementioned engagement; and, the Artist(s) further agrees to hold AMERICAN FAMOUS TALENT CORPORATION harmless and reimburse AMERICAN FAMOUS TALENT CORPORATION if it has to pay any other agent(s) a commission relating to the aforementioned engagement.
7. SPECIAL PROVISIONS:
a.) All riders attached hereto become a part of this agreement.
b.) Access to 220 outlets must be provided.
c.) Food and beverage SEE RIDER
d.)
e.)
8. The recording, reproduction, or transmission of Artist's performance is prohibited absent written consent of Artist.
9. We acknowledge and confirm that we have read and approved the terms and conditions set forth in this contract.

The "long, tall Marcia Ball" was one of Dom's favorite performers. Not only did she have tremendous skill in both her vocals and on the piano, she was also very loyal to The Decade. The pianist is a dear friend of Dom's to this day, and he has traveled all over to watch her perform, most recently at the Pittsburgh Blues Festival in the summer of 2015 and most notably on many occasions in New Orleans. According to Dom, she embodies New Orleans music.

Buddy Guy played The Decade many times and took his spot amongst many other traveling blues acts that booked the bar. Rock n' roll was a huge part of The Decade scene; however, blues acts were just as vital. Blues and punk were the two other genres that The Decade experimented with at both the local and national level. Pittsburgh sportscaster Mike Lange was a big fan of the blues scene and could often be spotted at the bar on a blues night.

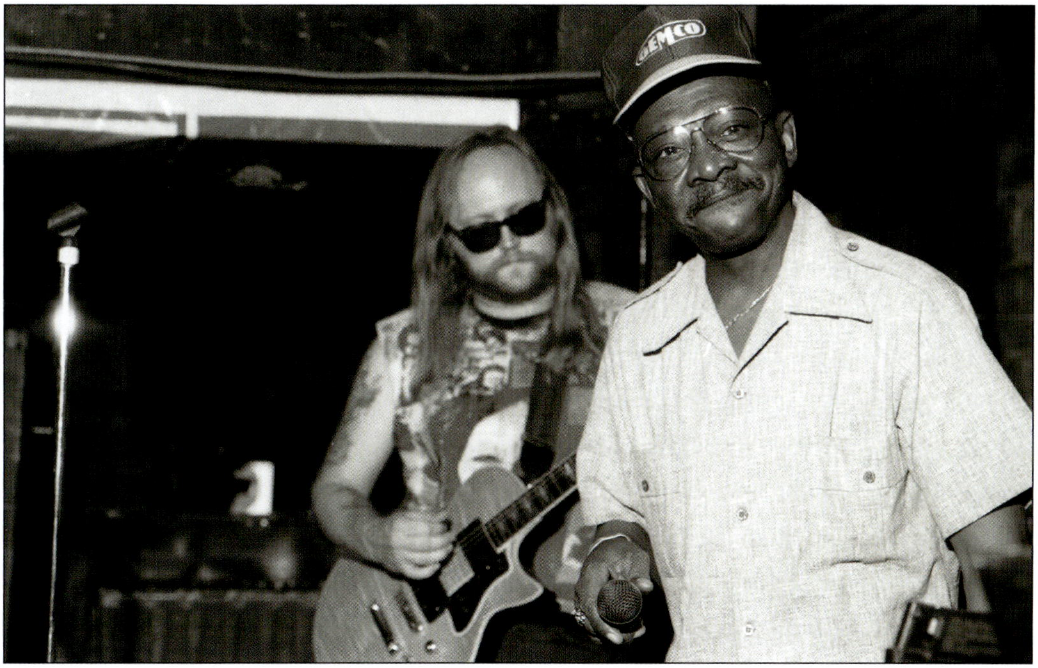

"Chizmo" Charles Anderson embodied local blues. Mystic Knights bandmate Gilbert Snyder referred to Chizmo as the "traveling troubadour' because he would walk out into the audience and could woo a crowd. He had an incredible memory for lyrics and an ability to color his blues with a tinge of comedy. When the musician passed away, there was a New Orleans–style accordion eulogy in the streets of Pittsburgh. Fellow Pittsburgh performers marched to the courthouse, where the mayor proclaimed it Chizmo Charles Day. Fitting, because Dom remembers him as "a true Pittsburgher." (Above, courtesy of Kurt Weber.)

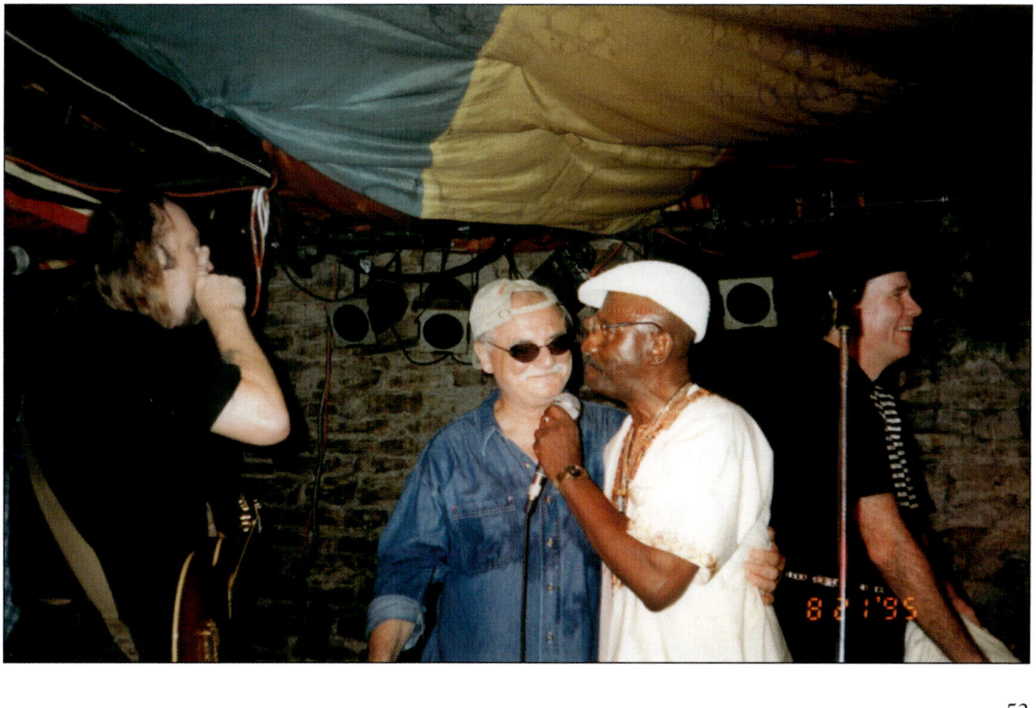

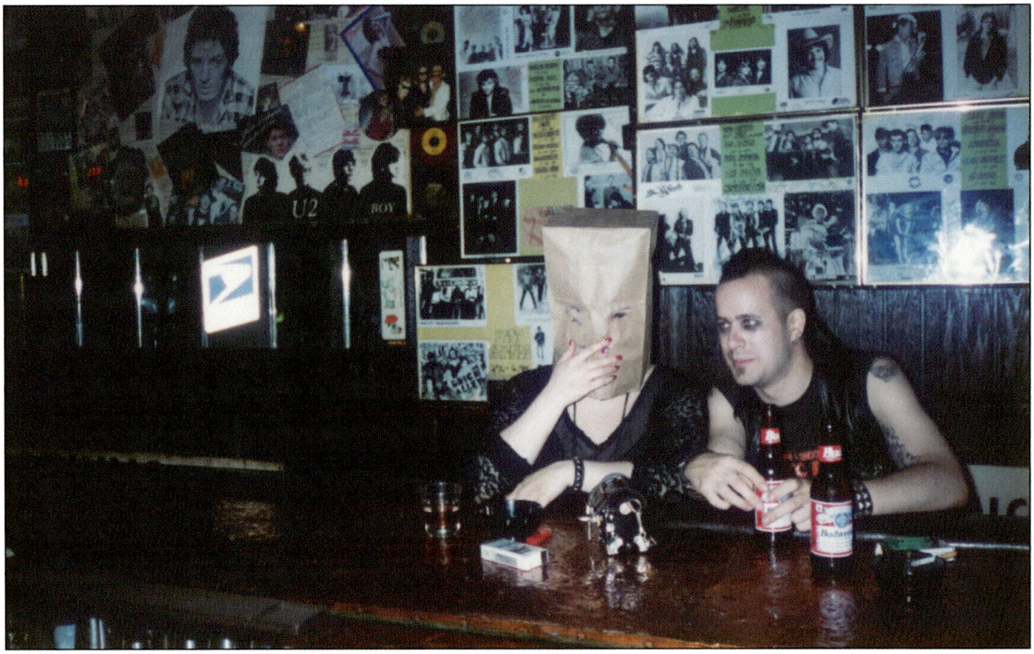

For a time during The Decade's history, the ever-changing Monday nights were deemed punk territory. Local punk legends Tommy Osh and Angelo Amantea were in part responsible for starting this trend, constantly making flyers advertising their bands. Joining together with Terry Thomas, the trio became the Addicts, a punk/rock crossover band; they would eventually become the Ultimatics. The Decade's rock 'n' roll crowd weren't the biggest fans of the punk nights. However, Dom made a point to ensure that various types of music, as long as it was good music, found a home under the parachute-covered ceiling. Above are Wiggy Walker and AJax Kennedy; below are Bobby LaMonde and Osh. (Below, courtesy of Kurt Weber.)

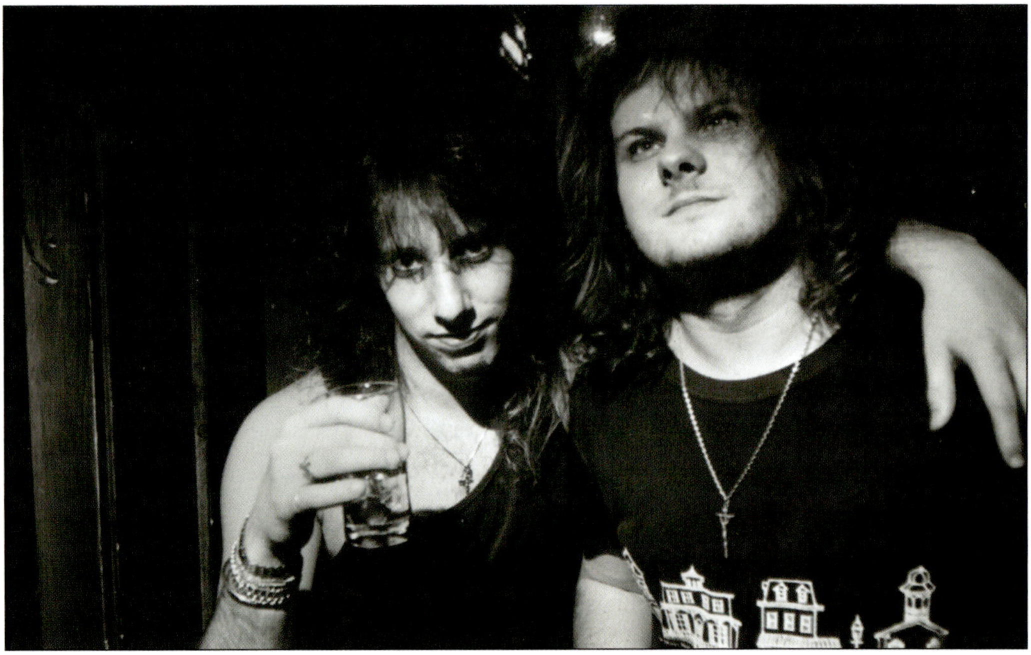

Four

The Island of Misfit Toys, or the Decade Family

One wife and five kids could not satisfy Dom's insatiable desire for family, so when he and Jan divorced in 1978, Dom remarried three years later. His new bride was a young, kind-hearted Pittsburgh native named Judy Bassett, sister to Wild Cherry's guitarist Bryan Bassett. Nineteen years after Dom's first child was born, Judy gave birth to the sixth of Dom's children: Briana Eileen DiSilvio. Judy and Dom eventually had two more children—Jacquelyn Danielle (named after Dom's favorite drink) and Gennaro Robert—before they too divorced. An odd *Brady Bunch* of sorts, Dom's entire family, made up of two ex-wives and now eight children, acted as one confoundingly functional unit. Yet, even this troop could not fulfill Dom's aching desire for an extended family.

At this time, while Dom's lineage outside the bar grew to unwieldy levels, a new family took shape inside The Decade. A band of oddballs came together to form what Decade regular Wiggy Walker referred to as "the island of misfit toys." A fusion of *The Breakfast Club* and *Cheers*, this random array of Pittsburghers found their home at the corner of Atwood and Sennott Streets. As the fearless "godfather" of this drunk—and often rowdy—crew, Dom did his best to make everyone feel at home.

On any given day, a mailman could be sitting with a punk rocker, who was chatting with a surgeon, who had earlier bought a drink for a college football player. All walks of life called The Decade home. The place certainly appealed to a specific type of person, one who could ignore the pungent smell of stale beer and appreciate the eclectic nature of the place, yet the bar did not cater to one particular crowd. Everyone who entered The Decade thought of it as home, and to this day, Dom considers the people who came to the bar his family.

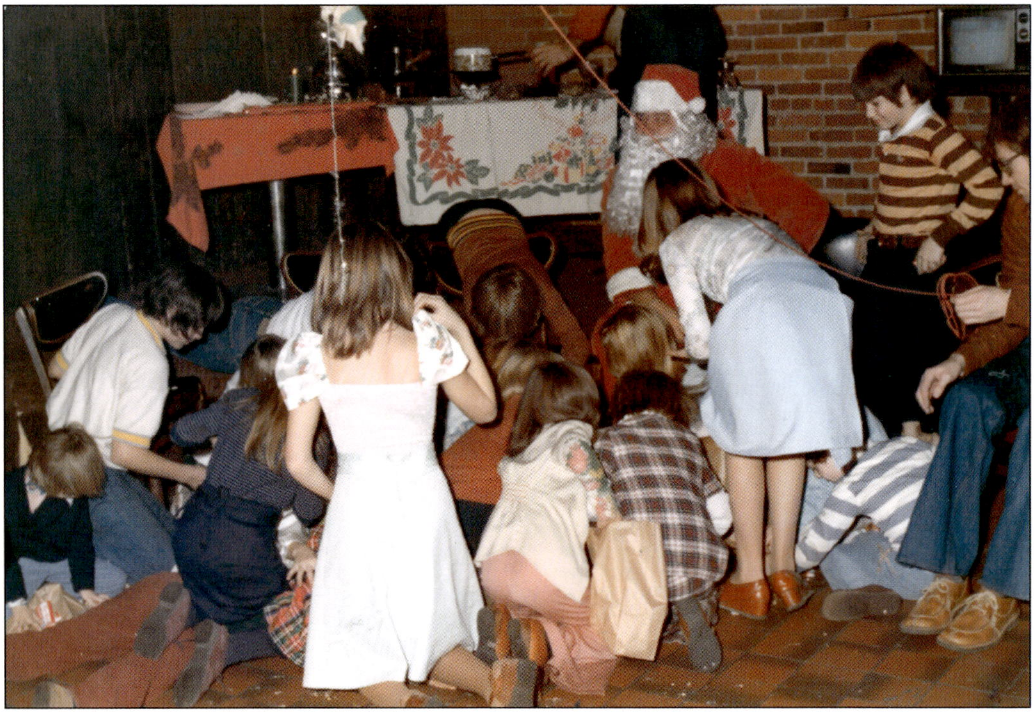

Dom and Jan often combined their home life and their work life by bringing their five children to the bar. Even at young ages, The Decade was occasionally the children's playground despite Dom's father, the surgeon, constantly warning that it would damage their hearing. In a manner quite characteristic of Jan, she would often set her children up on The Decade roof with straws and paper to shoot spitballs at unsuspecting customers below. At very young ages, the boys, Caesar and Dante, became extra roadies for the bands.

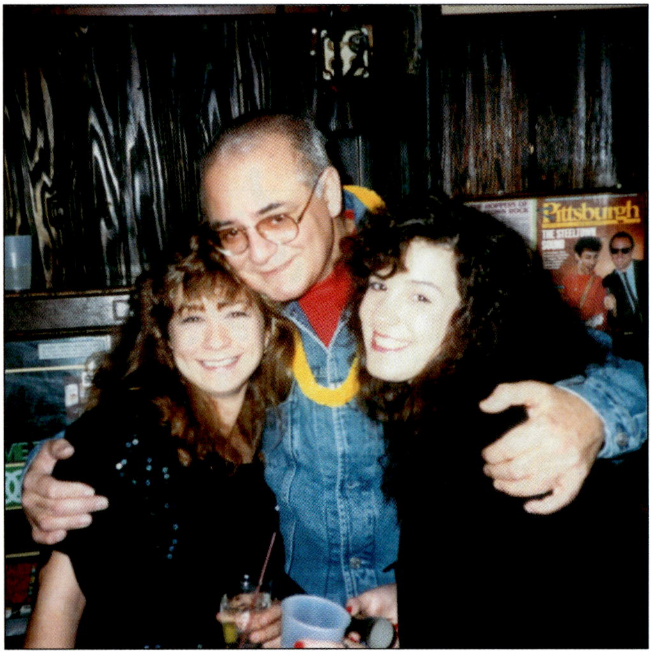

When the kids got older, they took jobs bartending or waitressing at The Decade while in college or over summer break. They used their position as children of a club owner advantageously by snagging all the fake IDs that remotely resembled them once the bouncers confiscated them from other kids. All of the DiSilvio children's underage friends were allowed in as long as they knew where the aprons were kept so that, in the event of a police raid, they could placate the cops by pretending to be members of the wait staff. Dom is pictured with daughter Domenique (right) and longtime family friend and waitress Angie (McClintock) Hay.

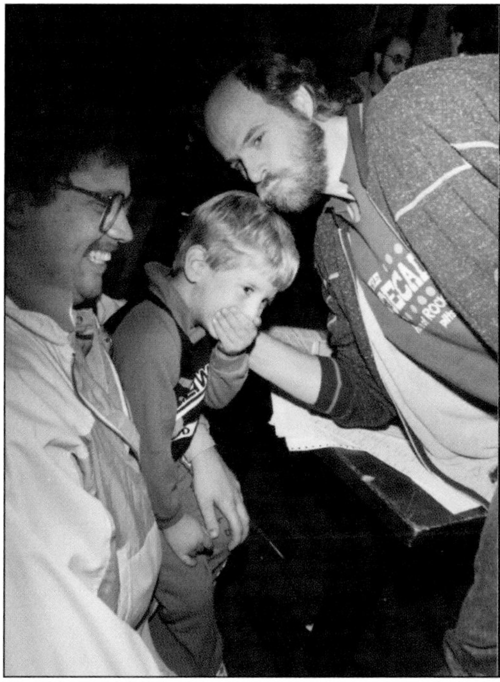

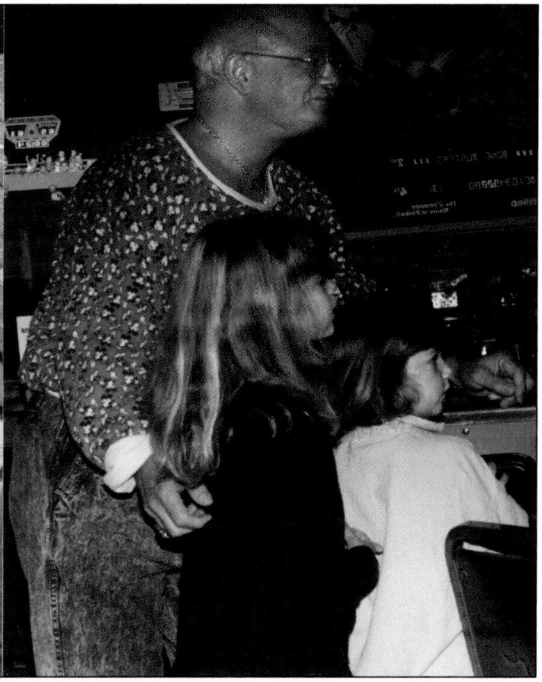

Dom's family did not stop growing once he had teenagers on his hands. Nineteen years after the birth of his first child, he found himself starting all over again with three new kids: Briana, Jacquelyn, and Gennaro. The trio provided an interesting generation gap within Dom's family that would help keep the ever-growing crew connected. Additionally, Dom's ex-wives got along well and kept the family unit dysfunctionally functional. (Courtesy of Kurt Weber.)

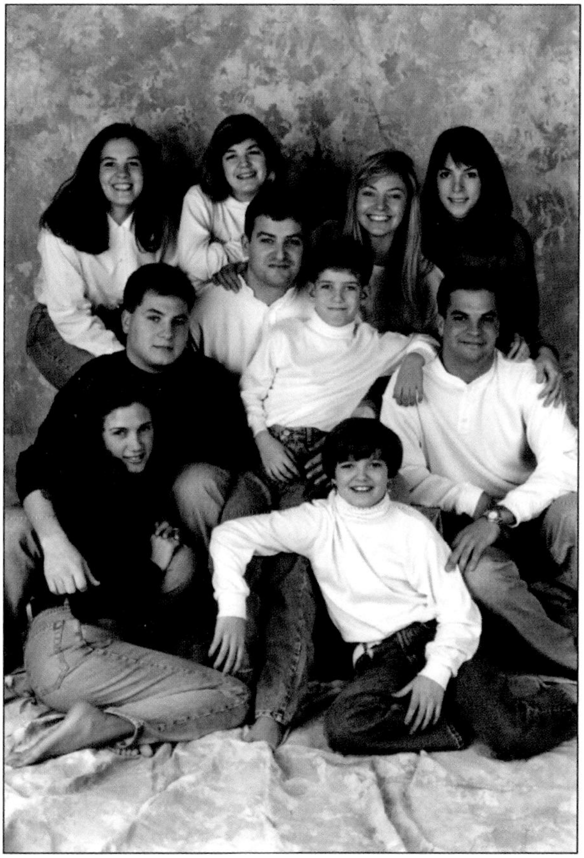

The final DiSilvio cast and crew at The Decade included Dom, Jan, and Dom's second wife Judy, Gina and her boyfriend (now husband) Danny, Caesar and his girlfriend (now wife) Ilene, Domenique, Dante, Juliet and her boyfriend (now husband) Dave, Bri, Jackie, and Geno. From left to right are (first row) Ilene and Jackie; (second row) Caesar, Dan, Geno, and Dante; (third row) Dommie, Bri, Gina, and Juliet. (Courtesy of Lynne Adelsheimer.)

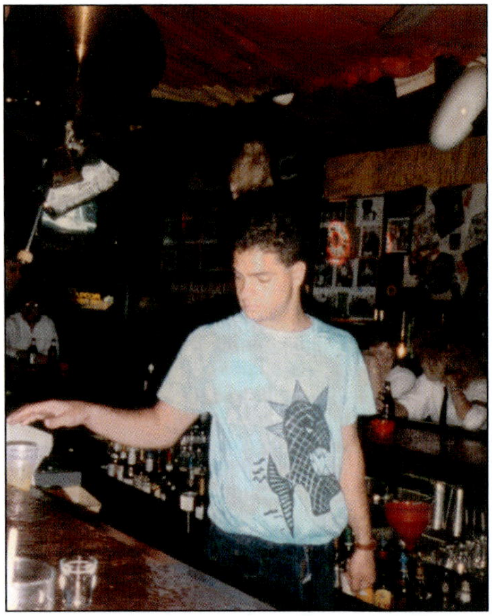

Dom's son Dante remembers that it wasn't always fun and games at the family-run bar; once, two guys were tormenting him while he was behind the bar. He took the name calling in stride for a while, but eventually, his hot-headed nature got the best of him, and he ended up getting into a fight with the men. Dom jumped in to defend his son. Eventually, the bouncers grabbed the two men and pulled them out of the bar. Dante realized that one of the men had left his glasses behind. He taunted them by stomping on the glasses, smashing them into a million pieces. "Those were my glasses, Dante," Dom grunted angrily.

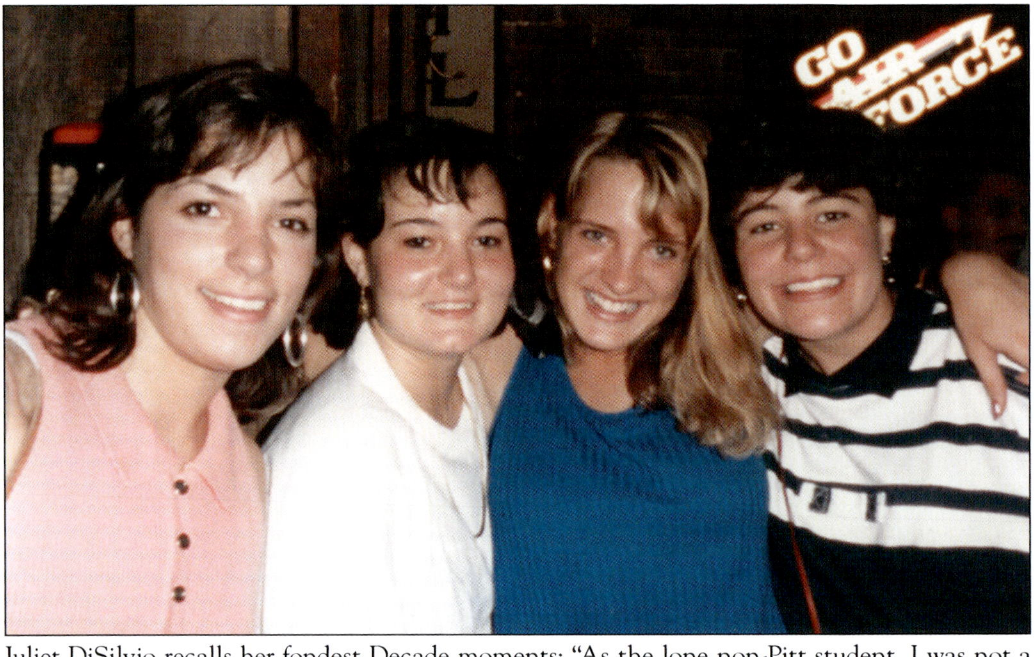

Juliet DiSilvio recalls her fondest Decade moments: "As the lone non-Pitt student, I was not a regular employee or patron during most of my college days. I worked as a lunch-time waitress while on my high school and college breaks and summer vacations. I used to mole my way to the front of the stage—my siblings and I felt that was our right. At school, my favorite State College band by far was Queen Bee and the Blue Hornet band. One night after enjoying them play at the Phyrst, I introduced myself to Mark Ross, the guitar player and sometime vocalist. I encouraged him to play at The Decade. So, Queen Bee and the Blue Hornet Band made their debut at The Decade on a Saturday night in November 1989 after a Pitt/PSU football game. Queen Bee, also known as Tanya Browne, and her band had won the hearts of my dad and the Decade crowd. They went on to play there regularly over the next six years, even during 'Dom's last call.' " From left to right are Juliet (DiSilvio) Black, Dana (Coyne) Goldcamp, Sabina (Romito) Berger, and Karen (Sproule) Pike.

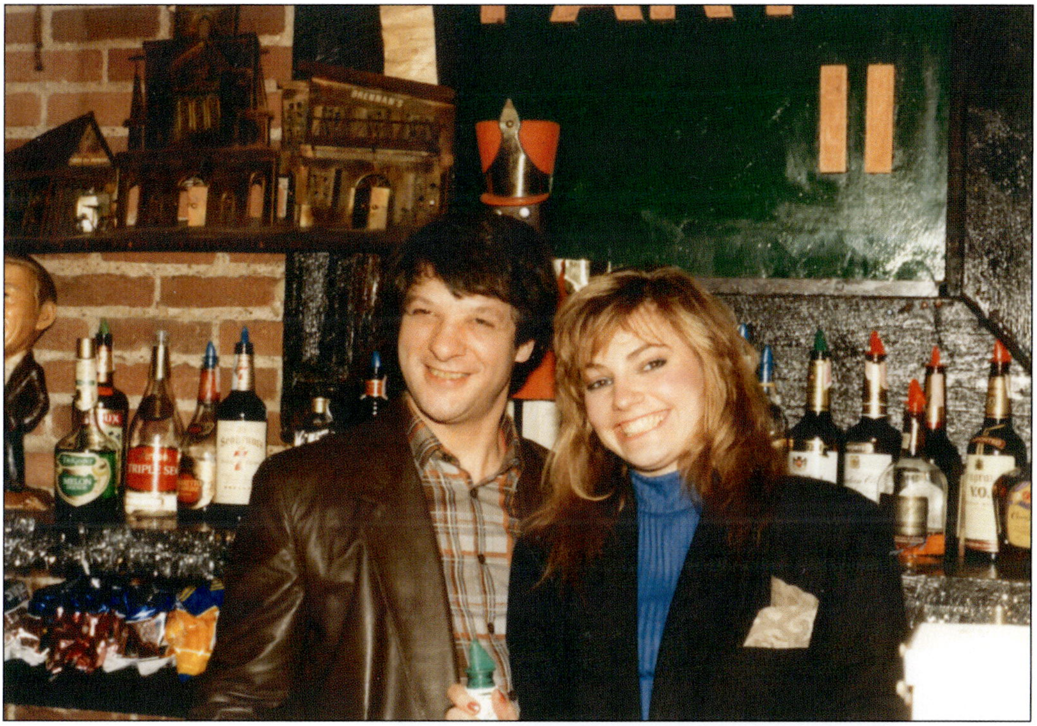

Dom's eldest daughter Gina is pictured above with her godfather and uncle, Dom's younger brother, Richard DiSilvio. Rich actually worked for a time as the Decade manager. Although being employed by his older brother was not always easy, Rich looks back fondly on his short stint as the bar's manager. Caesar DiSilvio and his now wife Ilene (right) spent many nights at The Decade but recall especially the time when their good friends Nick and Jen Wohlfarth decided to get married at the bar. A judge who was later arrested for public intoxication married them on the stage complete with all of the wedding essentials. The couple went on to get re-married outside of a bar, but Ilene and Caesar still think back on this fun, spontaneous night.

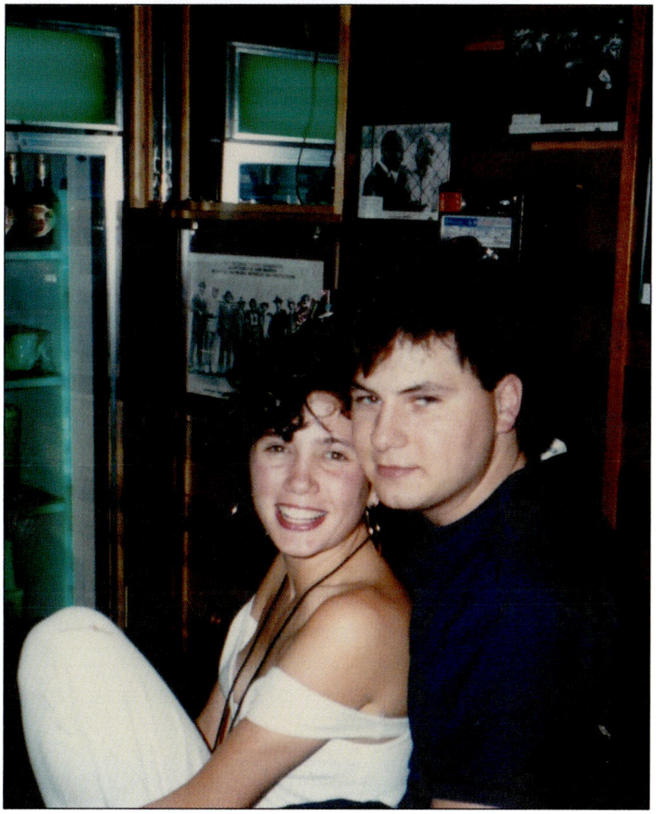

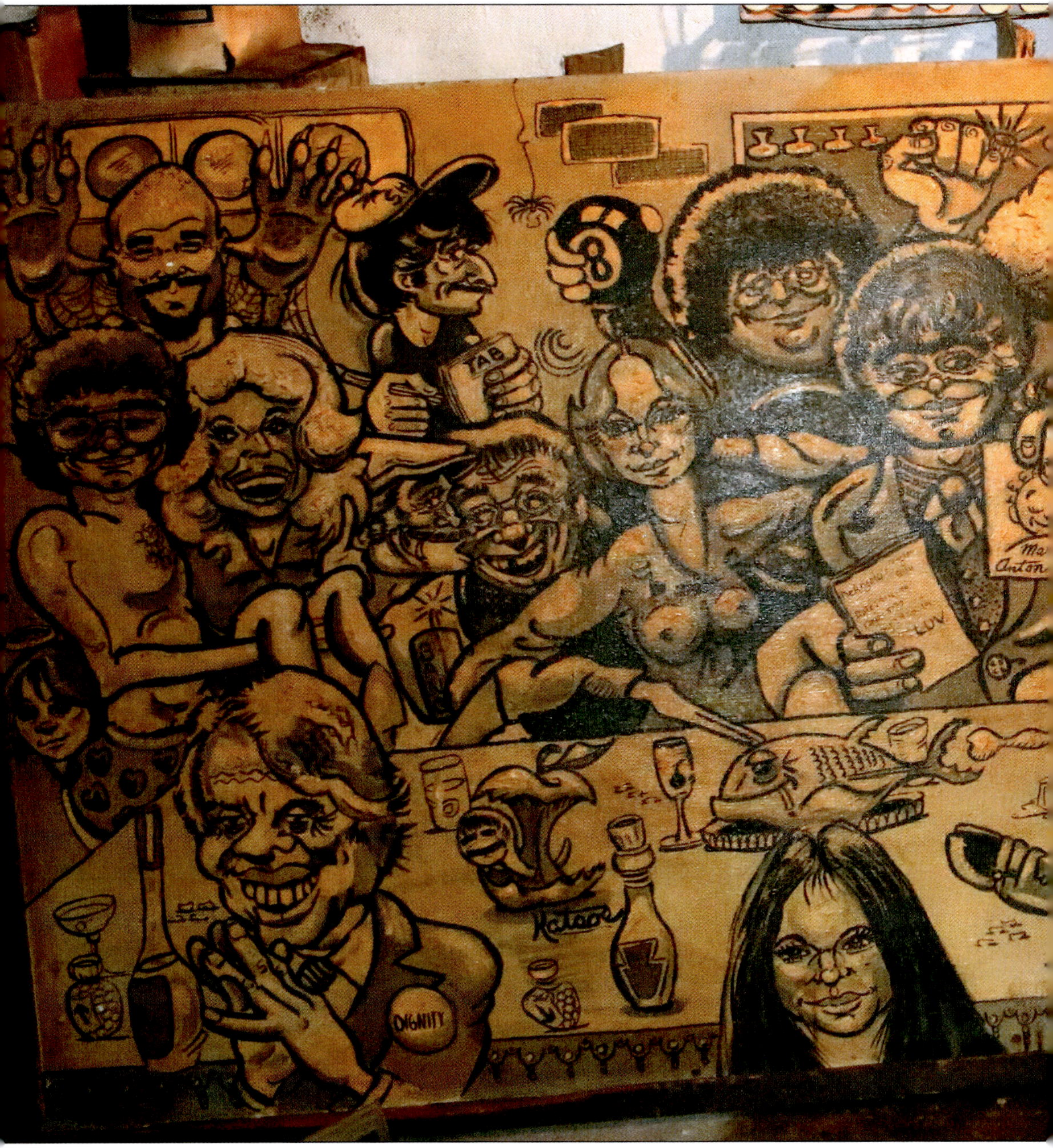

Located in the center of Oakland, The Decade catered to the college students who surrounded the bar. However, the loyal Decade employees and the regulars who packed the bar day and night became the lifeblood of the establishment. George Katsos, an occasional patron, had a unique

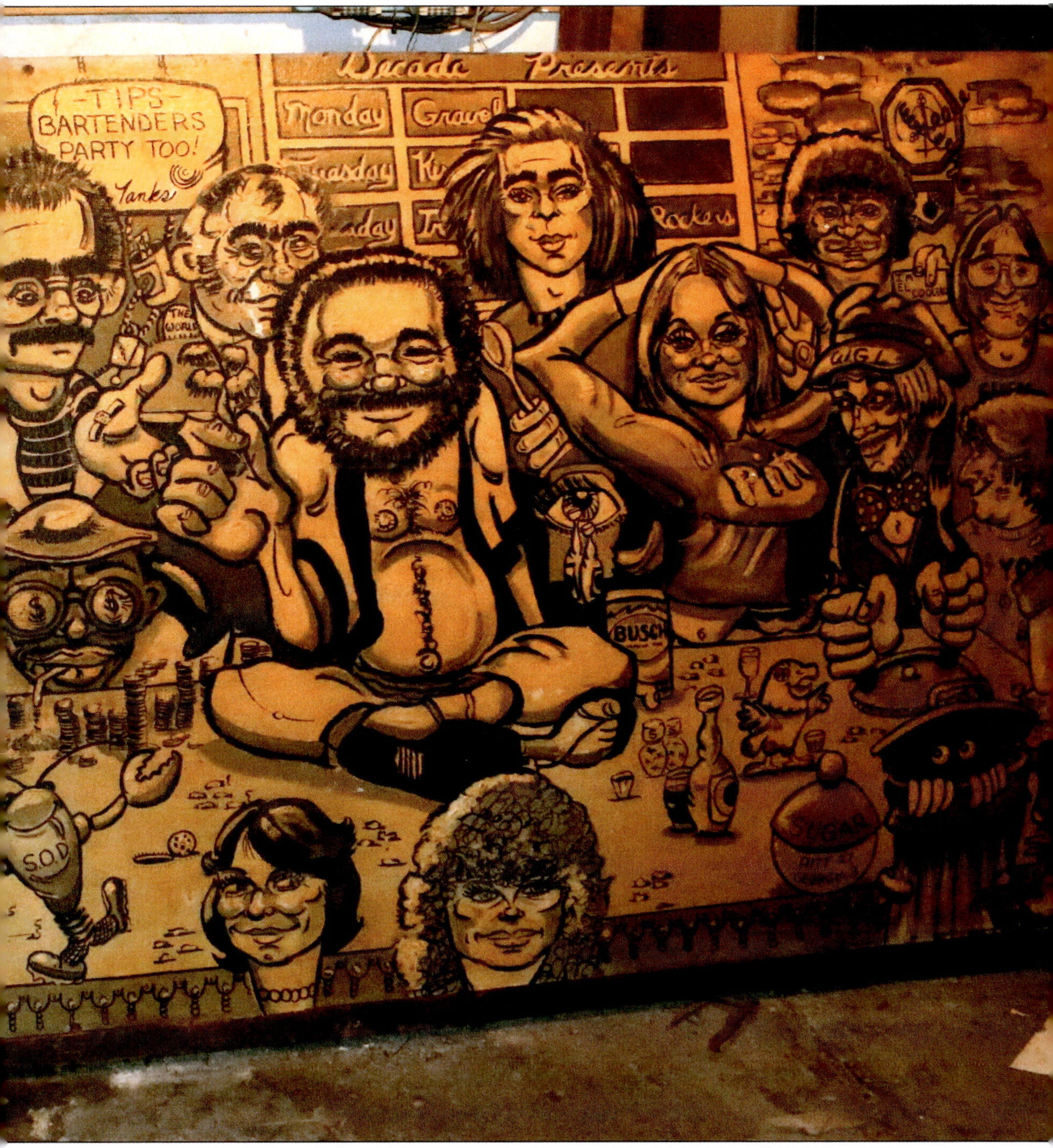

pastime: drawing caricatures of local bar patrons. Noticing his talent, Dom hired him to paint a mural commemorating some of his favorite regulars. When Katsos died suddenly in 1979, he had started several other murals, but the one for The Decade was his last fully completed piece.

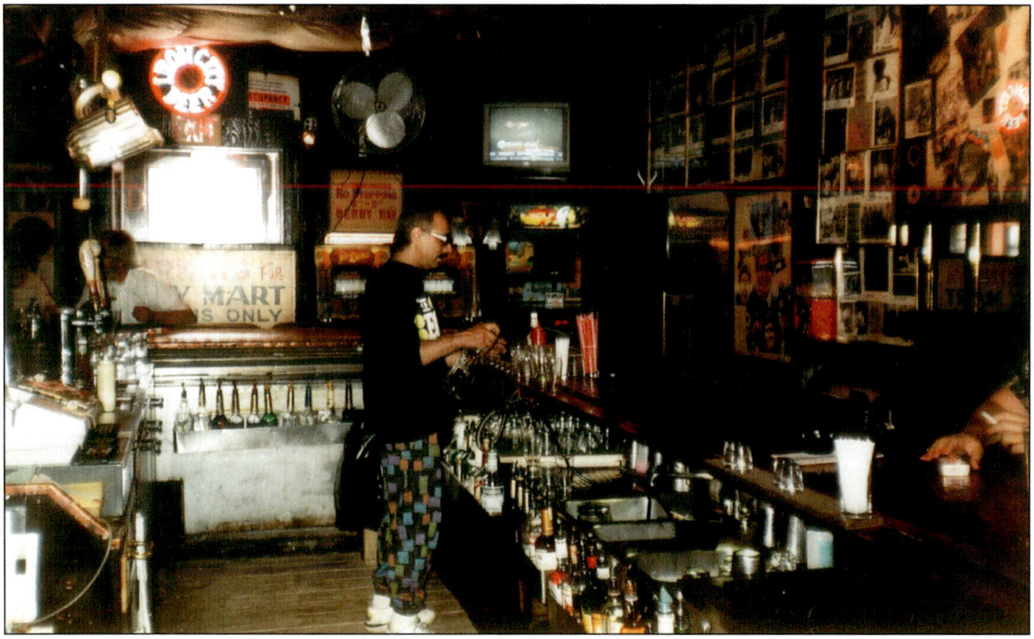

John Fareri began tending bar at The Decade around 1976 and continued on until its closing. Before that, he worked as a physical education teacher, but he preferred bartending. He was Italian, which appealed to Dom, and grew up with two brothers and a sister in Brookline, Pennsylvania. He served as the beloved daytime bartender for nearly 20 years and became a staple for those who packed the bar during daylight hours.

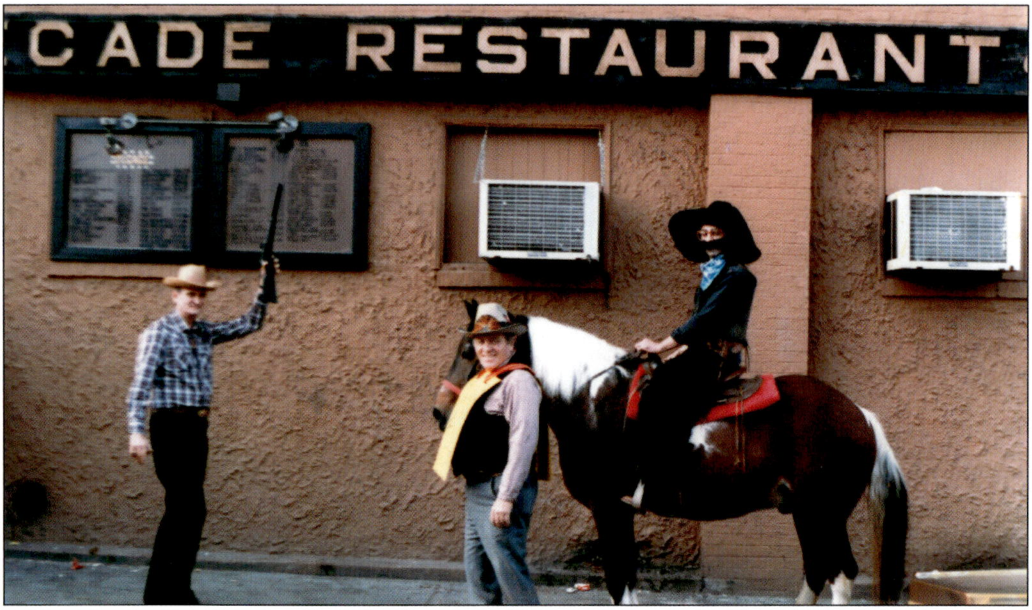

Taking artistic direction from Jan, John Fareri spent every Friday disguised as a pop-culture icon. No costume was off limits for him. The list includes, but is not limited to, Swish Larue (a fictitious, gay cowboy character who rode horseback through Oakland advertising The Decade), a University of Pittsburgh cheerleader (in an original uniform), the Tin Man, Charlie Chaplin, Groucho Marx, Pee-wee Herman, Father Guido Sarducci, the Energizer Bunny, and Gumby.

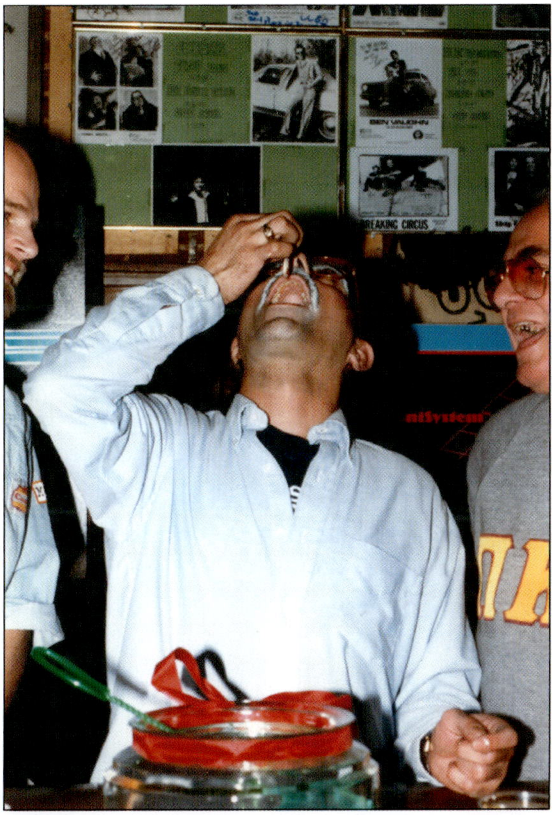

Known for his outlandish behavior, John participated in all Decade events and gained a special place in the hearts and minds of many Pittsburghers after consuming 50 goldfish, for a dollar donation each, at Jimmy Roach and Steve Hansen's seventh annual fundraiser for Children's Hospital of Pittsburgh. A Decade patron also recalls a time when Fareri revoked someone's restroom privileges due to their allegiance to Penn State; bathrooms were Pitt only. Above all, John was a character. Sadly, he passed away at age 60 on May 16, 2013. Dom considered him a phenomenal employee and an even better friend.

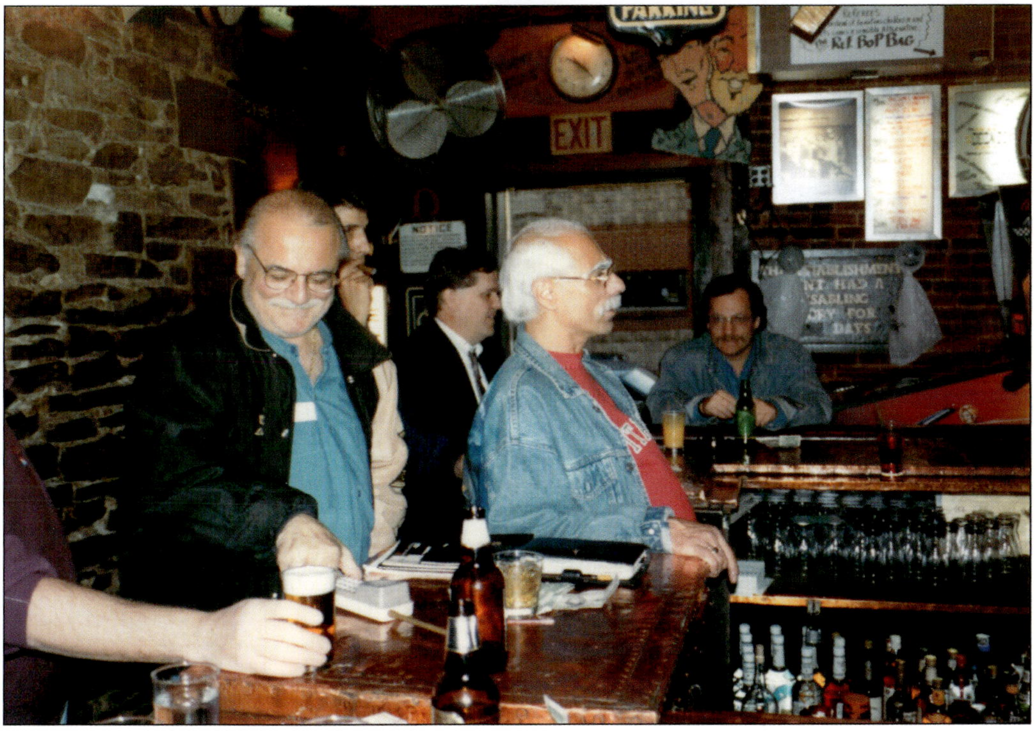

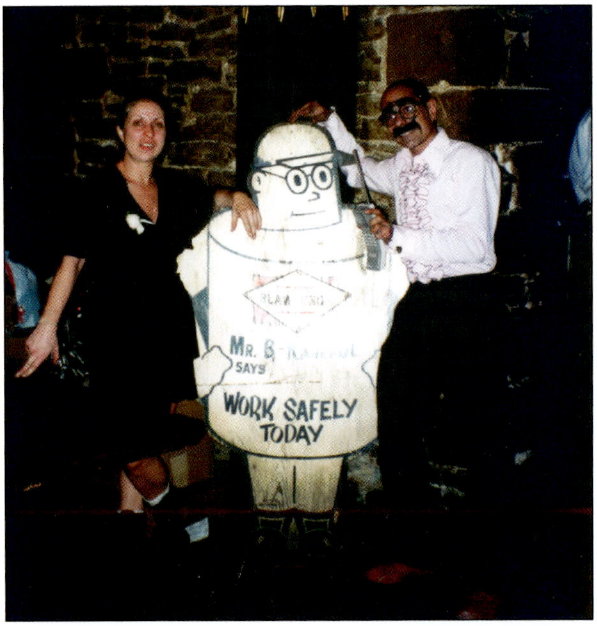

Waitress Irene Fine, pictured next to Fareri, held the longest tenure at the bar. With 22 years of service to The Decade, she outlasted even Dom and Jan, as both owners spent a year away from the place. Due to this, Irene quickly became a part of the family—she babysat all the DiSilvio kids and accompanied the family on their summer vacations. This was during the time when Dom and Jan would close the bar for a month and invite Decade employees to join them on their annual trip to the Jersey Shore.

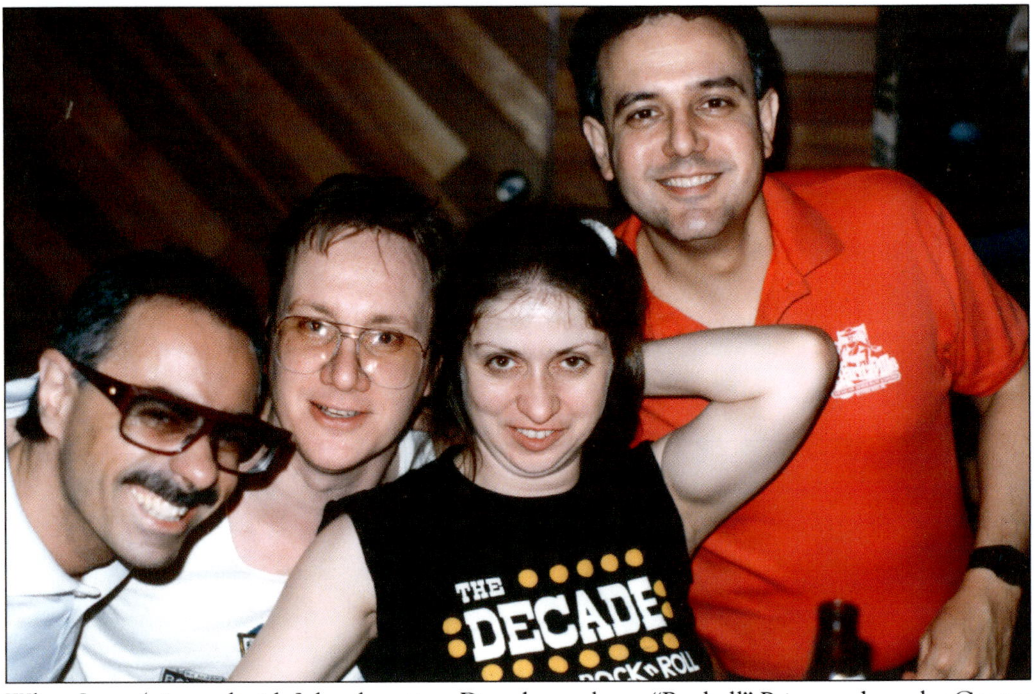

When Irene (pictured with John, longtime Decade employee "Rayball" Price, and regular George Sliman) started at the bar, the waitresses wore black dresses with gold striped tube tops; later on, there was no uniform besides the beloved Decade t-shirts. Her work was not limited to waitressing, as she worked six days a week and made all of the salad dressings, and in the role of head waitress, trained every new waitress. Irene additionally worked nights and served as an occasional bartender in the back bar when it opened in 1978. When asked if working at The Decade for 22 years of her life was time well spent, Irene explains, "I wouldn't trade in those years for anything because I met good people, ate good food, and watched good bands. It was like family there."

On November 17, 1980, the day of his 20th birthday, Billy Pascale became a daytime employee at The Decade. Attending college at Pitt and 300 miles from his parents, The Decade quickly became home. Pascale rose up to nighttime employee and eventually served as manager for 15 years. He insists that Dom and The Decade taught him vital life lessons: first, never mistake kindness for weakness, and second, you can't rock 'n' roll sitting down. When it comes to the closing night, Pascale said he "could've waited 10 years for that night." Pictured here is a young Pascale with friend and coworker Kelly McGough.

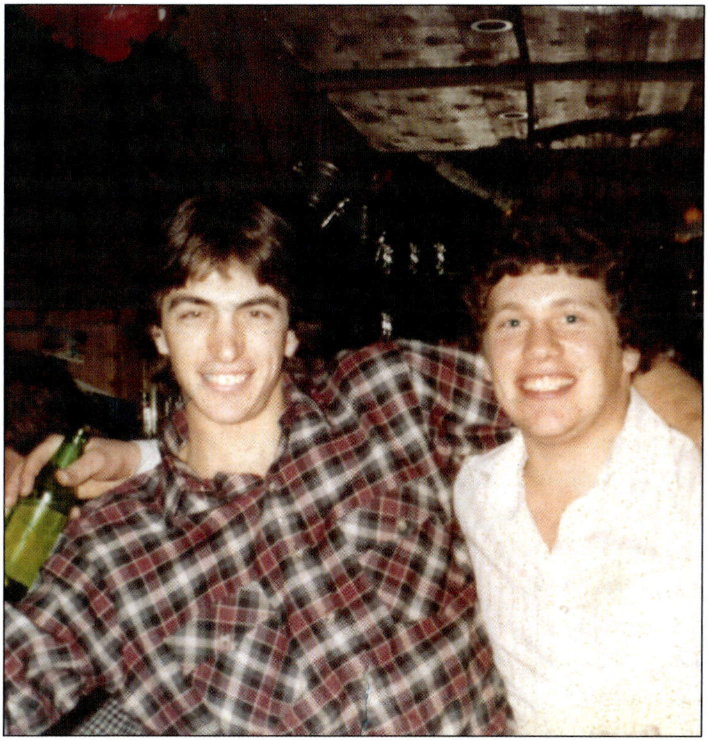

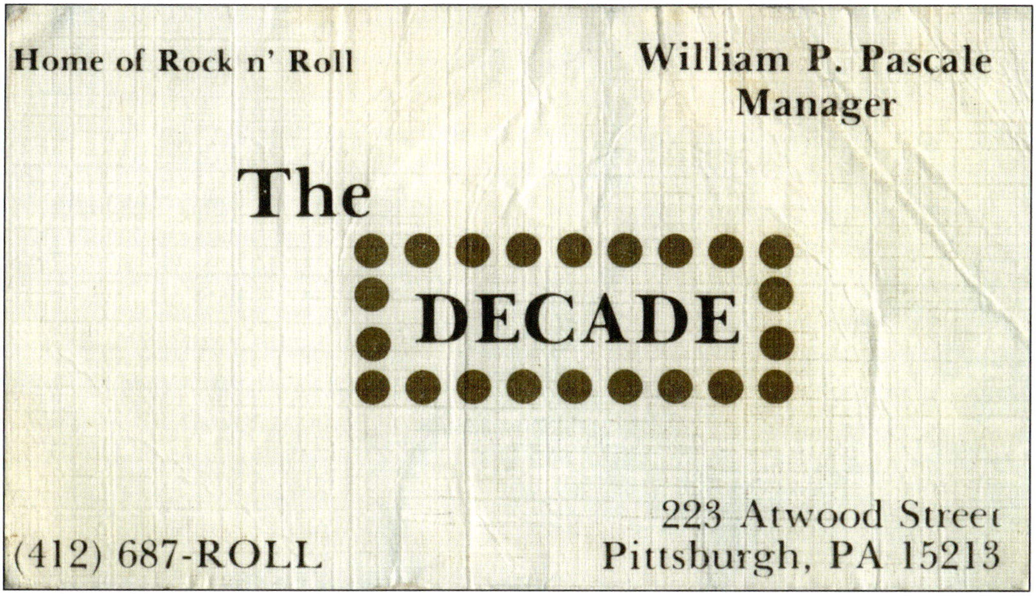

Billy Pascale witnessed a lot during his time at The Decade, yet most notable was likely one of his first nights, the night of the infamous "wig incident." Pascale dutifully manned his post behind the bar when two drunk men began making advances towards Dom's second wife, Judy. This provoked Dom, and a fight broke out. Pascale attempted to end the situation by pulling one man up by his hair; unfortunately, he had snagged his boss, and the hair ended up in Pascale's hand and off of Dom's head. Pascale had unintentionally revealed Dom's habit of wearing a hairpiece. Needless to say, Dom humbly embraced his hair loss after this night.

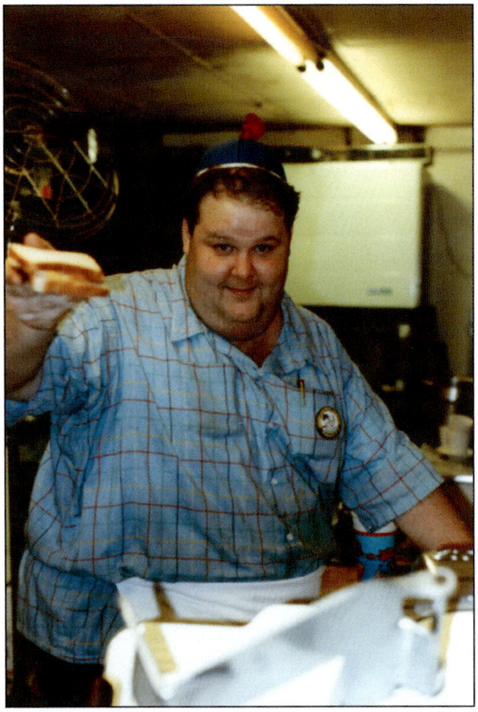

One of the main stalwarts of the kitchen staff was chef Chester Finkbeiner. He was an ideal bar chef; great at making staple bar foods, many of them from scratch. His soups, salads, and chicken salad sandwiches were all legendary amongst the Oakland clientele. By lunchtime, many regulars from the hospitals filled The Decade, including Dr. Thomas Starzl, a heart transplant pioneer, and Bruce Dickson, health director for the city of Pittsburgh at the time. Even after some hospital employees had been transferred out of Oakland, they would go out of their way to continue frequenting The Decade for lunch. Finkbeiner and Jan were a dynamic team in the kitchen.

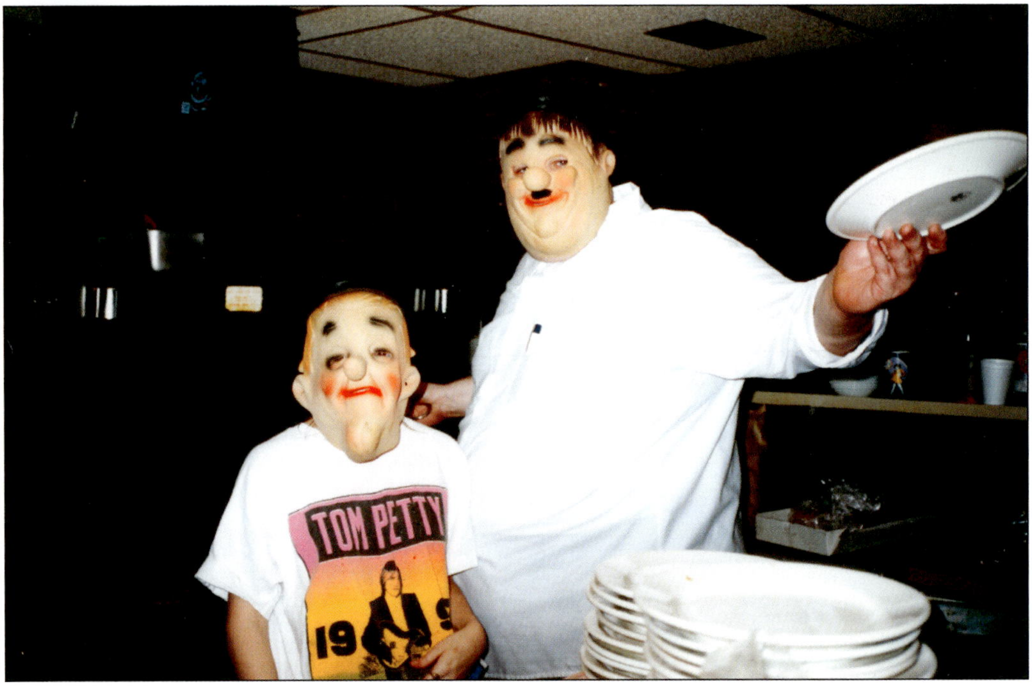

Chester was one of a kind. He stayed after hours and participated in all of the events that occurred in the bar. When forming his daily menus, he would include the specials of the day along with some off-color remarks concerning pop-culture news, employee antics, and some commentary on his boss. His menus were always very funny, very relevant, and often very offensive, but that was Chester. Pictured is Finkbeiner and his longtime assistant chef April Zottola.

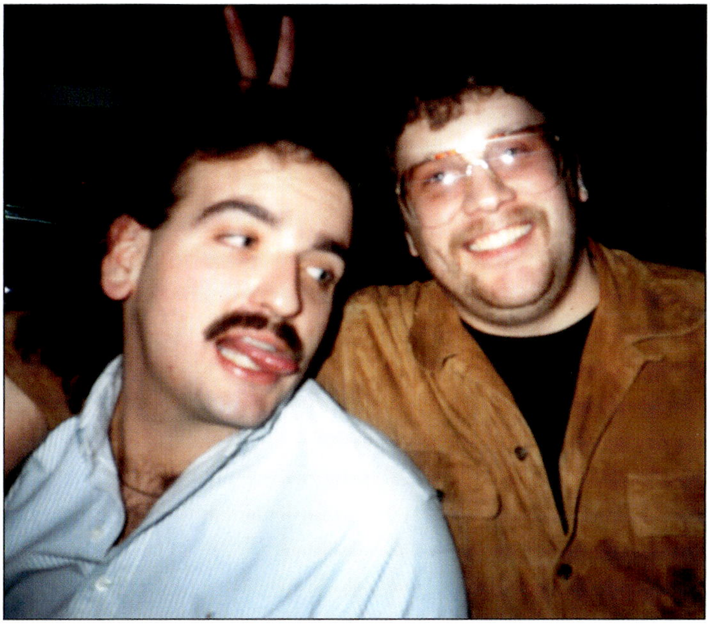

"The air never worked in that place but it was the greatest joint I've ever been to," longtime bartender Greg Nesbitt (left) began his interview. He then admitted that Dom deciding to close the bar broke his heart. In 1987, a young Nesbitt concocted a list of fake references because he wanted to work in the bar so badly. His first day of work was his first day bartending. One summer, Nesbitt claims to have worked 60 consecutive nights, yet on his first night off, he went to the only place he wanted to be: The Decade.

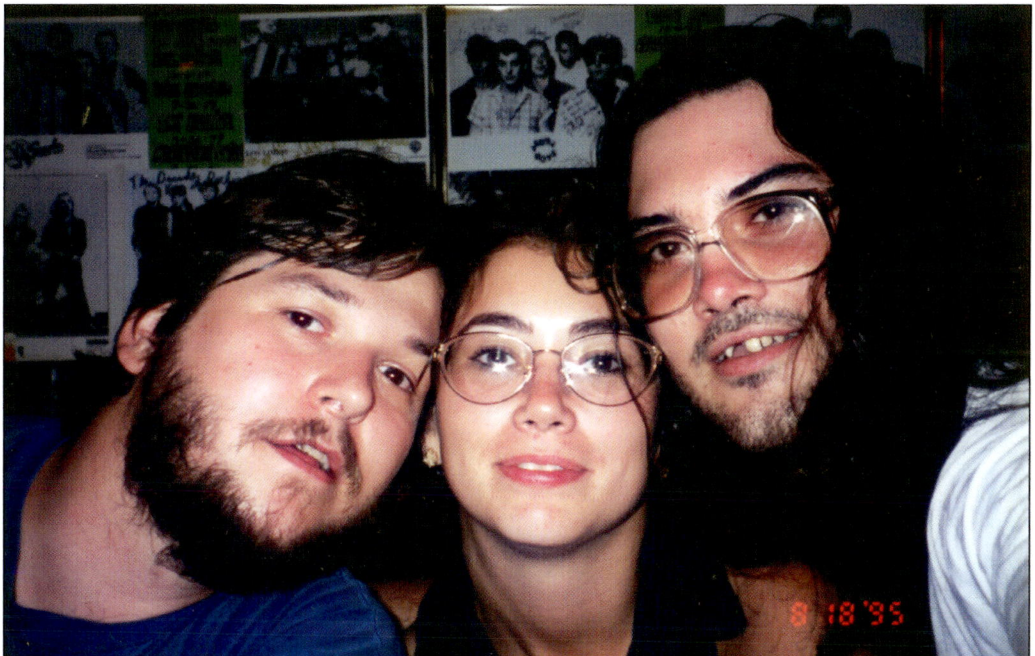

Some of The Decade's bartenders included Andy Casciato, Bobbie Jim DeAngelo, Bryan Presco, Caesar DiSilvio, Chuck Staley, Danny Casciato, Dante DiSilvio, Domenique DiSilvio, Flea McCavney, Fly McCavney, Greg Nesbit, Jimmy Capizi, John Fareri, John McCanowitz, Kelly McGough, Mike Fonas, Scooter, Stephen Bassett, Sue Hood, T.J. Spina, and Tim Acklin. This list is most definitely lacking, but these were just a few of the familiar faces who spent some time behind the bar. A few of them are pictured here.

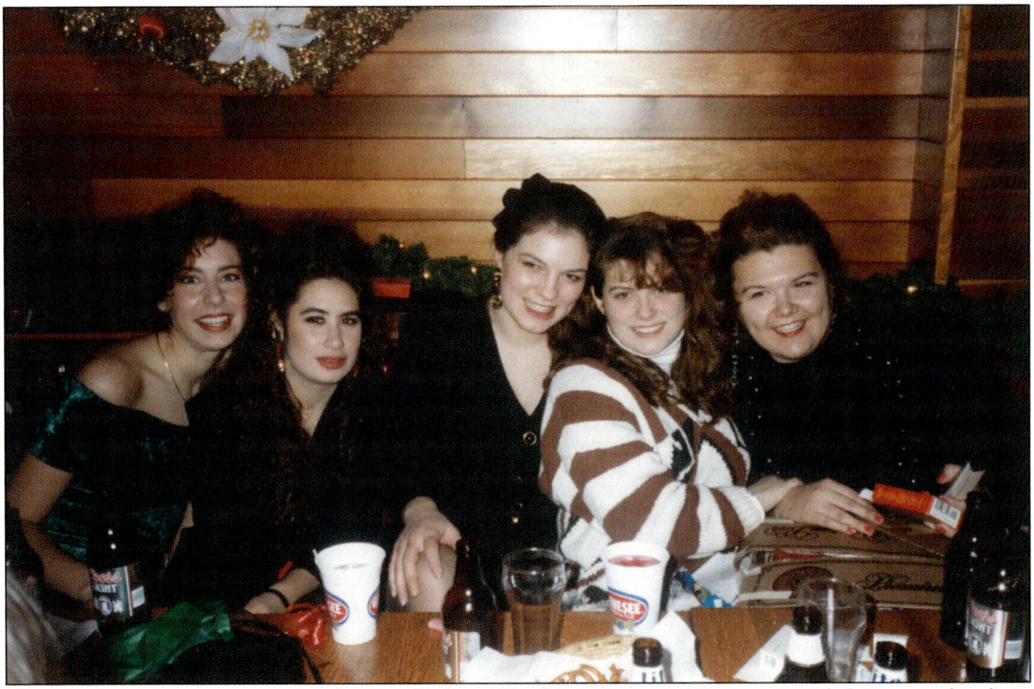

The waitresses were an essential part of life at The Decade, receiving a special shout out for their "polite" behavior in *Details* magazine. The wait staff, led by Irene Fine, included Amy Geier, Amy Boberg, Aimee Wenke Butch, Alyssa Schmitt, Avi Schmitt, Angie McClintock Hay, Lori Faiella, Sam Sheen, Lisa "Boom Boom" Booher, Michelle Becker, Little Gina, Theresa Leahey Van Ollefen, Bonnie Book, Christine Proto Danko, Dana Coyne Goldcamp, Scooter, Dawn Hedland, Dawn Waters, Denise, Gina DiSilvio Means, Juliet DiSilvio Black, Gracie, Jen Resutko Scalo, Jodi O'Brien, Jodi, Lisa Fonas, Maria Kuzma, Nancy "Sluggo," Natalie Kratsas, Sabina Romito Berger, Sharon and Maria, Samantha Steinmiller, Melody Macey, Kathleen Law, and many more. Several of them are pictured here.

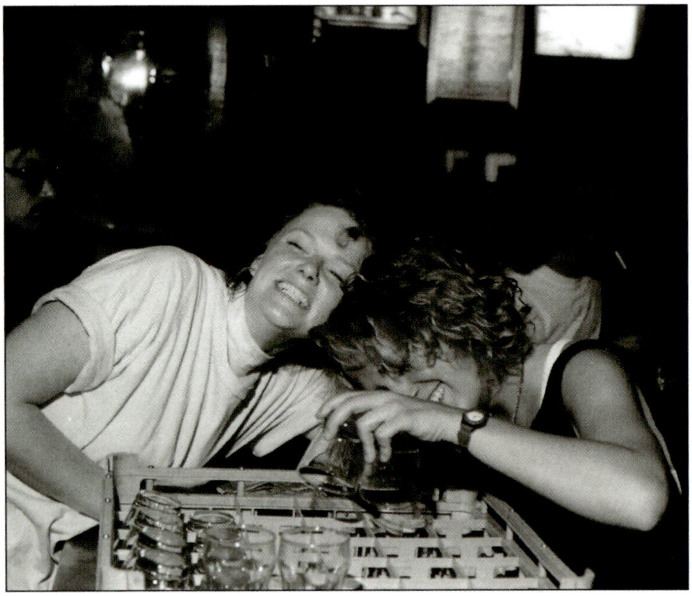

Decade waitress Amy Geier (not pictured) remembers going in to work on Monday mornings to collect any wooden chairs that weren't broken to set up in the dining room for lunch. This was before Dom made the smart business decision to switch to metal chairs. The place was rowdy back then. In an interview for the closing, John Fareri concurs, stating, "When I first started, it wasn't unusual at the end of the night to take all the bar towels and pass them out to wipe up the blood after all of the fights." (Photograph by Kurt Weber.)

Perhaps all of this fighting had to do with the tough bouncers at the bar. Dom's son Dante remembers returning to the bar anytime he got in a fight elsewhere because the bouncers would have his back. The Decade bouncers became notorious for being a crew of guys no one wanted to mess with. The list of bouncers includes, but is not limited to, Dan Means, Darryl, Greg and Dave from McKees Rocks, Eddie Casciato, Greg Brickl, Jim Fuller, Joe "Buster" Brown, John Eckert, John McClemonds, Mike Kosko, Mike Welch, and Steve Orlando. At right are Billy Pascale and Kelly McGough dressed in drag with bouncer "Big John."

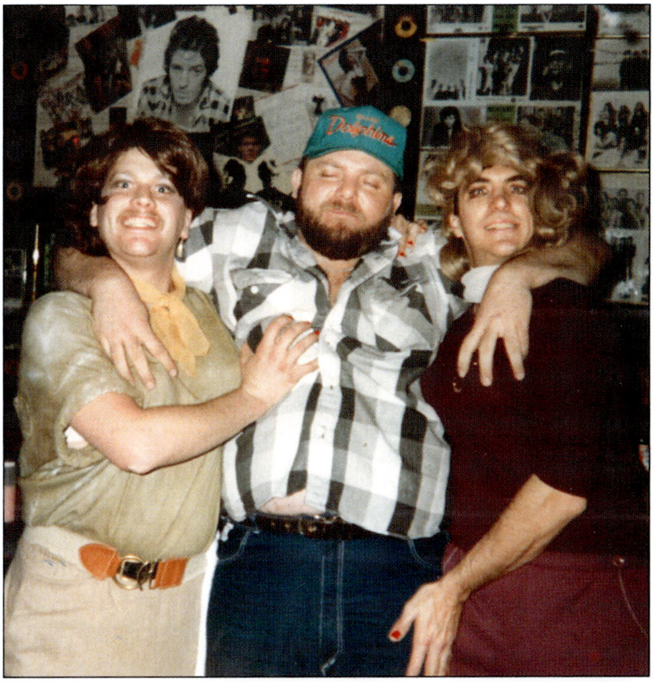

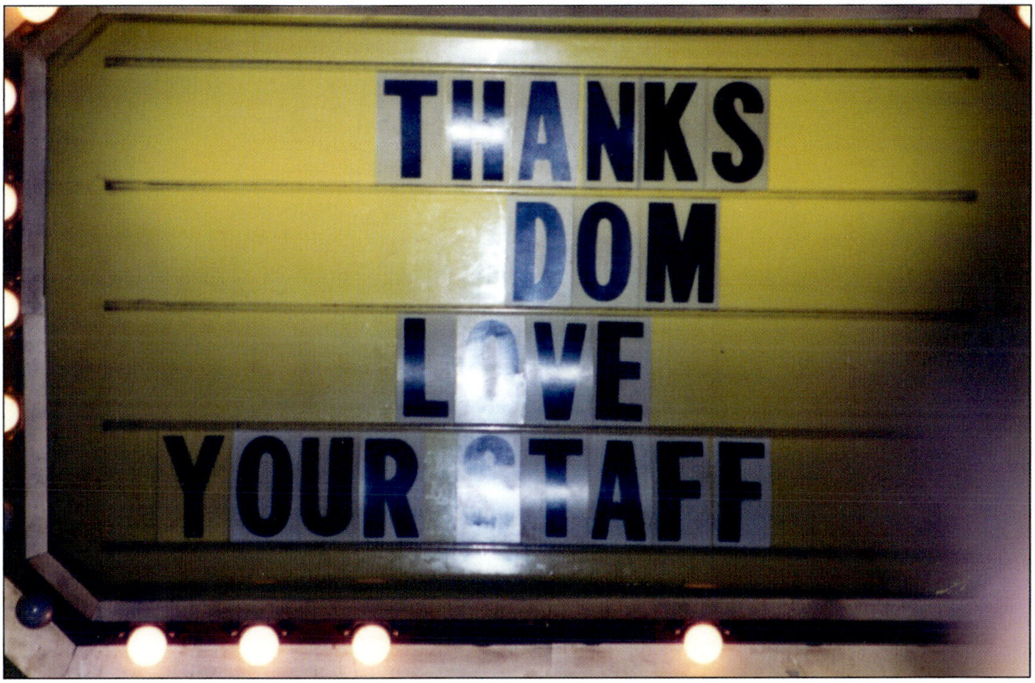

The Decade staff acted as a family. Thanksgiving dinner was served at the bar for anyone who could not go home or had nowhere else to go. In fact, the bar was open every day except Christmas Eve, which is part of the reason the employees became a family. On every birthday, the staff, whether they were working or not, would come into the bar to get pied in the face; it was a tradition. Christmas parties were also a huge event; all of the staff attended, and naturally, John dressed up as Santa. But the employees were not the only people who made up The Decade's family.

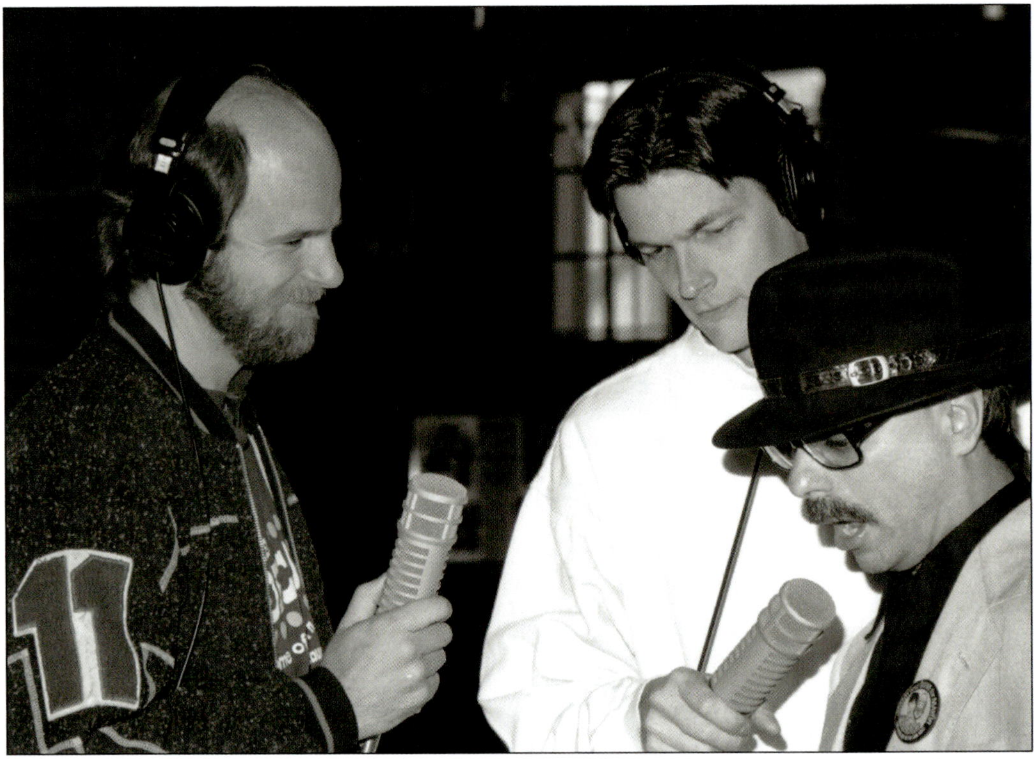

Local radio personas Jimmy Roach (right) and Steve Hansen paved the way for the "morning zoo" format with their comedic duo and satirical bits on WDVE. The two strived to promote local performers and often found themselves working closely with Dom, whether it be at their charity event Toys for Tots or during the times when they actually hosted their morning show from The Decade. Once, after a short hiatus from Pittsburgh, they made a triumphant return atop a bulldozer; Hansen donned an official Decade t-shirt. (Courtesy of Kurt Weber.)

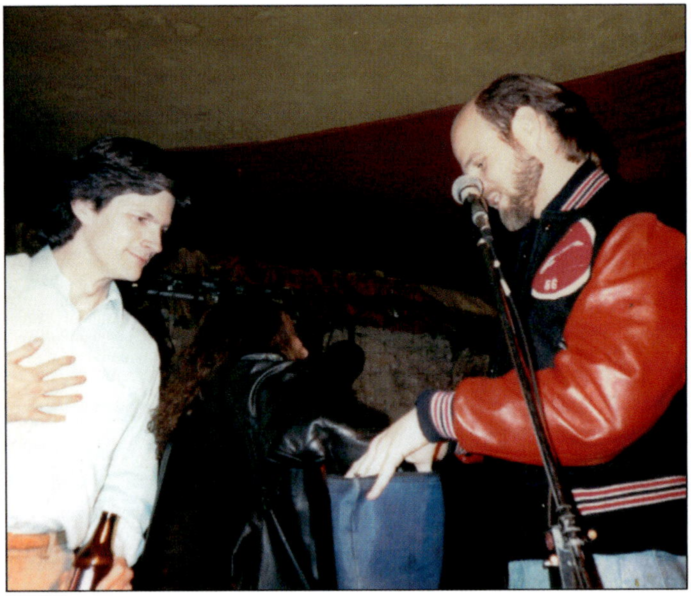

Jimmy (left) and Steve described their experiences seeing live music at The Decade, recalling the "hot zone," where people were focused on the music, and talking was not permitted. "The place was different. It was a way of life, not a club. It had its own persona; it was an alternate reality. It felt rock 'n' roll-y. It was in the heart of Oakland, under the shadow of the university. It legally fit 180 but could fit 500. It was claustrophobic." And yet they never had a bad time there. (Courtesy of Kurt Weber.)

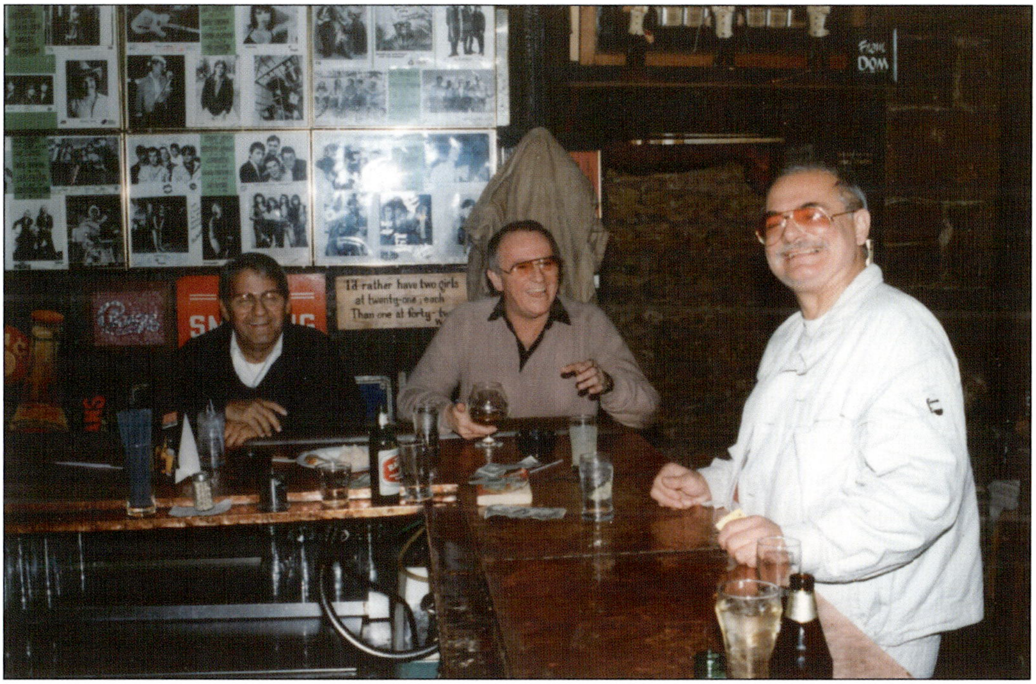

Dom's family and the employees made up a big part of the Decade clan, but the people who really added local color were the regulars who filled the bar. All walks of life considered The Decade home but, according to Scott Mervis, longtime Pittsburgh music reviewer and writer for the *Post-Gazette*, "to say they all got along was a myth; some of them got along, but others didn't. No one went to the other Oakland bars thinking there was gonna be a fight, but there were really some sort of over enthusiastic bouncers at The Decade."

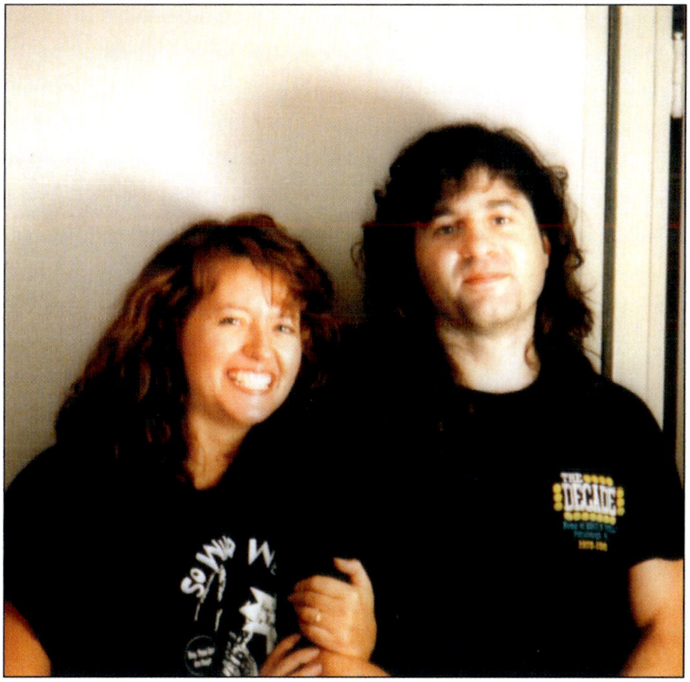

When Decade regular Katie Bicknell walked toward the infamous back bar one night, she noticed Pat Huwe—something about his presence struck her. At the time, she was dating the drummer from local band 8th Street Rocks and had situated herself ideally to watch them perform: on the ramp toward the sound board. She noticed Huwe next to her and promised that she would get him a beer if he saved her spot, and the rest is history. The two have been married since 1993 and are one of many couples who first laid eyes on each other within The Decade's smoky interior.

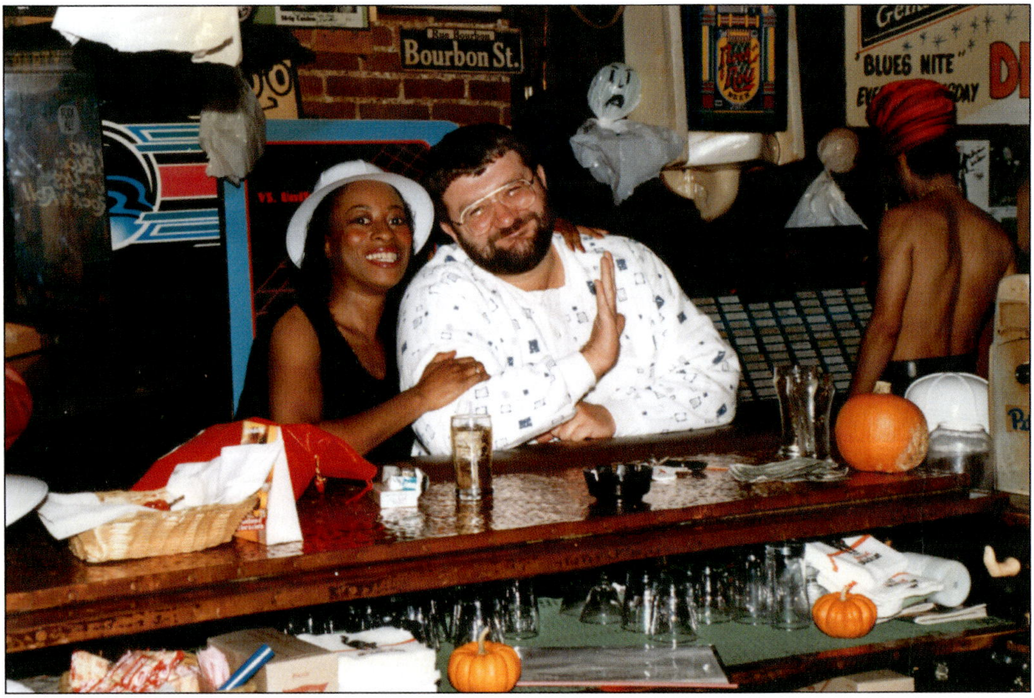

Jerry Weber, of Jerry's Records in Squirrel Hill, pictured with fellow regular Bee, worked previously as a mailman. He rose every morning at 6:00 a.m. to work at the post office across from The Decade. All of the postmen hung out at The Decade after 1:00 p.m. when the routes were finished. No matter how often they were reprimanded for being there during their shifts, The Decade was the mailman's home away from home; some wouldn't leave until 8:00 at night.

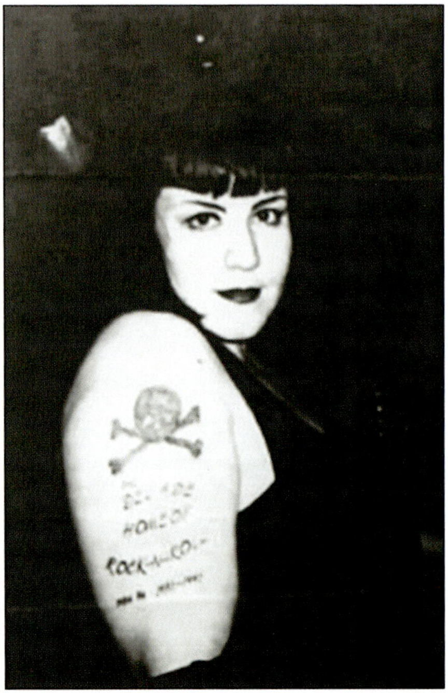

Michelle Walker, better known as "Wiggy," purchased an apartment above The Decade, unaware of how it would affect her life. A punk aficionado, she wandered downstairs one night to investigate the bar that once hosted the Ramones. Clad in her usual all black attire, Wiggy heard someone call her "Morticia Adams." She spat back, "Nice hat," to the culprit, Dom, who—for whatever reason—was wearing a sombrero that night. The two became friends instantly. For Wiggy, The Decade is the only place she ever truly called home, hence her tattoo.

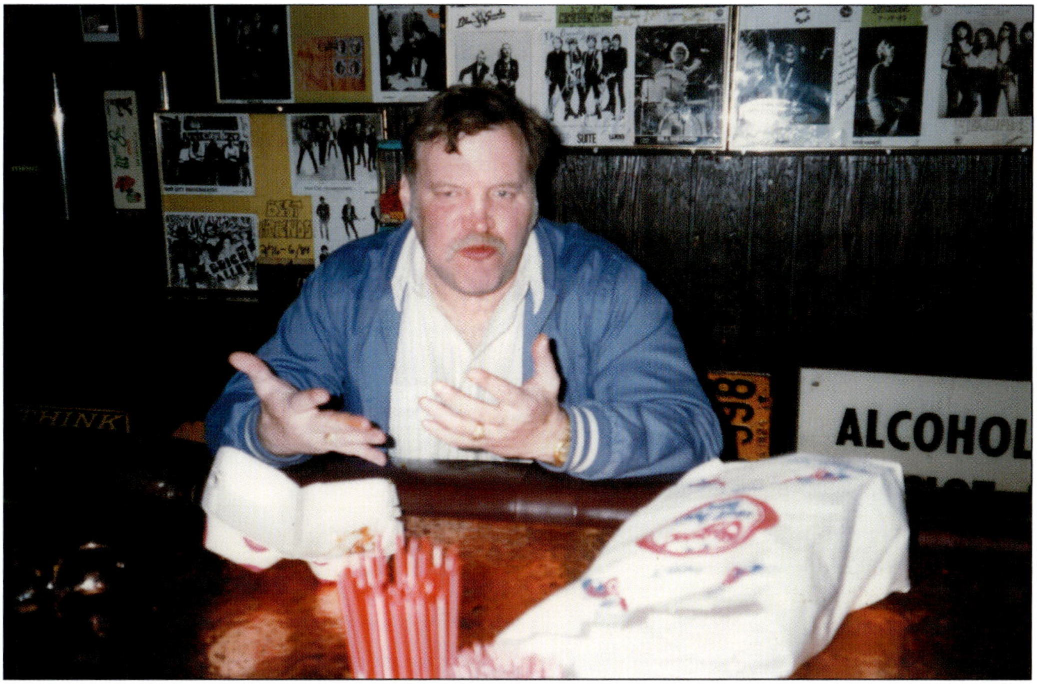

"Fire" was a regular who lived in an apartment near the bar; Dom can't remember why he was nicknamed that but does recall nicknaming his brother Smoke. He is a true example of a crazy regular who provided the local color Norm Nardini talked about. Other notable Decade frequenters included William "Boo" Connors (Pitt football equipment manager), along with football players Bill Fralic, Dan Marino, and Hugh Green.

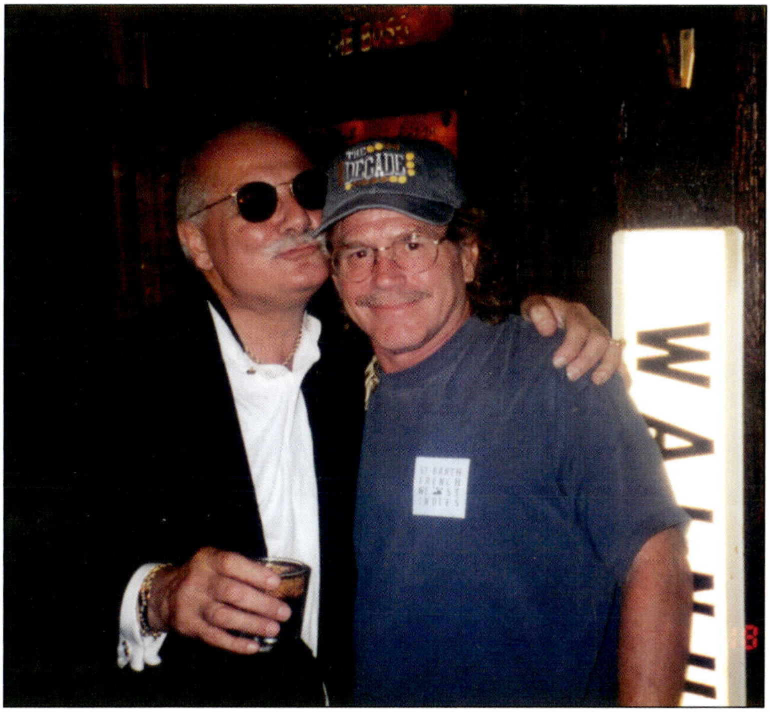

Longtime friend and regular Gary Zimmerman (right) was a prominent defense attorney in the city of Pittsburgh. He was introduced at many a family function as the "mouthpiece" for all of the DiSilvios. Not only was he a regular, but more importantly, he was a true friend of Dom's who has recently passed away. Dom misses him dearly.

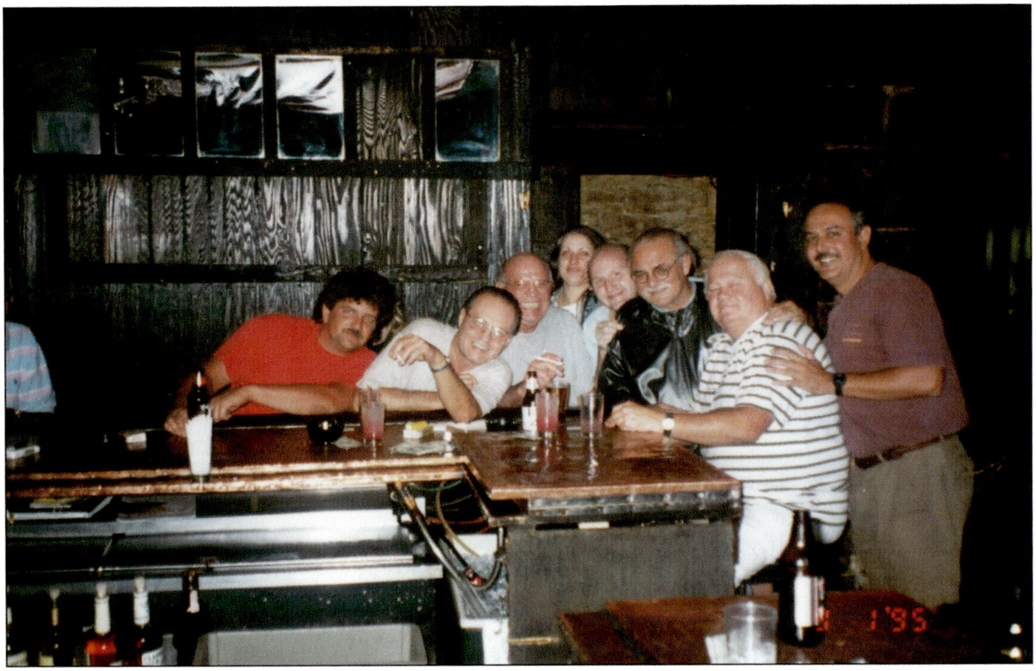

Many people considered The Decade a home. The employees, the regulars, and Dom's own family came together in an alternate reality of everlasting youth and extraordinary music, so it has become near mythical in the memories of those who spent their time there. Perhaps another reason for its mystical quality was the anticipation of what would happen there, because anything could happen at The Decade.

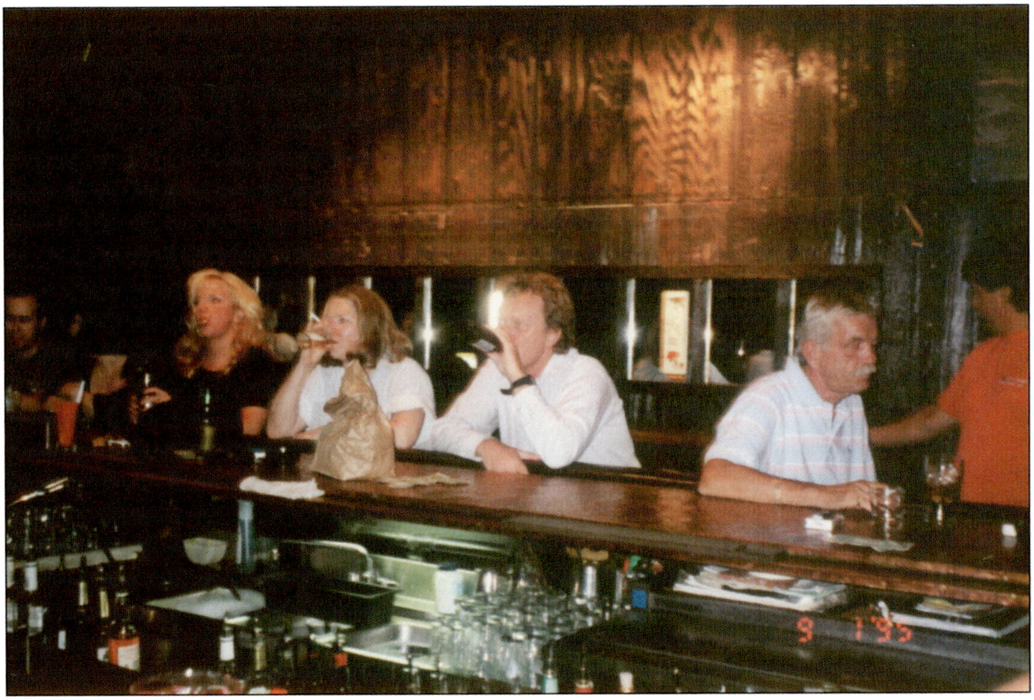

Five

Legendary Moments so Legendary, They may be Myths

Sure, the music was fantastic—that was a given. But there were a few other reasons people never wanted to leave The Decade.

With all of the bar's success musically and socially, it became the place people were talking about in the city of Pittsburgh. For visitors passing though, their friends made it a point to take them to The Decade. They just had to see it. Dom was lapping up the success as The Decade heralded a mention in the same sentence as places like the Stone Pony in Jersey. However, there was a singular element that differentiated The Decade from any other corner bar in the city. There was something different about the appearance, the smell, and the people. The Decade was very much its own unique place. Even still, a man was buried under the stage, mud wrestling occurred (much to the chef's dismay), a slew of celebrities chose to hit up the divey, smoky bar in Oakland, and to top it off, the place itself was covered in odd signage and paraphernalia while a large parachute covered the ceiling. The Decade was the stuff of legends. It is nearly too difficult to differentiate the mythical from the legendary, hence this chapter.

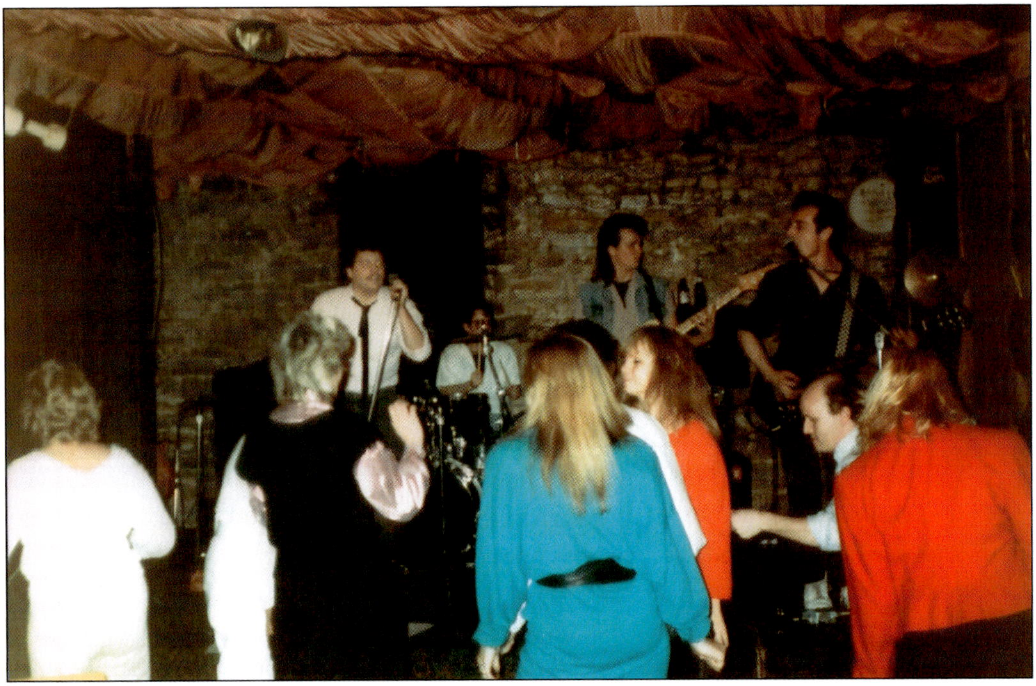

Many believe the parachutes were hung on the ceiling to enhance sound quality in the venue, but in reality, they were truly a display of Jan's resourcefulness. The landlord refused to fix the ceiling that was falling in, so Jan purchased some white parachutes and attempted to dye them red to hide the crumbling ceiling; however, they turned pink in the process. She got the idea from a photograph of a house of ill repute in Paris. Pieces of the ceiling would occasionally fall into the parachutes, and so they had to be emptied out from time to time. This do-it-yourself ceiling replacement made for impeccable acoustics in the bar, but it was all a happy accident.

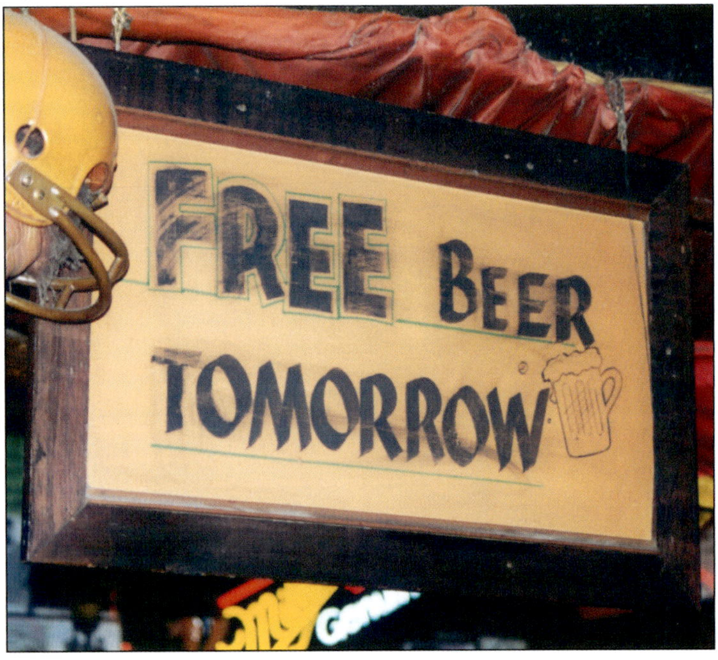

The rest of the decor on the walls of the bar was signage from Dom and Jan's travels. Included were signs from Dom's favorite places in New Orleans, New Jersey, and New York. There was a plethora of Pitt memorabilia, as The Decade served as a de facto University of Pittsburgh bar. At some point, customers began bringing in street signs that they wanted to hang forever in the bar, as a sort of offering to the Decade godfather. There wasn't an inch of empty wall space.

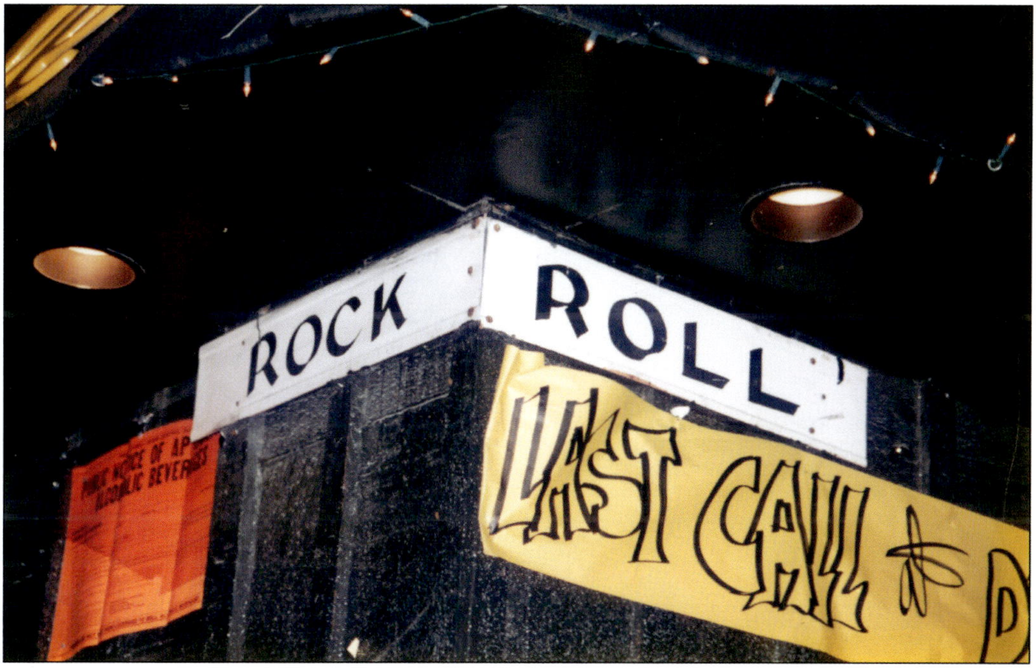

As Joe Grushecky recalls, there was a Halloween party at The Decade, and the place was packed. The Houserockers were the "hometown boys done good," having recently signed a record deal. Steve Popavich, who had signed them, was also involved with Meat Loaf, who was figuratively and literally (at six foot, six inches and 400 pounds) the biggest rock star at the time. The record company bigwigs and Meat Loaf were crammed in the greenroom, and since the green room was actually just the kitchen, it was packed. The staff were having difficulty serving food, and Dom had one of his characteristic meltdowns, demanding everyone leave the kitchen. Someone said, "Dom, don't you know who that is? It's Meat Loaf!" Dom yelled back, "I don't care if he's linguini and clam sauce—get him out of here!" This story has been told countless times, each with different foods, but Grushecky claims the original line was "linguini and clam sauce".

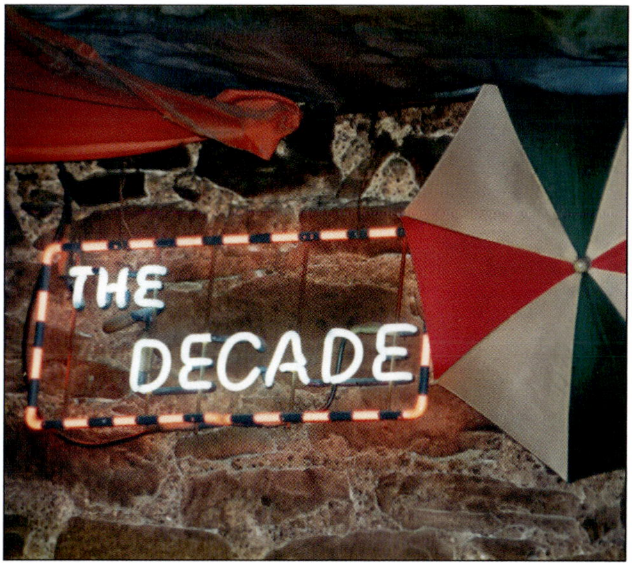

Once, the health department came in and found a plethora of issues (not surprisingly) and gave the staff 20 days to correct them. They only corrected a few, so in a hasty attempt to solve the problem, manager Tommy Cherabin chose this particular moment to paint the floors. When the health department returned, they could not get in because the floors were wet. They were then forced to pass The Decade. That was the kind of place it was, a place that needed to do anything it could to keep the health inspector out, and yet, people continued to eat lunch there every day.

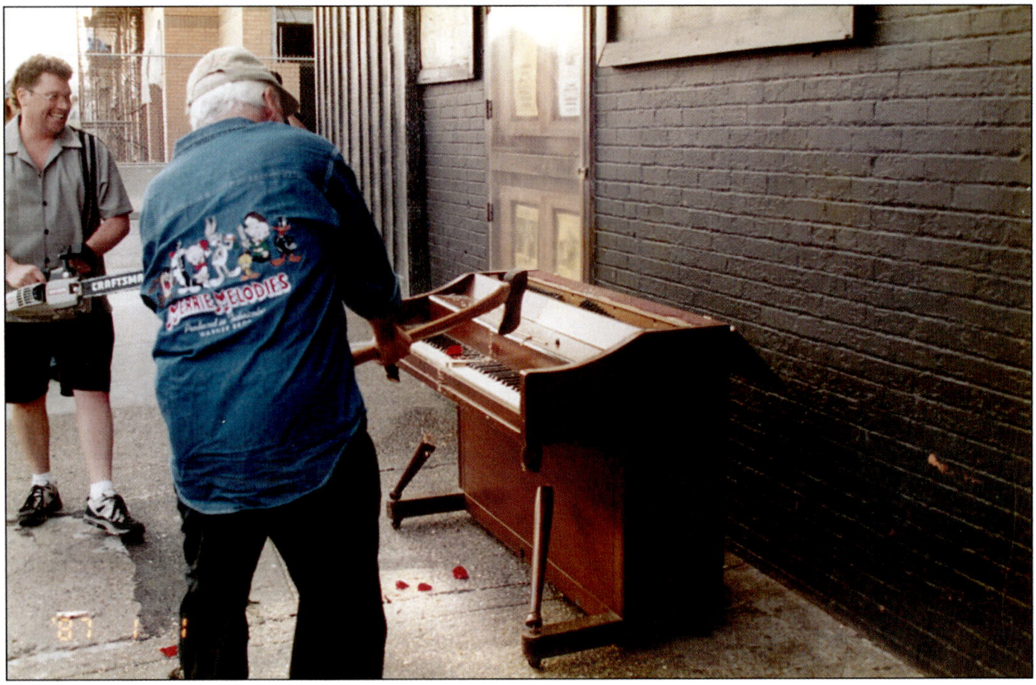

During an Iron City Houserockers reunion party at The Decade, Gilbert decided to chop a piano in half onstage. The next day, when Billy Pascale and Dom were moving the piano outside, they decided to chop it up some more to ease the load of the garbagemen—or just because they wanted to get in on the fun. Either way, the garbagemen witnessed Dom and Pascale and apparently stated, "Boy, these white people are crazy."

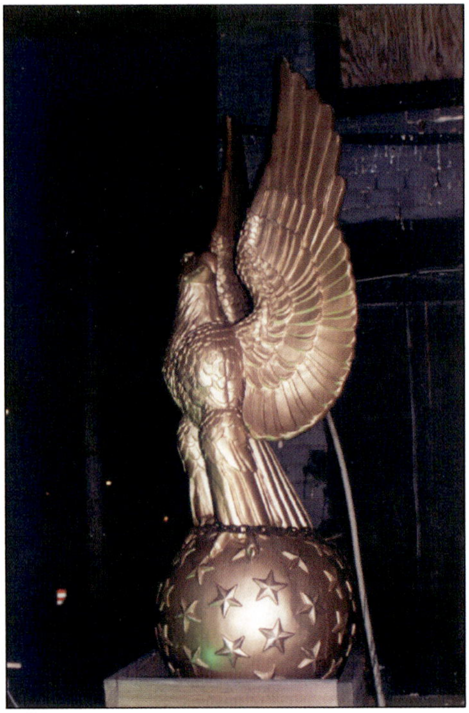

On the infamous last night at The Decade, there were many tears shed, many songs played, and many memories relived. On the same night, "the Decade Eagles," two large, golden eagle statues, were removed from their usual perch on the roof. The next morning, Wiggy Walker, who lived above The Decade, awoke to find the Eagles in her shower. She knew Dom would not be pleased if he found them at her place, so she decided to ride the statues down the stairs and leave them in the laundry room, where they were eventually found. To this day, Wiggy will not reveal the identity of the eagle thieves, except to say, "It was someone who really loved the place."

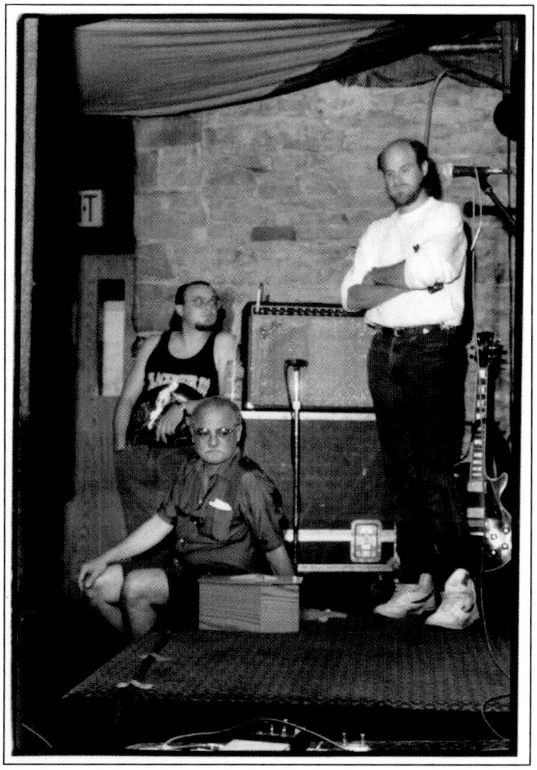

Was there someone buried under that small Decade stage? Yes, there was indeed. Bob Boyer—Iron City roadie, soundman, and songwriter—passed away without a family, so Dom and his Decade family paid for his funeral. He was cremated, and Dom decided to bury his ashes under the Decade stage. He was quite a talented songwriter who co-wrote a few songs for The Houserockers, one of which is about Dom and The Decade. The opening lyric is "I'm going down to Dom's cafe, just to have a beer." However, later lyrics "Old man bar is where I am and where I'll be," seemed to suit the beloved roadie perfectly, and so they were written on his memorial plaque on the Decade stage. Pictured at right are Gilbert Snyder, Dom, and Steve Hansen at Boyer's burial. Below is Norm Nardini onstage beside Boyer's plaque.

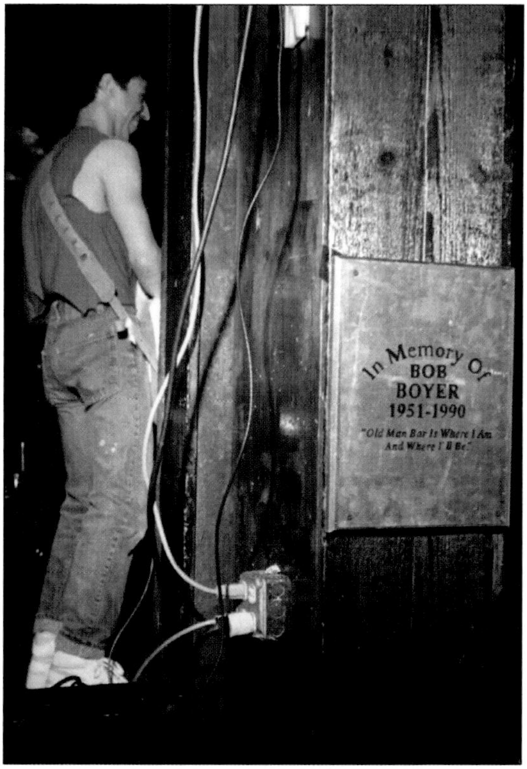

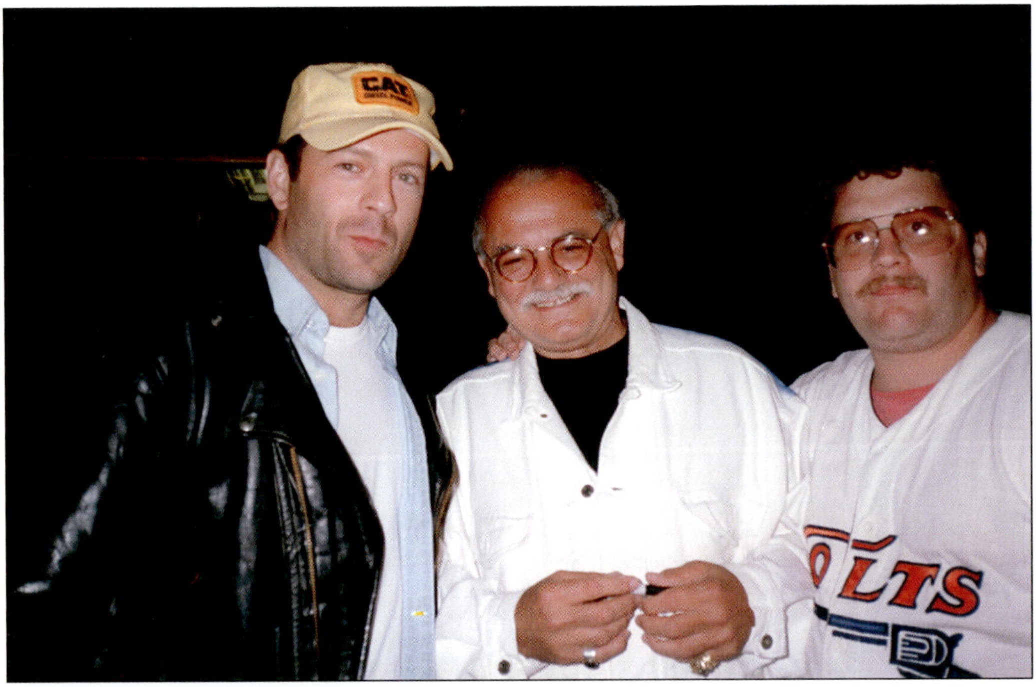

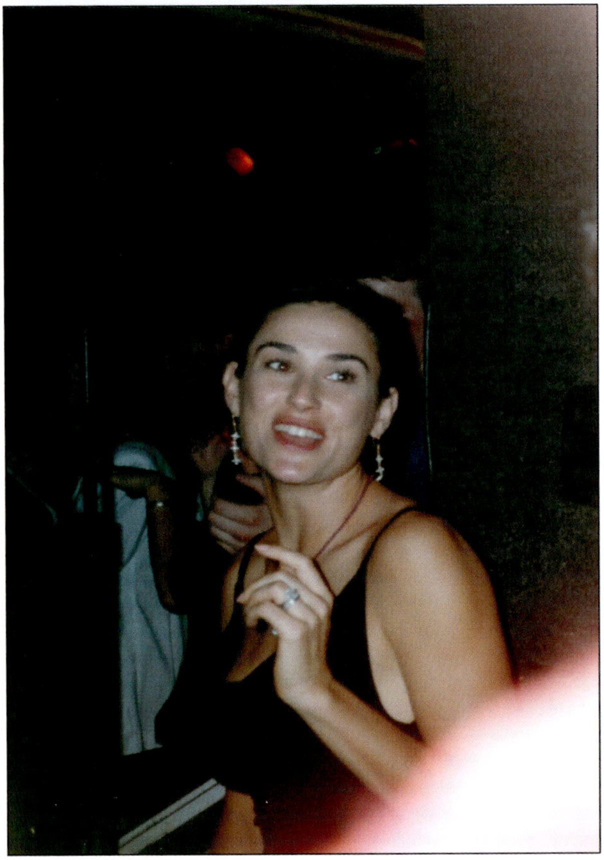

Dom got a call one day from Bruce Willis's manager, asking if the *Die Hard* star could perform at the bar with his LA–based blues group. Dom agreed to allow Willis to play but refused to pay the actor. The band arrived with Willis's then wife, Demi Moore, and were rushed to the dressing room to avoid being mobbed—Demi specifically asked that no photos be taken of her. As seen at left, no one thought much of her request. In the dressing room, the band requested a rider—a list of gratuities—and Dom agreed to a few cases of beer but "nothing else." After the performance, the couple hung around the bar and chatted with employees. When Willis finished up his gig, Dom told him to "keep his day job." Pictured above with Willis are Dom and Billy Pascale.

Eddie and the Otters decided to throw a beach party at The Decade. To go about this, Dom and Billy Pascale brought in sand and a huge water pit. The place was a mess, and as usual, the whole bar had to be cleaned up to serve lunch to customers the next day. Pascale claims, "If the people who ate there in the day knew what happened at night, the daytime staff wouldn't serve nearly as many fish sandwiches." Another event that may have dissuaded Decade diners was the mud wrestling tournament. Dom procured contestants, prizes, a small wading pool, and even two regulars in proper referee attire. Dom realized one could either purchase clean or unsifted mud; he went with unsifted because it was cheaper and he had no plans of getting into it himself. He dressed as boxing promoter Don King in a white suit and maintained his distance from the pool. At the end of the night, mud coated the bar and clogged the sewers on Atwood. Infuriated by the state of her kitchen, Jan shoved Dom into the pool of mud.

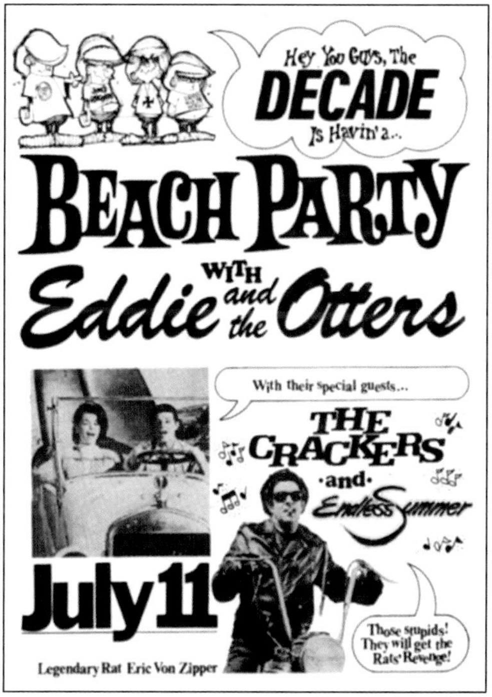

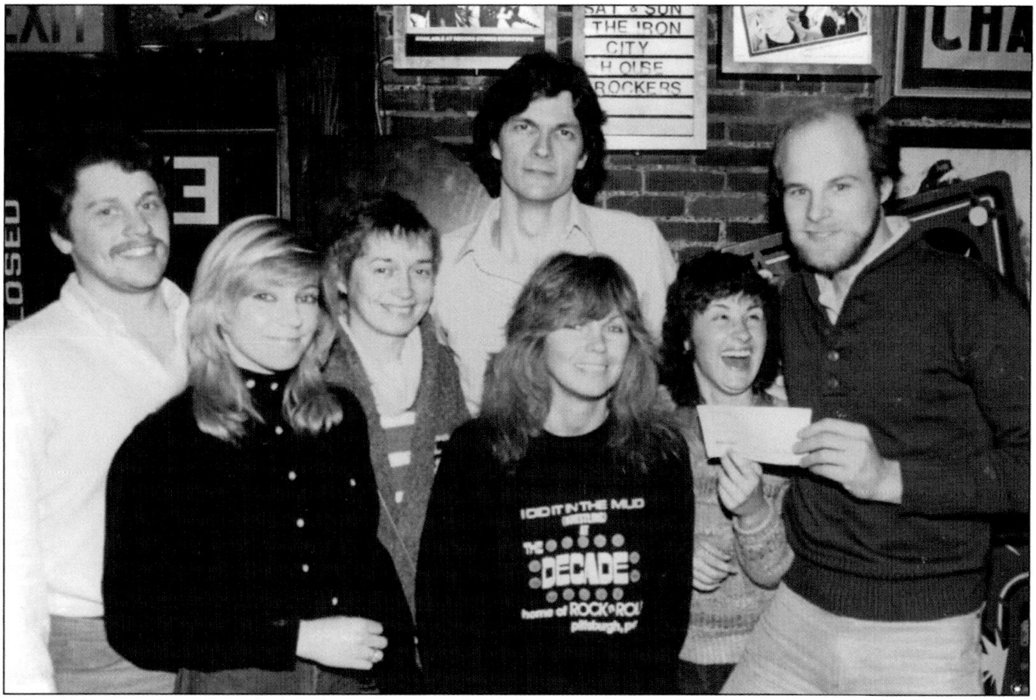

The infamous Pittsburgh death pool started at The Decade, and Dom, Jimmy Roach (center) and Steve Hansen (far right) were all willing participants in its mechanics. The saying went, "When your man goes, you get the dough." In a morbid version of a lottery, participants would choose what celebrity they thought would kick the bucket before the rest. Dom claims to have had to call England once to verify that a celebrity there had died.

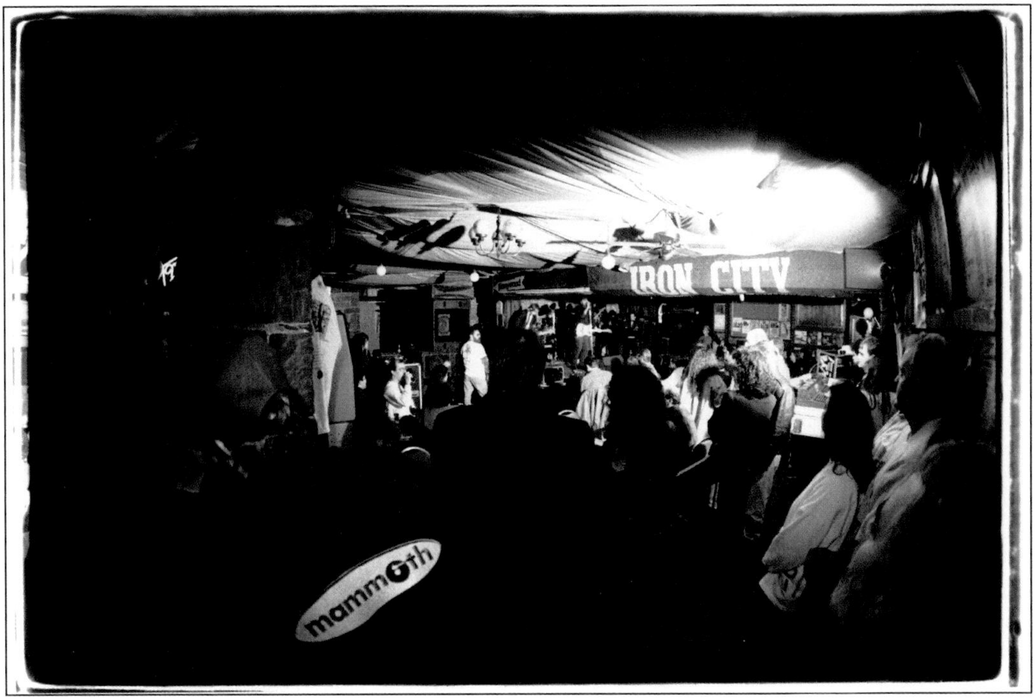

THE TATTLER
GEORGE ANDERSON

Stars soak up local nightlife

The Joker and the Penguin at the Decade: All work and no play might make Jack a dull boy, so "Hoffa" star **Jack Nicholson** and his director and co-star **Danny DeVito** went to the Decade on Sunday night. They were with a party that included **Robert Curran** of the Pittsburgh Film Office. They stayed for the whole first set by Chicago rhythm-and-blues artist **Otis Clay. Billy Price,** a fan of Clay's, joined him for a number. Our spy reports Nicholson and DeVito drank tequila and Iron City beer.

At The Decade's height, it was not unusual for a popular musician to jump onstage with whatever band was playing; however, one night, three celebrities showed up, and their presence shocked everyone in the place. Jack Nicholson, Danny Devito, and Armand Assante, all of whom were shooting *Hoffa* in Pittsburgh at the time, sipped Jose Cuervo and Iron City while watching Billy Price and Otis Clay jam out onstage. The maximum capacity at The Decade was around 165 people legally, but on a good night, there could be about 500 people crammed inside. However, every single person in the city seems to have had an interaction with the three stars that night. Legend has it that at the end of the night, Nicholson said, "You've got a nice place here, Dom." (Above, courtesy of Richard Kelly.)

Six

Last Call

"A music utopia," "massive energy," "headquarters for Pittsburgh music," "an integral part of rock 'n' roll history," "funky," "alive"—these are just a few of the things people said about The Decade in interviews for this book.

When Dom and Jan opened the bar, they had no preconceptions of the cultural phenomenon they would build. Each step of the way was a chance interaction, a happenstance that went incredibly well in their favor.

However, 22 years after they opened the bar, the entire DiSilvio family was at a much different point in their lives. Dom and Jan's children were grown, and most were married; the DiSilvios were ready to start their lives beyond The Decade. Since the kids all had their own unique ambitions, no one particularly wanted to take over the family business. This disappointed Dom, but as he always says, "Bars are bad for livers and marriages," so he accepted their disinterest. With a few grandchildren on the way, Dom and Jan decided the bar had run its course and that it was better to get out on top.

The last month at The Decade was packed with events, but the final month not only provided a great time for all the fans, it truly helped cement The Decade in Pittsburgh music history.

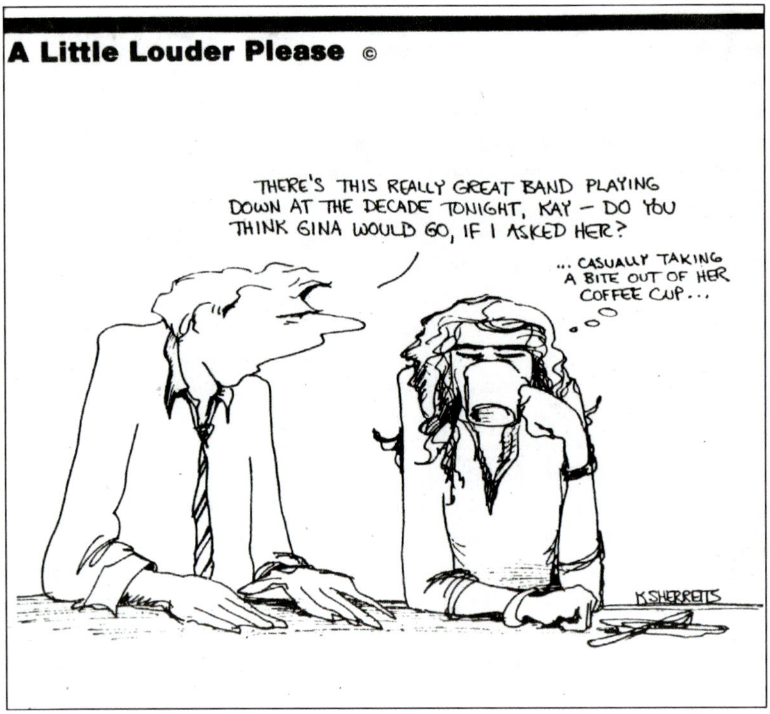

The Decade became a piece of Pittsburgh pop culture and a household name amongst college students and everyone in the Oakland area. Not only did it appear in many newspapers and magazines over the years, it also showed up in this comic strip by K. Sherretis. The comic even mentions the name of Dom's eldest daughter, but that might have just been a coincidence.

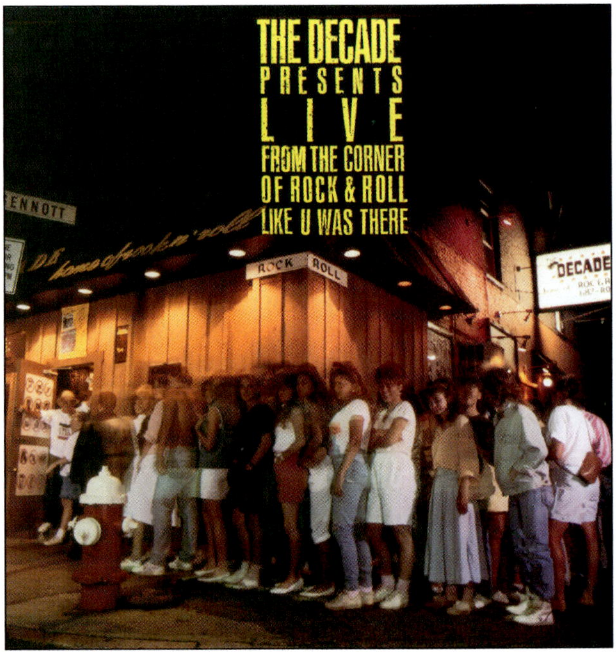

A Decade album was made to feature some of the best local Decade favorites. It captured the life and energy in the bar and was aptly named *The Decade Presents LIVE From The Corner Of Rock & Roll "Like U Was There."* The album, produced by Xayne Berlinski for On a Roll Productions, features an intro by radio personality Steve Hansen, "Slippin' And Slidin'" by Frankie and the Contenders, "Make Our Own Music" by the Eight Balls, "Boom Boom Out Go the Lights" by the Pep Boys, "Hideaway" by Joey G and the Rockers, "Bad Case of Love" by Room To Move, "99 1/2" by Frankie and the Contenders, "Sittin' Pretty" by 8th Street Rox, and "Last Call For Alcohol" by Bon Ton Roulet.

Not only did The Decade support itself through many years of business, it constantly participated in charity events. Jimmy Roach and Steve Hansen remember a time when they held their Toys for Tots event at The Decade, and at the end of the night, Dom handed them a paper bag full of cash. They proceeded to party at the bar for the rest of the night and ended up leaving the bag at a Winky's Hamburgers restaurant. Luckily, when they returned, the bag was still there. This ticket stub is from another charity event called The Decade All Stars Rock for Life cancer benefit.

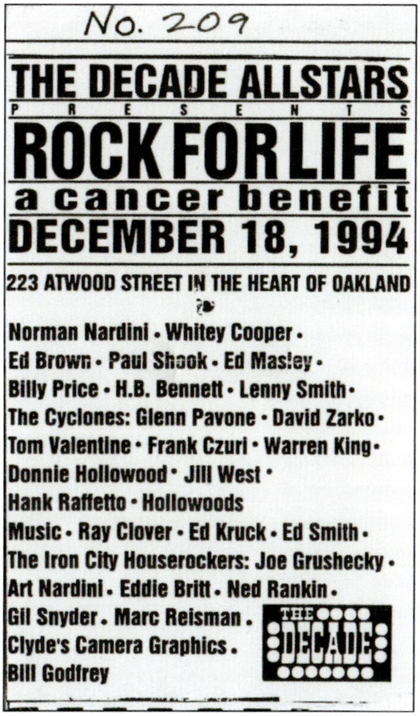

No. 209

THE DECADE ALLSTARS

PRESENTS

ROCK FOR LIFE

a cancer benefit

DECEMBER 18, 1994

223 ATWOOD STREET IN THE HEART OF OAKLAND

Norman Nardini • Whitey Cooper • Ed Brown • Paul Shook • Ed Masley • Billy Price • H.B. Bennett • Lenny Smith • The Cyclones: Glenn Pavone • David Zarko • Tom Valentine • Frank Czuri • Warren King • Donnie Hollowood • Jill West • Hank Raffetto • Hollowoods Music • Ray Clover • Ed Kruck • Ed Smith • The Iron City Houserockers: Joe Grushecky • Art Nardini • Eddie Britt • Ned Rankin • Gil Snyder • Marc Reisman • Clyde's Camera Graphics • Bill Godfrey

THE DECADE

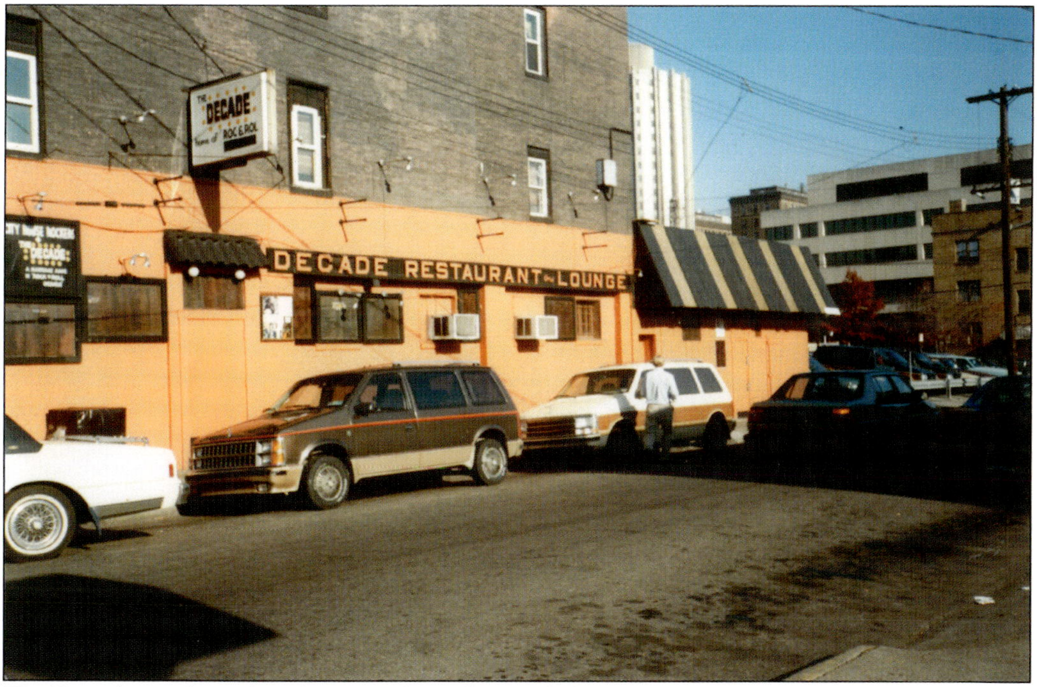

The Decade was legendary, but Dom knew he needed to close; he explained that despite the fact that the bar was still making money, he was tired. Joe Grushecky called Dom when the closing was finalized and insisted that the Iron City Houserockers play the final note on the Decade stage. Dom explains, "Obviously, Joe Grushecky played the last note of the last night," continuing on to say he "wouldn't have had anyone else do it."

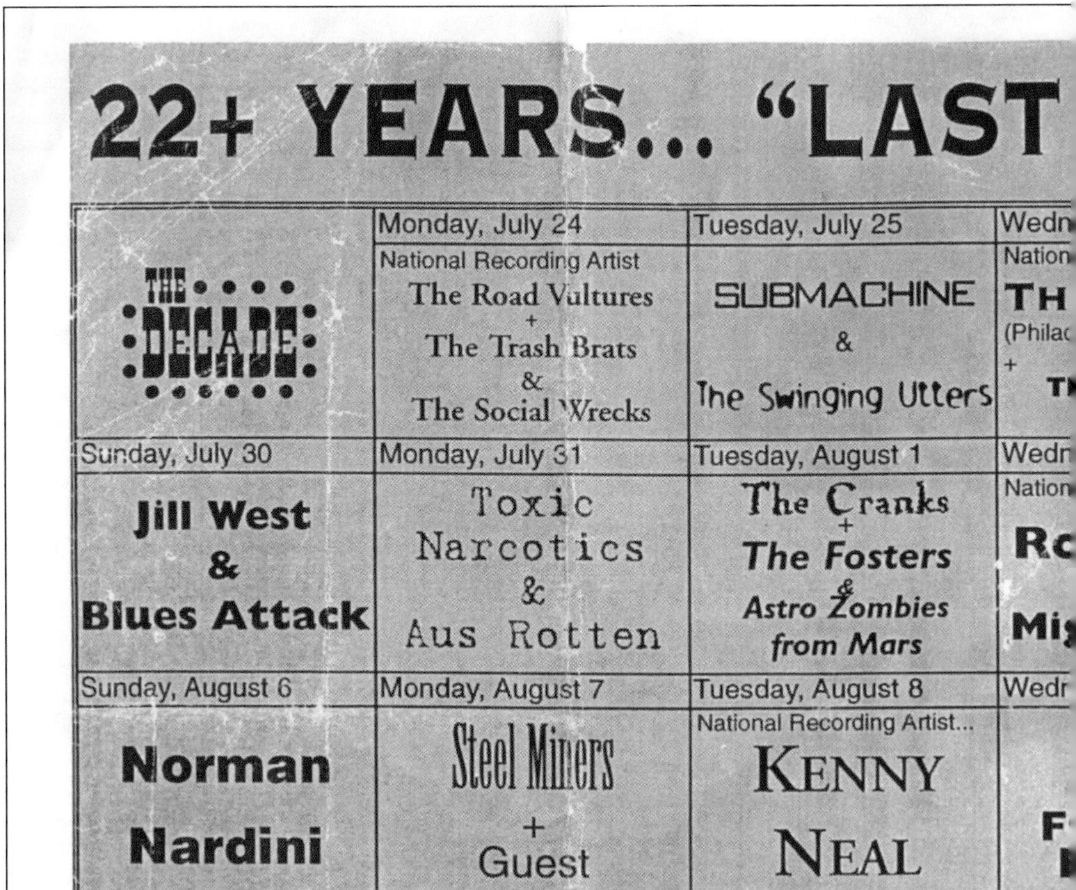

22+ YEARS… "LAST

THE DECADE	Monday, July 24 National Recording Artist The Road Vultures + The Trash Brats & The Social Wrecks	Tuesday, July 25 SUBMACHINE & The Swinging Utters	Wedn Nation TH (Philac + T
Sunday, July 30 Jill West & Blues Attack	Monday, July 31 Toxic Narcotics & Aus Rotten	Tuesday, August 1 The Cranks + The Fosters & Astro Zombies from Mars	Wedn Nation Rc Mi
Sunday, August 6 Norman Nardini	Monday, August 7 Steel Miners + Guest	Tuesday, August 8 National Recording Artist... KENNY NEAL	Wedr F
Sunday, August 13 the Silencers & Diamond Rio	Monday, August 14 ALTERNATIVE ALL STAR NIGHT ALL MUSICIANS WELCOME FOR FINAL GIG	Tuesday, August 15 TBA	Wedr G
Sunday, August 20 Red Hot & Blue The Mystic Knights w/ special guests Warren King & Billy Price	MONDAY, AUGUST 2 IRON CITY		

It was decided that the Iron City Houserockers would close out the old bar, but figuring out who should play during the last month was a difficult task. Dom wanted to honor both the local acts that The Decade grew up with and also the national acts he had come to love. It was also short

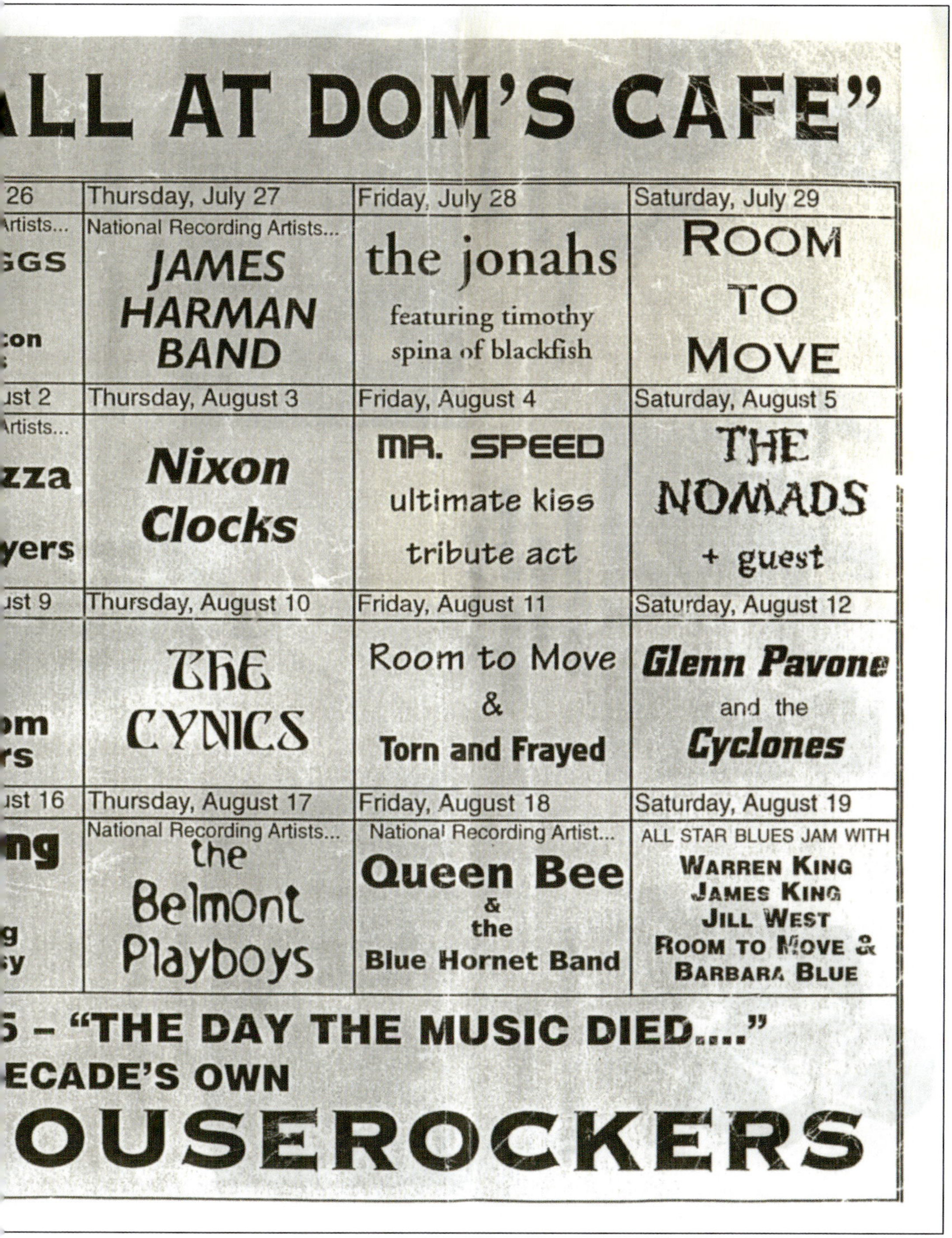

notice, as Dom sold the place faster than he had anticipated, so it was difficult finding national acts that could be there in time.

The DECADE

Home of Rock n' Roll

223 Atwood Street
Pittsburgh, PA 15213

(412) 682-1211

July 24, 1995

Dear Pittsburgh,

Since 1973, we've had a mutual relationship that has been very special. It is extremely difficult to express in a letter how we at THE DECADE feel. The accomplishments, hardships, friendships and sentiments have all formed a mosaic that is super-glued by two facets.... LOVE AND MUSIC!

We here at the home of "Rock 'N' Roll" hope that the 'Burgh and THE DECADE will always cherish and remember what we have accomplished together.... for DECADES to come!

Love always,

The Decade

In classic Dom fashion, he wrote a letter to the fans of The Decade explaining the closing. Many Pittsburghers bemoaned this fact, but both Dom and Jan knew they had made the right decision. Luckily, the bar was allotted a month-long farewell. The month was famously referred to as "Last Call at Dom's."

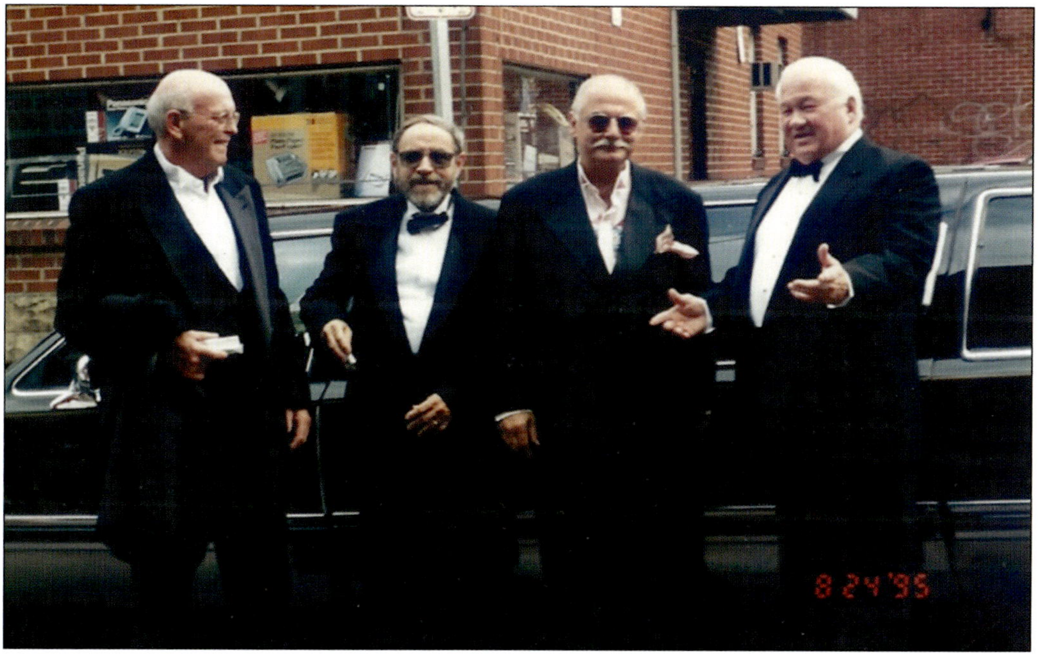

Dinners were often held in the Decade dining room, and during the last month at The Decade, Dom held one final dinner, calling it "The Last Supper." Regulars, Dom's friends, and employees showed up in final celebration of The Decade's kitchen. Ed Barrett decided that he, along with the rest of Dom's cronies, would wear tuxedos to the final dinner out of respect for the bar.

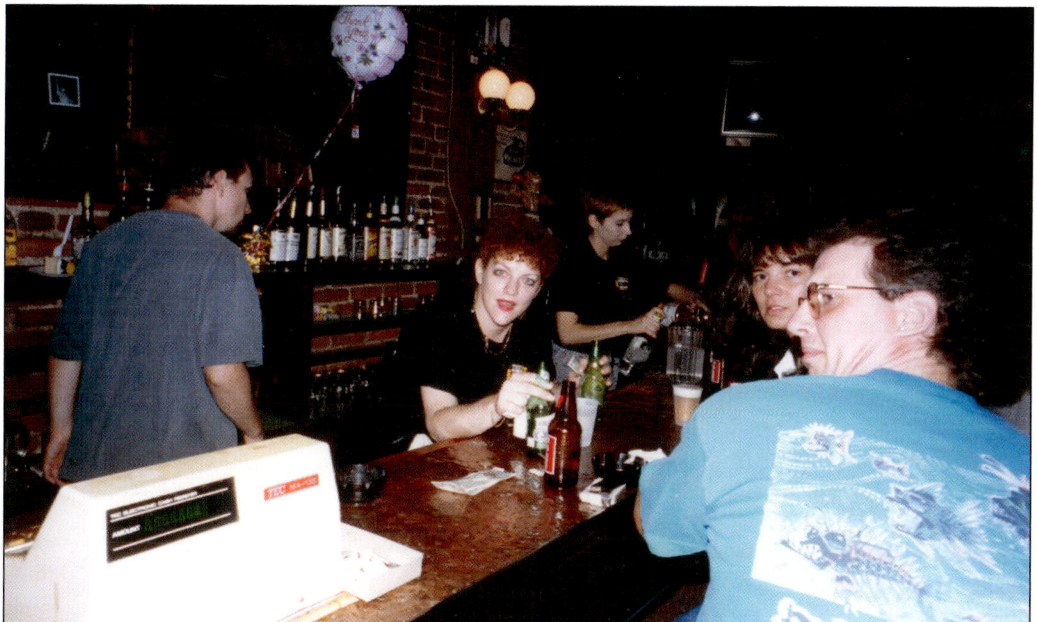

During the last month, in the sweltering heat that douses Pittsburgh in the summer, Sue Predis was hired as an extra staff hand. She recalls that Dom rehired anyone who had tended bar at any time in The Decade's existence for the huge blowout and that they all donned Decade shirts that read, "What are you gonna do, fire me?" on the back. The last few weeks were like a family reunion.

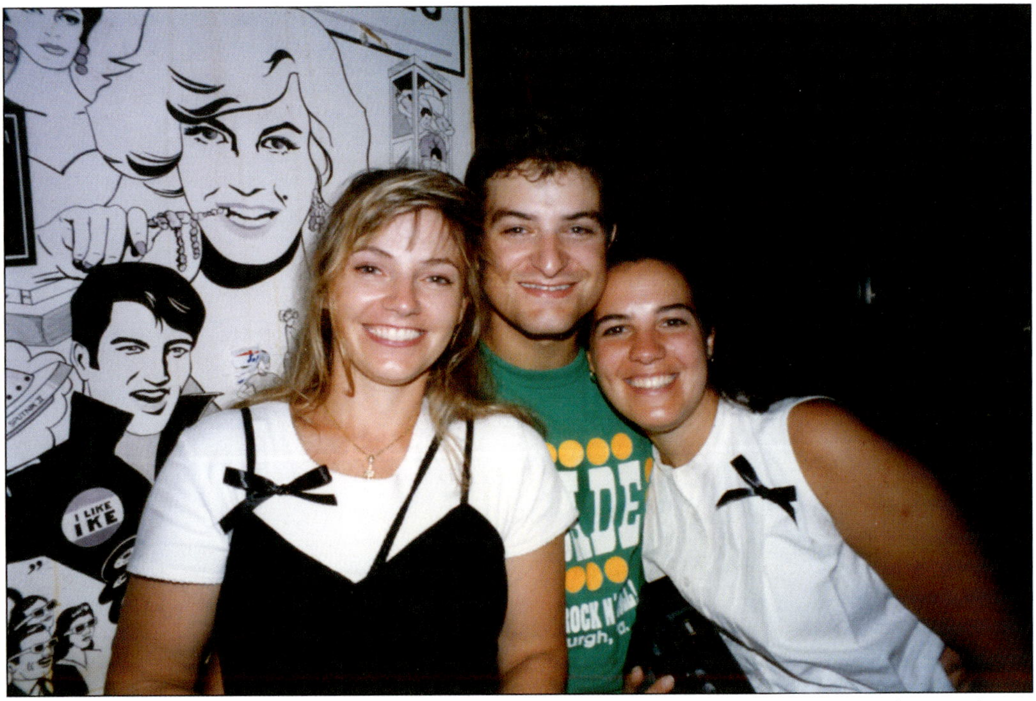

On the last night at The Decade, everyone drank, Dom's treasured bands played, and a couple got married onstage. It was a perfect example of the insanity that had occurred within The Decade for all 22 years leading up to the closing. That night, the staff wore black ribbons in mourning of their beloved bar; this melodramatic touch was Dom's idea. Pictured here with their black ribbons are Dom's eldest daughters Gina and Domenique, as well as Gina's husband, longtime Decade bouncer and the author's father, Danny Means.

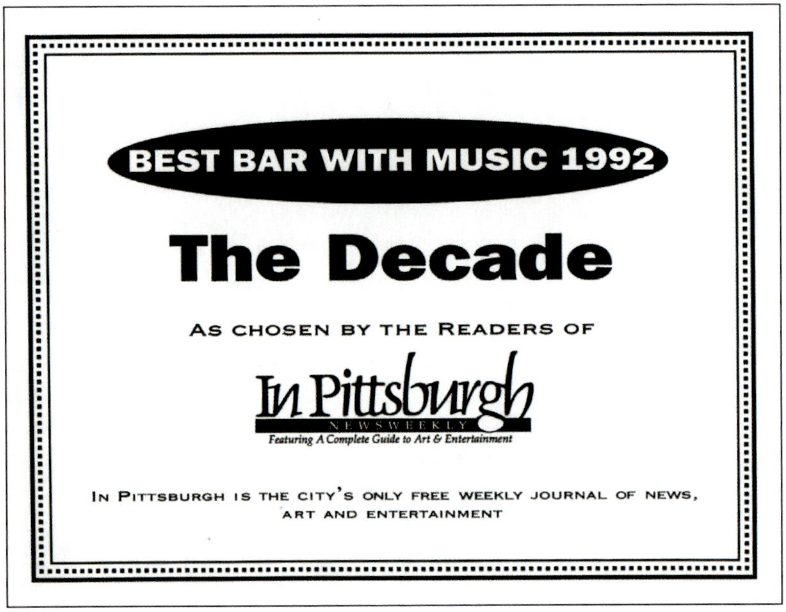

The Decade won the award for the Best Bar with Music several years in a row by the readers of *In Pittsburgh Newsweekly*. It wasn't a shock, as many Pittsburghers claim it was the only place of its kind then and now. Nothing has come along to replace it and its closing has left a large hole in the Pittsburgh music scene.

This "Almost a Landmark" sign on the side of the building is the last physical reminder of the bar. A proclamation signed by the mayor of Pittsburgh designated August 21, 1995, "The Day of The Decade."

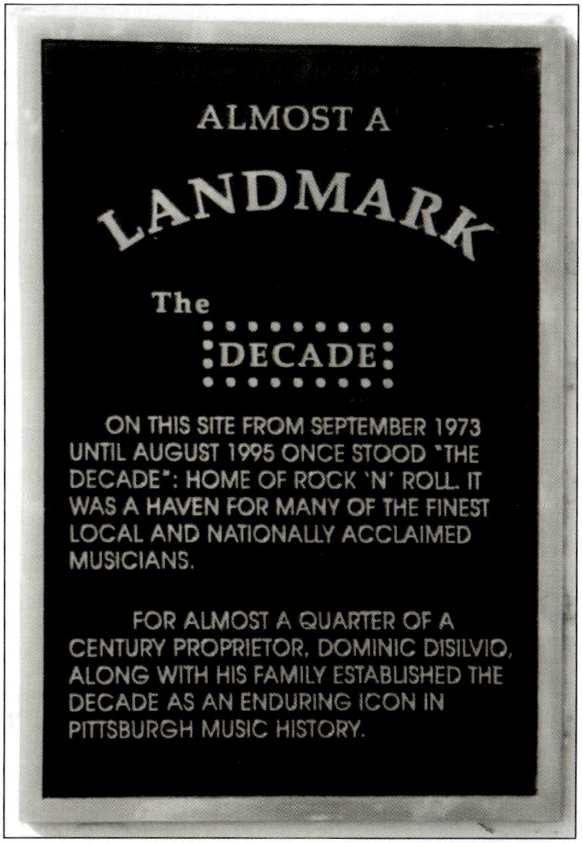

The night after they played the last show, Grushecky brought his kids down to the bar and told them that he wanted them to remember the place. Not only was it the stage that helped launch his career, but it was the place where Joe met his wife; she came in one night, and according to Grushecky, she was "the most beautiful woman in the place."

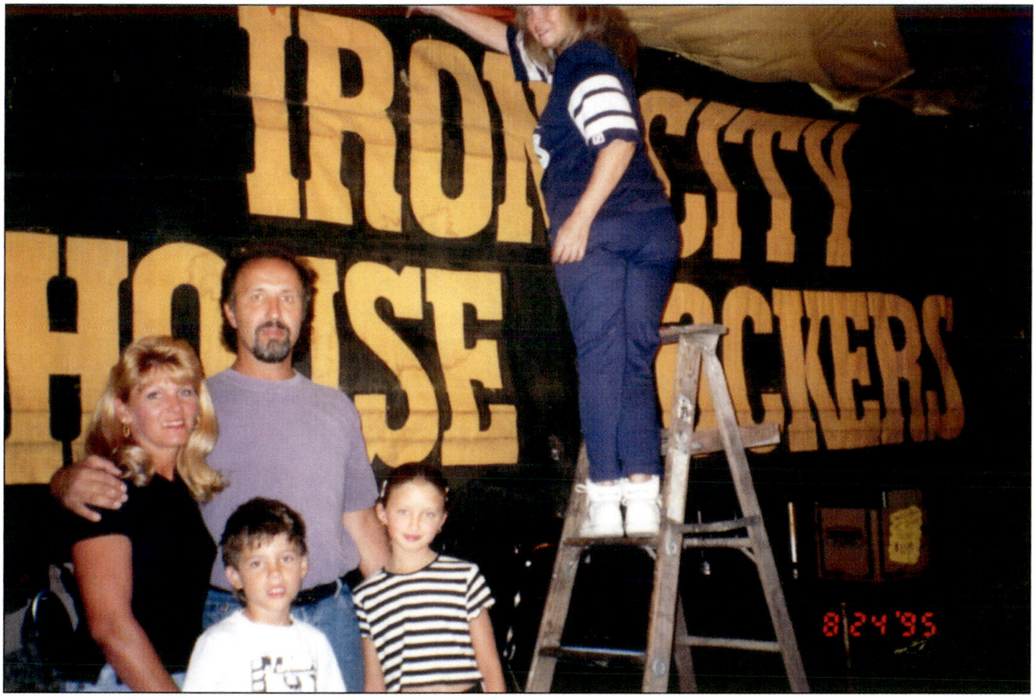

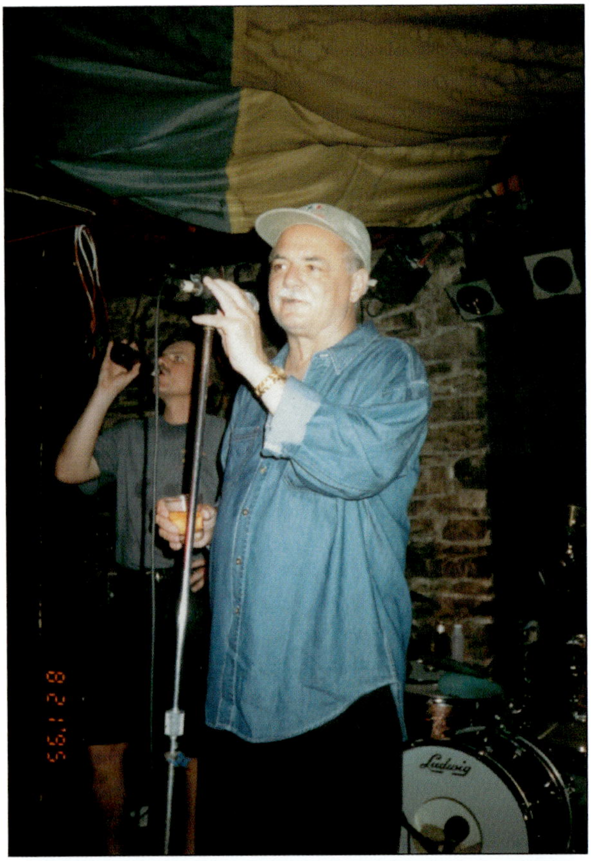

Dom loved The Decade more than a lot of things in his life. The bar not only allowed him to pursue his lifelong passion, but was also the place where he had found a family of people that he loved. He provided a space and fostered the dreams of many musicians, while they were simultaneously helping to foster his. The closing saddened him deeply.

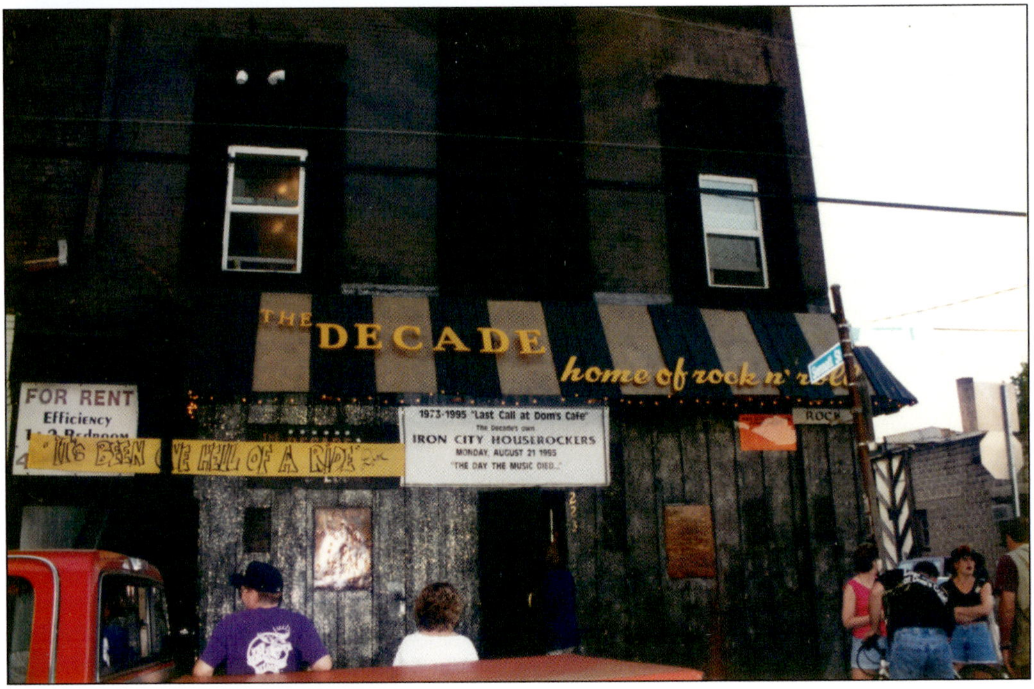

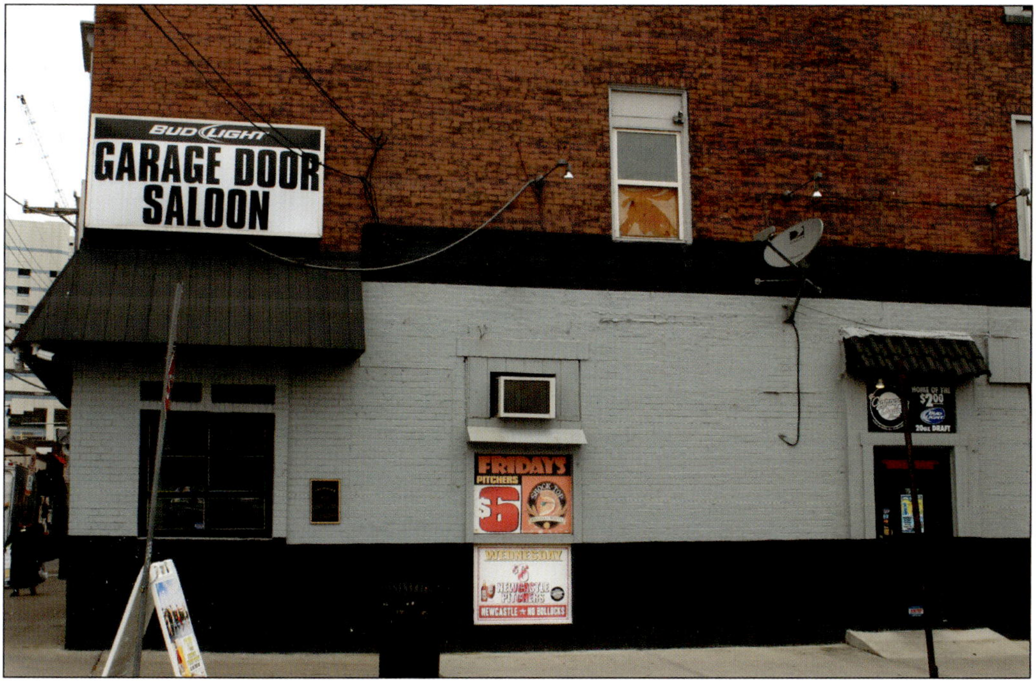

The property at 223 Atwood Street is currently Garage Door Saloon. To the local Oakland students, it is known as the place that is very strict on IDs and, therefore, the go-to place to celebrate after a 21st birthday. It is no longer the bar where underage kids could get in by simply disguising as a waitress or playing operation on their cardboard licenses. Saloon owner Mark Welshonse says that people come in on a regular basis and ask about The Decade. It has been gone for 20 years, but that does not stop customers from asking Welshonse why he decided to stop having live music. Clearly, some people are a bit confused.

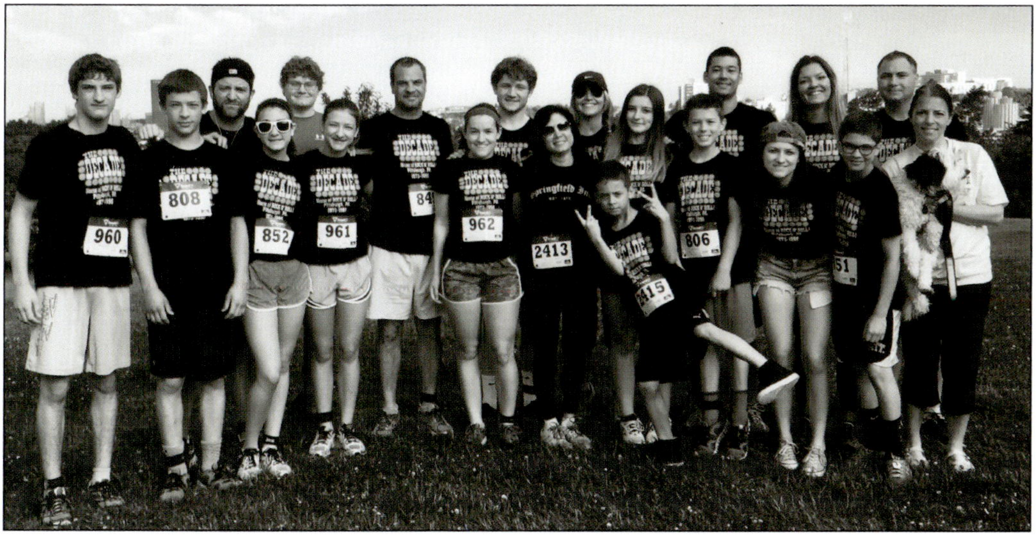

People still constantly ask the DiSilvios about The Decade. The family recently wore new Decade shirts while participating in a run as a team in honor of their grandmother. This new generation spends less time in bars and has a penchant for running, sweeping most age divisions of the race and coming out on top.

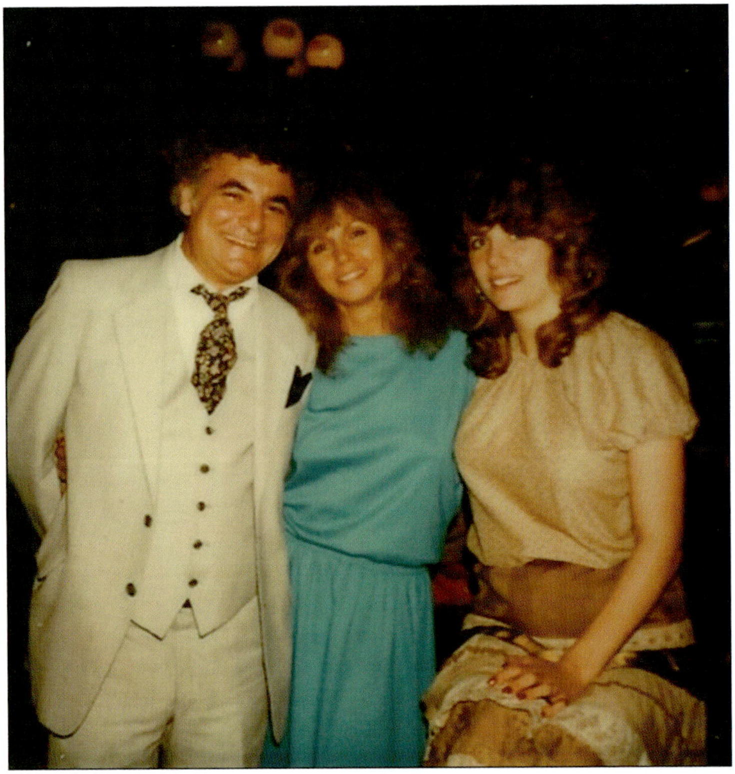

After the bar closed, Dom and Jan remained very close. Their large, ever-growing family, along with Judy and Dom's children, hold Sunday dinner every week, with Jan cooking dinner for everyone. Over the years, their children had their own children. Dom's current grandchild count is 16. Of this horde of grandchildren, the author is the oldest and one of only two to have ever set foot in (actually, been carried into) The Decade.

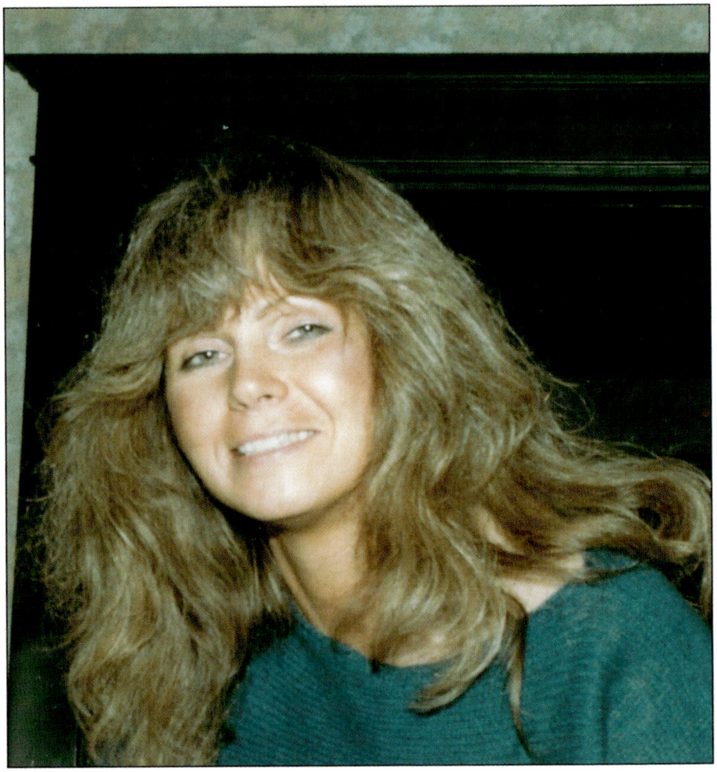

This book contains the stories of many great people whose time came too soon. Janet Chepes passed away from cancer on November 6, 2014, at the age of 73. She is missed dearly by everyone she touched, especially her business partner and life counterpart, Dom. Her spirit lives on through any of the family's acts of selflessness, because if there is one thing that reminds the DiSilvios of Jan, it is a selfless nature.

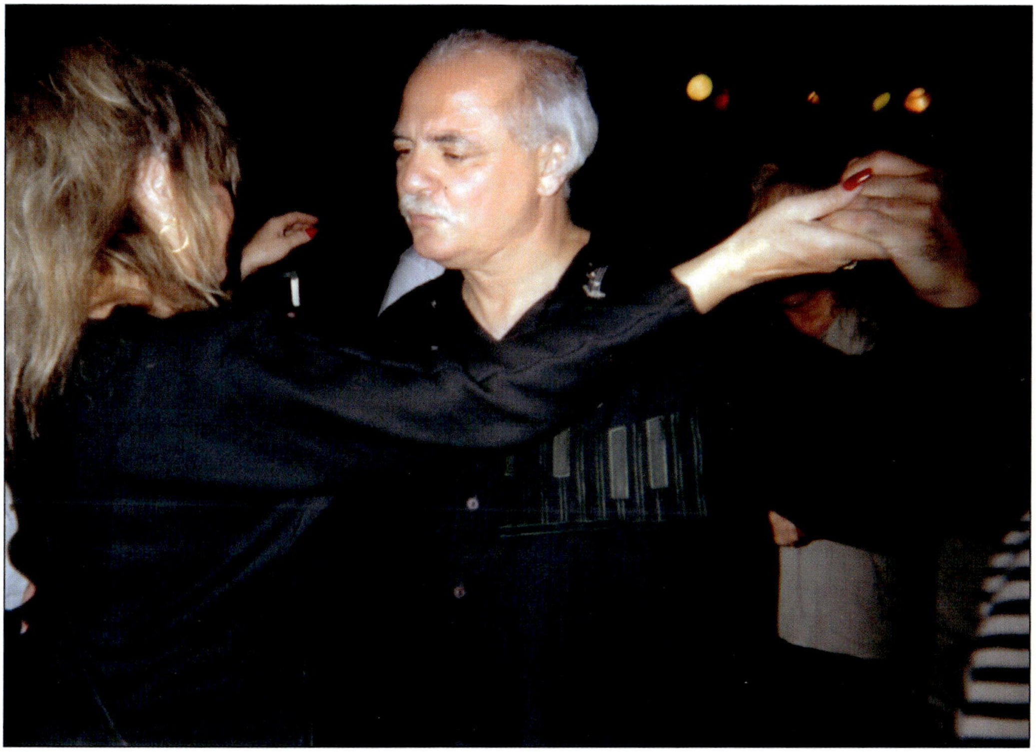

Dom and Jan had achieved their American dream. With a lot of hard work, dedication, a fantastic team dynamic, and a supportive family, they were able to make their mark on the Pittsburgh music scene. Their efforts will forever be remembered by those who enjoyed the fruits of their labor.

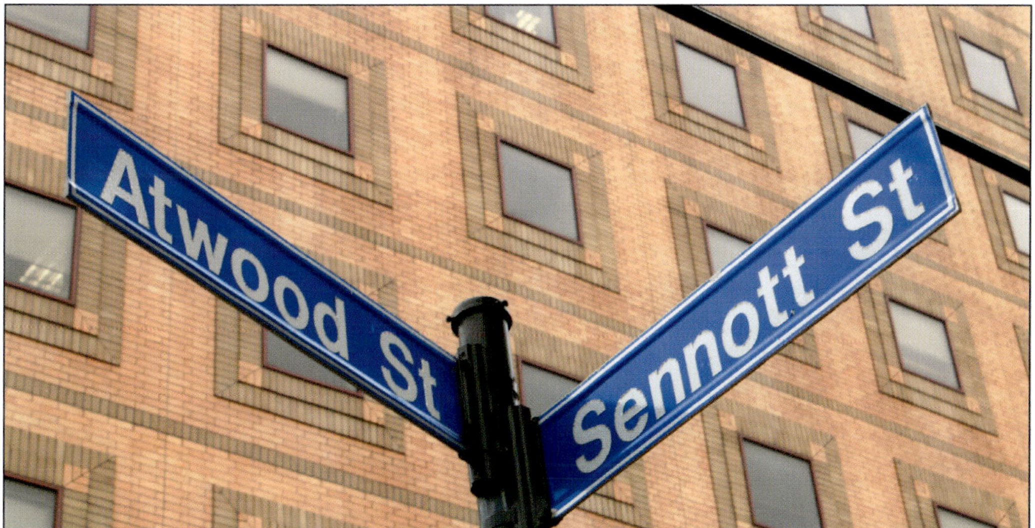

For a lot of people, the corner of Atwood and Sennott Streets will forever be home to the legendary Decade: Home of Pittsburgh Rock 'n' Roll. It is the place where they spent their youth and where dreams went untarnished and potential seemed overabundant. Dancing, singing, drinking—it was a time that will never be again but is forever locked in the memories of those who were there. And for those who were not there—well, they missed out.